DEADLY
DOCTORS

DEADLY DOCTORS

Max Marquis

Macdonald

A *Macdonald* Book

First published in Great Britain in 1992 by
Macdonald & Co (Publishers) Ltd
London & Sydney

Copyright © 1992 by Max Marquis

A CIP Catalogue record for this book is available
from the British Library

ISBN 0 356 20254 2

Photoset in North Wales by
Derek Doyle & Associates, Mold, Clwyd.
Printed and bound in Great Britain by
BPCC Hazell Books
Aylesbury, Bucks, England
Member of BPCC Ltd.

Macdonald & Co (Publishers) Ltd
165 Great Dover Street
London SE1 4YA
A member of Maxwell Macmillan Publishing Corporation

CONTENTS

DEADLY
DOCTORS

DR BUCK RUXTON

Oh, blood, blood, blood!
Othello

O, what a rash and bloody deed is this!
Hamlet

I am in blood
Stepp'd in so far, that, should I wade no more,
Returning were as tedious as go o'er.
Macbeth

There was a *grand guignol* element in the Ruxton murders of which nightmares are made. It was a bloodsoaked double crime; blood, blood was everywhere – on Dr Ruxton's clothes, on the bath, on walls, stairs and carpets. Fire and water could not get rid of all of it. Compared with Ruxton's real-life double killings Hitchcock's *Psycho* with its murder in the shower was mild. But the sheer gory horror of the Ruxton case was not the only reason that made it notable.

There were other factors which raised it far above the average family murder: the wildly flamboyant major figure, Bukhtyar Ruttomji Ratanji Hakim, later known simply as Dr Buck Ruxton; the only slightly less extravagantly behaved Isabella Ruxton; and the pathetic, tiny twenty-year-old Mary Rogerson.

Ruxton's trial lasted eleven days, including a sitting on a Saturday. Some 213 exhibits were produced, including such diverse and unexpected objects as a model of the Ruxton home, a full-sized bath, a vinegar bottle (to show that fingerprints from one of the severed hands were to be found in the Ruxton home), a chamber pot from Mary Rogerson's room, pieces of newspaper, a lavatory seat and pieces of woodwork from the house.

Exhibits 135–143 were books containing a total of 126 photographs of Isabella Ruxton and Mary Rogerson in life and after the necessarily sketchy re-assembly of the various remains. These books were divided into three groups: Body No. 1, Body No. 2 and a grimly entitled 'Miscellaneous Parts'.

More than one hundred witnesses gave evidence for

the prosecution, while only Ruxton himself gave evidence for the defence, and there were times when he seemed bent on bolstering the prosecution case by his extravagant behaviour and claims. The case against him was overwhelming. Yet Norman Birkett KC, later Lord Justice Birkett, put up a masterly defence which almost raised a reasonable doubt about Ruxton's guilt in the face of this great mass of evidence.

The forensic pathologists Professors Brash and Glaister did some brilliant, albeit grisly, reconstruction work and invented a technique to help in the identification of bodies which is still used more than fifty years later.

Finally, after Ruxton's life had come to an abrupt end at the end of a rope there was another startling development.

Yet perhaps the most fascinating features of the case were three minor incidents which first pointed to the guilty man and then helped to convict him. It is tempting to believe that these random occurrences were really the deliberate acts of a fate which was determined that Ruxton should not escape the consequences of his acts.

As far as the general public was concerned the opening chapter of the story was on Sunday 29th September 1935. Miss Susan Johnson, a holiday-maker from Edinburgh, was out for a stroll on a cool autumn morning. When she crossed the road bridge over the ravine of Gardenholme Linn in Dumfriesshire, she glanced down and saw a parcel at the edge of the river. She looked at it casually, then with a shock she regarded it more intently. When she was convinced that her eyes weren't playing her tricks she scurried back to the hotel where she was staying with her brother Alfred.

She blurted out what she had seen, which sent him hurrying to the ravine. There Alfred Johnson found that his sister hadn't exaggerated. A human arm was sticking out of the parcel.

Some three miles from the point of this discovery is an area with the sinister, but apt, name: The Devil's Beef Tub.

The police were called and that afternoon Police Sergeant Robert Sloan clambered down into the ravine. The life of a country policeman in the mid-nineteen-thirties was usually fairly placid, with nothing much more exciting than cases of straying cattle, bicycles without lights and the odd drunk, with poaching as the most serious of local crimes.

Sergeant Sloan must have had mixed feelings about this departure from the routine and familiar. He found four parcels in all, containing a total of two heads, three thigh bones, two forearms with hands from which the tips of the fingers and thumb were missing, several pieces of flesh and skin, two upper arm bones, the lower parts of two legs, the chest part of a human torso and some thirty-odd pieces of flesh.

The first of the unforeseen incidents which helped send Ruxton to the gallows had already occurred. There had been heavy rain storms in the area on the 18th and 19th of September, which caused flash floods in Rusholme Linn and the River Annan. These threw the package, and others which were discovered later, high on to the banks of the rivers. When the water level fell again, the packages were left high and dry. Had it not been for this unexpected torrent the parcels of human remains might well have been swept away for ever.

This incident had further effects, of course. It was obvious that the dismemberment had taken place before the 18th September, so the police were able to concentrate their enquiries on missing persons who disappeared before that date. They had no success at first. It was also fairly evident that the remains had been transported to the Linn by car, so the police tried to find out if there had been any unusual movements made by cars registered in Dumfriesshire – again with no result.

The gruesome find triggered a further search along the banks of the Linn and the River Annan. More human remains were found: a left forearm and hand, a left thigh, a pelvis and various pieces of flesh. In the following month, the 28th of October, a left foot was discovered at Johnstonbridge, some nine miles south of Moffat on the Edinburgh–Carlisle road, and six miles north of Lockerbie. The last find was on the 4th of November, on the Edinburgh road south of the bridge over the Linn: a right forearm and hand.

We are nearly finished with the macabre accountancy. The total pieces of persons found consisted of two heads, two parts of torso, 17 pieces of limb and 43 items of soft tissue, including three female breasts, two pieces of female exterior sex organs and a uterus.

Among the wrappings of the remains were pieces of various newspapers, *Sunday Graphic, Daily Herald* and *Sunday Chronicle*. This was the second innocuous-seeming incident. As we shall see, it was a particular issue of the *Sunday Graphic* out of the millions of copies that were printed, which pointed the finger unerringly at the Lancaster area.

The third incident concerned torn pieces of bedsheet which were in the packages. It might seem that one piece of bedsheet is very much like another of the same make. But not in this case. Again, as we shall see, a million to one chance made this particular piece of sheet as identifiable as a fingerprint.

There is one final detail about the discovery of the remains which has to be said: they were badly decomposed and infested with maggots. This last fact proved of considerable significance in the pathological examination, and gave rise to a (then) new technique for determining the time elapsed between death and the examination of human remains. The work of the pathologists on the jigsaw puzzle of an awful pile of human debris was nothing short of brilliantly inspired . . . and, to the layman, stomach-churning.

I discussed the case with Professor Glaister some years ago. I remarked that the case was exceptionally unpleasant even for an experienced forensic patho- logist, and I asked him how he could bring himself to deal with the remains, and whether doing so affected his everyday life. His reply was simple, and tinged with a certain surprise.

While trying to identify the remains as parts of particular bodies, the professor said, he was preoc- cupied with the problems and hardly thought of the specimens as parts of corpses. And when he closed the laboratory door behind him, the whole operation was totally shut out of his mind. It was a detachment that most people would envy and few could equal.

The central figure in this story is Dr Buck Ruxton, who was thirty-six years old at the time of the murders. He was born to a wealthy Parsee family in Bombay and came to England to study. Later he returned to Bombay where he qualified as a Bachelor of Surgery and subsequently took a commission in the Indian Medical Corps, in which he served in Basra and Baghdad. He returned to Britain in 1927 where he added the degree of Bachelor of Medicine of the University of London to a similar degree of the University of Bombay, but he failed the examination for a Fellowship of the Royal College of Surgeons in Edinburgh.

It was while he was in Edinburgh that he had the literally fatal encounter with his future common law wife and victim, Isabella Van Ess, née Kerr. She was the manageress of a restaurant in Princes Street where

Ruxton was a frequent customer. She also called herself Isabella Stewart for a period, and at the same time Ruxton was styling himself Captain Gabriel Hakim. Isabella acquired the name Van Ess by marrying a Dutch sailor when she was eighteen years old. This marriage was later dissolved.

In 1928, when Ruxton was twenty-nine years old and she two years younger, she went to live with him in London, where Bukhtyar Hakim changed his name by deed poll to Buck Ruxton. She called herself Mrs Ruxton, and although they lived together until her death in 1935, they never legally married. However, they went through a form of marriage in London despite the fact that Ruxton had a Parsee wife back in India. In those days some people still believed that 'living in sin' was a fate worse than death. In Mrs Ruxton's case, it wasn't.

Two years later the Ruxtons, who now had a child, Elizabeth*, settled at 2, Dalton Square, Lancaster, a house with a semi-basement, ground floor and two upper floors, and a back yard with an outside w.c. It was in this house that the third person in the drama entered on the scene: poor little Mary Rogerson. She was 18 when she entered the Ruxton household as a maid mainly concerned with taking care of the children. She was tiny, barely five feet tall, and she had a cast in one eye, but she had a cheerful disposition and a strong sense of loyalty to Mrs Ruxton and the children. Other servants came and went, but Mary stayed, despite all the violent rows, threats, screams and shouts.

She didn't have much of a life. She was paid fifteen shillings (75p) a week, and on her days off she invariably went to see her parents in Morecambe. The one week she didn't go home was when she took the Ruxton children to a farm for a fortnight, but her

---

* Some accounts of the trial give her name as Kathleen.

parents knew of the trip and she wrote to them almost every day.

She was a couple of weeks short of her twentieth birthday when she was murdered.

The house at Dalton Square soon reflected the doctor's flamboyant character and uncertain temperament: it was bright red and white on the exterior, green and yellow on the interior. In a town of sober – if not plain drab – houses then it stood out like a football shirt at a funeral. The furnishings were an uneasy mixture of East and West, although the decor of the reception room suffered no indecision of choice and was completely Indian, with heavy furniture and thick tapestries.

Unhappily, excessive flamboyance was the least of Ruxton's failings. He certainly had a persuasive charm at times, but his highly volatile and complex character was also heavily charged with bombast, egotism, vanity, and overweening self-confidence; yet nor were these features the most serious. Dr Ruxton was easily moved to terrible rages and suffered from an acute pathological unreasoning jealousy which by comparison made Othello seem a model of tolerance, and Ruxton had no need of an Iago to stimulate his sick suspicions.

Men found Isabella Stewart Ruxton interesting, but it took a Buck Ruxton to find her desirable. It strains politeness even to call her face toothy and plain, and the rest of her ordinary at best. At Ruxton's trial it was stated that her legs were the same thickness from knee to ankle. She compensated for this lack of physical attractiveness with a determined flirtatiousness. Ruxton could hardly have become infatuated with a more dangerous partner: the compound of their temperaments made an explosive mixture. A bloody and violent outcome was inevitable.

The Ruxtons were far from ideal neighbours. Life in their home was frantic and noisy almost from the outset. They both seemed to be prone to turbulent rages. Isabella often instigated screaming matches by deliberately starting a quarrel with her husband because making up was so much more passionate afterwards. She would go into his surgery with a smile on her lips and say, 'I wonder how I could pick a row with you . . . '

The trouble was she didn't seem to know just where to draw the line between teasing and goading. The price she paid for her lack of judgement was high. Ruxton, indifferent to the presence of witnesses, gave way to extraordinary emotional outbursts, furious threats and actual violence against Isabella. Once when she left him he said, 'She will not come back alive. I will bring her back to the mortuary.' People remember remarks like that. Domestic servants who preceded Mary Rogerson in the Ruxton household spoke of Ruxton grabbing his wife's throat, threats with knives, and a revolver being kept in the bedroom.

Ruxton himself described their relationship as: 'We were the kind of people who could not live with each other and could not live without each other. He who loves most chastises most.'

Apart from her flirtatiousness, Isabella Ruxton had another weakness: gambling. Ruxton claimed he gave her £12 a week housekeeping money every Monday – a very generous allowance in those days – and there was no reason to doubt him. However, he found that cheques he gave her were endorsed over to bookmakers, so he paid all the household bills himself and gave Isabella a whole pound a week for herself to spend as she liked.

The Ruxton upheavals were like Mediterranean storms, violent, but usually brief. Nevertheless, even the deliberately provocative Isabella finally had more than she could stand. In addition to the emotional turmoil of living with Buck Ruxton, Isabella became increasingly disenchanted with Lancaster. Though some consider Scotland to be dour, Lancaster couldn't compare with Edinburgh as far as Mrs Ruxton was concerned.

As a result of the turbulent relations between the Ruxtons, the police got to know the couple quite well. Twice Isabella fled the house to the local police station for protection. At that first visit Detective Sergeant Walter Stainton found Ruxton and took him to the station. The doctor was in an almost-gibbering rage and accused his wife of being unfaithful. He would be justified in murdering her, he said. Stainton suggested instead a more traditional line of action and recommended Ruxton to give the offending man a good hiding. The next day Buck Ruxton followed Isabella to the station and repeated the murder threat.

Next, the police were called to the house because of Ruxton's excesses. Stainton was the unlucky officer to get this call. This was pretty much a repeat performance. Ruxton was in one of his hysterical moods. He accused his wife of being unfaithful again, and went on to elaborate, 'I feel like murdering two people in Dalton Square.'

Stainton again recommended a rather more traditional course of action and suggested that Ruxton give the man a good hiding. Ruxton would not be pacified and elaborated and said of her alleged lover, 'I feel like murdering him.'

Mrs Ruxton, who was afraid to say much, nevertheless commented quietly, 'He may kill you.'

'Well, if he does, I will kill him and there will be two murders,' Ruxton said. The situation may have been tragic, but the dialogue was hardly classic Greek drama.

According to contemporary reports, he behaved like a madman on several occasions, becoming so excited that he was incoherent, looking as if he was going to have a fit, and then burst into tears.

By the end of 1931, if not before, the Ruxtons were occupying separate bedrooms on the top floor of the house. Ruxton had one, Mary another, and Isabella Ruxton and the children the third. At the end of that year Ruxton sent a wild telegram to Isabella's sister, Mrs Jeanie Nelson, a 49-year-old widow, living in Bothwell Street, Edinburgh. This sent her rushing to Dalton Square. Ruxton took her into his consulting room and told her that Isabella had tried to commit suicide by gassing herself. 'Are you at fault in any way?' Mrs Nelson asked him.

Ruxton replied indignantly that he most certainly wasn't, he was a kind and loving husband; Isabella was trying to get him into trouble and ruin him by gassing herself, which was a pretty fanciful explanation, even by Ruxton's standards. Eventually Jeanie Nelson persuaded Ruxton to let her go upstairs to the bedroom to see her sister.

'Now, tell your sister the truth,' Ruxton ordered his wife.

'It was an accident,' Isabella said, whereupon Ruxton slapped her face while she lay in bed and shouted, 'Come on, now, the truth, the truth. You must tell the truth.' Isabella continued to insist that the gassing had been an accident. She turned to Mrs Nelson and asked her to take her home with her to Edinburgh. Ruxton immediately said that if they left, taking the children with them, he would cut the throats of the lot of them.

By the next morning the storm had passed. Isabella, Jeanie Nelson and the three Ruxton children, aged six, four and two years, left for a short holiday. Ruxton was calm and considerate, and drove the party to the railway station. Mrs Ruxton and the three children stayed with Mrs Trench, another of Isabella's sisters, and after a week or so Ruxton drove to Edinburgh and returned to Lancaster with his family.

It is sad but not altogether surprising, in view of the tumultuous life of the Ruxtons, that Isabella had a stillborn child in April 1932. After another two years of stormy life with Buck Ruxton in Lancaster, which she so firmly disliked, Isabella packed her bags and went to stay with Mrs Nelson, again. This time she left their three children behind her.

'I've finally left Lancaster and I'm not going back,' Isabella said determinedly.

Ruxton arrived in Edinburgh a few days afterwards and demanded that Isabella go back with him. From demanding he moved to pleading, telling her that he would be ruined if she left him, that he could not live without her and the children needed her. Maybe it was this last plea that made Isabella begin to weaken, and her sister Jeanie added her voice to Ruxton's. Perhaps it was because Jeanie Nelson simply didn't want Isabella living with her; or, more likely, it troubled her sense of propriety to have a sister separated from her husband and abandoning her children. That mid-thirties, middle-class Edinburgh morality was demonstrated in court at Ruxton's trial. When Norman Birkett pressed Mrs Nelson whether Isabella Ruxton was 'fond' of Mary Rogerson, the maid, she eventually replied, 'She admired her. I cannot say fond; Scotch (*sic*) people do not be fond of people like that . . . ' i.e., a servant.

Whatever it was that made her encourage her sister to return to Lancaster with Buck Ruxton, she undoubtedly regretted it to the end of her days.

On 7th September the following year, 1935, occurred the last incident which finally pushed Ruxton over the borderline to uncontrollable rage, and murder. Isabella Ruxton went to Edinburgh with some friends, the Edmondson family: the parents, a daughter Barbara, and a son, Robert James Edmondson, who was an assistant solicitor in Lancaster Town Clerk's department. They travelled in two cars. The original plan was for Mrs Ruxton to stay overnight with her sister, Mrs Nelson. In the event, the entire party stayed at the Adelphi Hotel. They occupied four rooms: Mr and Mrs Edmondson in one, Isabella Ruxton, Barbara and Robert Jr separately in the three others.

Ruxton had been unreasonably jealous of young Edmondson for some time and made many unfounded allegations about his relationship with Isabella Ruxton. The insubstantial suspicions seemed to evaporate quickly, and Ruxton remained quite friendly with Edmondson. Nevertheless, Ruxton hired a car and followed the party to Edinburgh. He pasted brown paper over part of the windscreen so that he would not be recognised. In those days 'staying in a hotel' could have a suggestive ring about it. Despite the fact that all the Edmondsons were at the hotel and had separate rooms, Ruxton was convinced that the whole thing was a plot to allow Bobby Edmondson and Isabella to sleep together.

He seemed – and 'seemed' is the operative word – to have calmed down and dismissed the suspicions from his mind during the following week. However, the following weekend Isabella behaved thoughtlessly again. Whether she intended deliberately to provoke Ruxton, whether it was mischance, or whether she was just bored with life in Lancaster we can never know. This time she pushed her luck too far.

On Saturday 14th September Mrs Ruxton drove in her husband's car alone to Blackpool, about twenty-two miles away, to meet Jeanie Nelson and another sister, Mrs Eleen Madden and her husband to see the illuminations, a trip they made regularly. After their sight-seeing tour the party returned to the boarding house where Mrs Ruxton's sisters were staying and had a meal. Finally, Mrs Ruxton left brilliantly-lit Blackpool at about 11.30pm to drive back to sombre Lancaster.

From that moment she was not seen alive by anyone outside the Ruxton home in Dalton Square.

It is impossible to be absolutely certain to the last fine detail what happened when Isabella Ruxton returned to her home. After all, the principal actors in the tragedy are in no position to give their own versions. However, the broad pattern is clear, and there is a great deal of evidence painstakingly assembled by the brilliant pathologists and scientific experts; there are also the incidents before and after the night of Saturday 14th–Sunday 15th September to provide material for us to reconstruct the events of that night so we can be sure we are very near to the exact picture.

When Isabella opened the front door at something like half an hour after midnight, she walked straight into another wild row with the doctor, who was practically babbling with rage. The row continued upstairs, into Ruxton's bedroom away from the children, where the argument became even more incendiary; wild accusations were met with mocking. Ruxton's rage finally boiled over and rushing to Isabella, he punched her hard several times and then grabbed her by the throat – as he had done so many times before.

But this time was not like the others. This time there would be no apologies and sweet words, followed by impassioned reconciliation. This time Dr Ruxton had gone to where there could be no turning back. In an unparalleled paroxysm of fury he kept up the pressure on Isabella's windpipe – he squeezed, and squeezed . . . until she stopped struggling and fell to the floor, dead.

At last all his previous threats of murder had been fulfilled. Yet there was worse to come.

Mary Rogerson, woken by so much noise, came to see what was happening, and why the tumult had stopped so abruptly, so ominously, so finally. She may even have arrived in time to try to stop Ruxton strangling his wife. She fell to her knees and vainly tried to revive Isabella. At last she turned to Ruxton and said, 'Oh, doctor! You've killed her!'

At that instant, time was crystallised in one immeasurable moment. A new relationship between the ill-assorted couple was born: they shared the secret that Dr Ruxton had murdered his wife.

Mary suddenly realised the danger of her own position and a glance at Ruxton's face confirmed it. His blood was still running hot. God knows he often had an almost insane temper, but now he was in the grip of an intense madness the like of which had never seized him before. They both knew that if Ruxton was to have any chance of living, Mary Rogerson must die.

She turned and bolted headlong for the stairs and the front door where she might find safety. Ruxton snatched up a brass candlestick and rushed after her. She had just reached the top of the stairs when the heavy brass crashed down on to her head . . . and again, smashing in the top of her skull.

But Mary Rogerson was not dead. Not yet. Ruxton went downstairs to his surgery to fetch a knife to complete the night's ghastly work. He went back upstairs and plunged the weapon into the still figure. Blood started to well out on to the stairs.

All the while Elizabeth, age six, Diane, age four and Billie, age two, slept peacefully in their mother's room. It is impossible to imagine what effect it would have had on them if they had woken and come to see what had happened. At least they were spared that.

At last Ruxton, looking down at two dead bodies, one of them pouring blood on to the stairs, managed to bring himself under some semblance of self-control. He knew that the human body is difficult to destroy and unwieldy for one man alone to move. So, with an inhuman logic he came to the conclusion that his best course was to reduce the two corpses to manageable proportions.

He dragged one of them into the nearby bathroom and dumped it into the bath, the other into his bedroom, where he locked the door before beginning his ghastly work.

(At the trial the prosecuting counsel, Mr J. C. Jackson KC, suggested that Ruxton dismembered the bodies on the Sunday morning, but almost certainly he at least started the process the previous night.)

Ruxton had studied the human body for years in order to cure his patients' sicknesses. Now, with an iron will born of unbalanced desperation he turned his knowledge and training to a massive labour of dissection and mutilation to save his own life – mutilation to conceal the cause of death and the identity of the victims. It is a wry compliment to Ruxton's surgical skill that he reduced two bodies to relatively small pieces with only a scalpel with changeable two-inch blades.

The dissection of the bodies was not all. Although Ruxton was no longer in the grip of the insane hyper-active fury which had pushed him to a double murder, he must have been suffering a quiet, unfeeling madness of dissociation for he was able to undertake the massive task of cutting away parts of the two dead bodies which might help to identify them. The catalogue compiled by the pathologists of the butcheries he performed make horrific reading and outdo some of Jack the Ripper's mutilations for ghastliness. The full list is better left unsaid; a few examples will be more than enough.

Isabella Ruxton's legs, it was reported, were practically the same thickness from knee to ankle. One pair of legs had all the flesh sliced from the bones. Mary Rogerson had a slight cast in one eye. Ruxton cut her eyes from her skull.

The third operation he carried out almost defies imagination and evokes an allegedly true ghost story by the late American writer and journalist Alexander Woolcott.

A young doctor was invited to spend a weekend with some old friends at an old house in Kent. He arrived at night while his hosts were out, so he let himself in and went to bed. In classic ghost story fashion a storm was raging which caused a power failure. A peal of thunder woke him, and in the corner of the room he saw a ghostly seated figure which appeared to be stitching, or doing embroidery.

He leapt out of bed and ran downstairs, just as his delayed hosts turned up in their car.

The doctor and friends started on a cold meal that had been laid out for them and the doctor told them of the ghost he had seen. No one believed him. The hostess went into the kitchen for some wine. She screamed; the other rushed in. On the floor was the body of the woman cook. The body, but not the head. It had been hacked off with a cleaver.

Suddenly the doctor realised what he had seen.

> 'Clutching a candle in one hand, he dragged his host to the room from which he had fled, tiptoeing the final steps. The precaution was wasted, for a regiment could not have disturbed the rapt contentment of the ceremony still in progress within. The lunatic had not left his seat . . . Between his knees he still held the head of the woman he had killed. Scrupulously he was plucking out the grey hairs one by one.'

Dr Ruxton decapitated Isabella Ruxton and then drew fourteen of her teeth so that her mouth wouldn't match her dental records.*

* There was medical evidence that fourteen of her teeth had been recently

Ruxton worked swiftly through that unimaginable night, but necessary haste made him careless. The house was in an indescribable condition. Blood was everywhere: on the stairs, on the bathroom walls, floor and fittings. The bathroom looked like a slaughter-house, and the bath itself was stained with blood to within a few inches of the top. Some of it was Ruxton's own. His hand, made slippery by his victims' blood, lost its grip on the scalpel and he accidentally cut his hand to the bone.

His heart must have been pounding so hard that it seemed that it drowned out every other sound, and yet he was listening intently for the tiniest sound from his children's bedroom. If one of his children woke and came out on to the landing while he was moving around the bodies he would be lost.

Which one of the two women he dissected first is uncertain, and not really important. What we can be fairly sure of is that he carried into his bedroom the parcels of flesh, now largely drained of blood, that had once been a human being and dumped them on to the bed, next to his second victim. He carried this woman's body into the bathroom without difficulty, the great surges of adrenalin into his bloodstream giving him unnatural strength.

The first streaks of daylight began to lighten the sky before he had finished his butchery. And with a shock he remembered that although it was a Sunday (15th September) the charwoman Mrs Agnes Oxley was due

---

extracted, although the dental expert said it was impossible to say whether this had been done just before or after death. However, there was no evidence that Mrs Ruxton had recently been to a dentist or had ordered false teeth. In view of the other mutilations Ruxton carried out on the bodies, there is an irresistible presumption that he pulled the teeth as well. At the trial, among the exhibits from his house was a pair of dental forceps.

to arrive at 7.15 a.m. She came to the house every day to do most of the heavy cleaning and some cooking. She worked all the hours God and Dr Ruxton sent.

Ruxton locked the doors of the bathroom and his bedroom, and left his children alone in the house with the tangled mass of flesh and bone that had been their mother and nursemaid. He now set out on the horrendous, Sisyphean task of cleaning the house of all traces of blood. For his misdeeds on earth Sisyphus was condemned in Hades to roll a heavy stone to the top of a hill. When it reached the summit it rolled back down again, making his punishment eternal. Ruxton must have felt that his own task was equally never-ending: as soon as he cleaned up one set of bloodstains he found more.

He arrived at the Oxley home at about 6.30 a.m. A surprised George Oxley opened the door to him: Dr Ruxton had never called at their house that early.

'Tell Mrs Oxley not to trouble to come down this morning,' he said. 'Mrs Ruxton and Mary have gone away on a holiday to Edinburgh and I'm taking the children to Morecambe; but she should come as usual tomorrow.'

Mrs Oxley was on the stairs at the time and she overheard the brief exchange between her husband and the doctor. It was her turn to be surprised, for she hadn't missed a day's work since she had been employed by the Ruxtons.

Dr Ruxton hurried back home where he soon would have to help his children get up and to give them their breakfasts. It defies comprehension how Ruxton managed to get through the rest of that day without breaking down completely. He had spent a sleepless night of ghastly activity that few men could have survived and remained sane – if indeed Ruxton *was* sane at that time. He was walking the most slender of tightropes. Now all he wanted to do was finish without

interruption the awful task of dealing with the remains
of the two women he had murdered.

It wasn't going to work out that way.

At 9 a.m. Miss Winifred Roberts rang the bell at 2
Dalton Square to deliver the *News of the World, The
People* and the *Sunday Pictorial* for Graves News-
agents. These were, of course, precisely the kinds of
newspapers that would be most interested in subsequent events of Dr Ruxton's life. There was no answer,
so Miss Roberts went away for about ten minutes
before returning to ring again. She persisted in trying to
get an answer because she had to collect payment for
two weeks' papers. After some three minutes her
knocking was answered. To her surprise Ruxton
himself opened the door. He was wearing a pale cream
shirt and light grey trousers, and kept his right hand out
of sight. Miss Roberts thought it was because he was
holding up his trousers with that hand before she
realised that he was wearing braces. She commented,
'He appeared to be very agitated.' Understandably; it
takes no great feat of imagination to guess what the
doctor had been doing.

Miss Roberts apologised for disturbing him, and
Ruxton explained why he had opened the door himself:
'My maid is away with my wife in Scotland.'

At about 10 a.m. Mrs Margaret Hindson arrived as
usual to deliver four pints of milk. She, too, was
surprised when Ruxton himself answered the bell, for
normally Mary Rogerson or Mrs Oxley took in the
milk. Ruxton then told her that his wife and the maid
had gone away *with the children*.

First contradiction.

He added that he had 'jammed' his hand.

Mrs Hindson entered the house and made for the
scullery at the end of the passage on the ground floor,
but Ruxton stopped her and told her to put the milk on
the hall table.

Less than a quarter of an hour later there was another knock at the door. The effect on Ruxton's overstrung nerves can easily be imagined. This time it was Thomas Partridge, a labourer who also delivered newspapers, for another newsagent. Partridge knocked several times in vain, so finally he slipped a copy of the *Sunday Graphic* under the door. This innocent-looking newspaper turned out to be a vital link in the chain of evidence that was to bind Ruxton.

A quarter of an hour after this, the frantically busy Ruxton drove his Hillman car to the Midland Station Garage, where he was only an infrequent customer. He bought two two-gallon tins of petrol which the attendant put in the back of the car. From there Ruxton drove to another garage in Nelson Street – again, not his usual garage – where he had four gallons put into the tank. If Ruxton thought that by using unaccustomed garages he was leaving no trail he was being extremely naive. He was well-known in the town, he was an Indian in a time when Empire immigrants were very few, and his manner on this morning after a night of murder was far from being unremarkable.

He returned home, but had hardly drawn breath when there was yet another knock on the door. Mrs Isabella Whiteside, her small son Ronald, and a friend, Mrs Gilbert were on Ruxton's doorstep. Mrs Whiteside had an appointment for a minor operation on her son.

Ruxton opened the door about a foot and looked round it. 'I'm sorry, Mrs Whiteside,' he said, 'but I can't perform the operation today as my wife is away in Scotland and there is just me and *my little maid*, and we're busy taking up the carpets for the decorators in the morning.'

Second contradiction.

'Look how dirty my hands are,' he added, holding out his left hand.

Dr Ruxton's next problem was to get his children out

of the house while he cleaned up, as best he could, the bathroom and bedroom. Fortunately for him he was very friendly with the Andersons, a dentist and his wife who lived in Morecambe, some three and a half miles away. They had known each other for about eighteen months, in which time Herbert Anderson developed a high regard for the doctor. Ruxton drove over to the Anderson home with his three children, where he was received by Mrs Ethel Anderson. 'Will you do me the favour of keeping the children with you for the day?' he asked. 'Isabella has gone away with Mary for a few days.'

'Of course,' Mrs Anderson replied. She noticed that his right hand was bandaged. 'What's wrong with it?' she asked.

'I cut it with a tin opener this morning, making breakfast for the children. I've got one or two cases to deal with, and I'll be back later for the children,' Ruxton said gratefully.

Back home in Dalton Square Ruxton was able to take a calm – a relatively calm – and lengthy look at the house. When he fully realised just how much blood there was he must have been appalled. He worked at cleaning up for four hours, but there was still so much to do that he decided to seek help.

It was now that he made one of the first of his major blunders in trying to cover his traces.

The next reasonable step he could have taken was to get either Mrs Oxley or Mrs Elizabeth Curwen, another charwoman who normally worked every day at the doctor's house, to come and give him a hand. Unaccountably he went to a Mrs Mary Hampshire, a woman who had been his patient for six or seven years, but who had never worked at the house. What he said to her on that day after the murders and on subsequent occasions went a long way to help put the noose round his neck.

Ruxton drove to Bulk Road, where Mrs Hampshire lived. Her son Alwyn was standing outside the house when Ruxton arrived. He shouted to Alwyn to ask if his mother was in. 'If she is I want her to come to my house and clean up a bit. I'm having the decorators in and I've pulled the carpets up. I need some help because I've cut my hand.'

Alwyn went inside the house and gave his mother the message. A few moments later she came out, got into Ruxton's car and went with him to Dalton Square. On the way she enquired how he'd cut his hand, and Ruxton gave her the same explanation he had given the others: he had cut it badly opening a tin of fruit.

'Where's Mrs Ruxton?' Mrs Hampshire said next.
'She is in *Blackpool*.'
Third contradiction.
'What about Mary?' Mrs Hampshire went on.
'*She's gone on holiday*.'
Fourth contradiction.

When they got to the house Mrs Hampshire must have been rather taken aback to find how the other half lived. The wireless was blaring away although there was no one in the place. The stair carpet had been taken up and the stairs themselves were 'very, very dirty', she later told the court. More: there was *straw* from the hallway right up to the top story of the house. 'It was just as if someone had been carrying an armful of straw and bits had fallen off as the person had walked up the stairs,' she explained with rare insight.

Ruxton said he would pay her 7s 6d (37p) to scrub down the stairs. Next he showed her into Mary's room, and then into the bathroom.

If a blaring radio and dirty stairs with straw on them hadn't surprised Mrs Hampshire, the condition of the bath certainly did. It was very dirty yellow, right up to about six inches from the top. She scrubbed at it hard with hot water and Vim, but the stains would not come

off. There was so much work to be done that Dr
Ruxton agreed that she could get her husband to come
and help her.

Dr Ruxton left her working in the house while he
went off, to go back to the Andersons in Morecambe.
While he was out Mrs Hampshire made some
interesting discoveries. If she had realised their
implications she would have been out of the house like
a greyhound out of its trap. There was straw sticking
out from under the doors of the two bedrooms. She
tried to open the doors so she could get at the straw to
sweep it up, but they were both locked and the keys
weren't to be seen. All the other doors in the house
were unlocked. Beyond those locked doors were the
dismembered bodies of Isabella Ruxton and Mary
Rogerson. When Mrs Hampshire finally learned how
near she had been to discovering the ghostly secret of
that house she must have had nightmares.

On that Sunday afternoon of 15th September she
went out into the yard where she found several carpets,
staircarpets and landing carpets. They were all stained
with blood, one of them heavily stained. On these
carpets were a number of equally unusual objects.
There was a bloodstained shirt and some badly stained
large towels, which were partly burnt. Later Ruxton
told her that he had tried to burn the towels using
petrol, but they were too wet. In the doctor's waiting
room were some more rolled-up carpets and stairpads,
and a suit.

Ruxton, meanwhile, was at the Andersons' home.
He invited them to go for a drive, but Herbert
Anderson was still in bed. He suggested that the
Ruxton children should stay with them overnight
because of Ruxton's cut hand. Ruxton gladly accepted.

He drove Mrs Anderson and his children to
Lancaster to pick up the children's night things,
stopping on the way at the home of Mary Rogerson's

parents in Thornton Road, Morecambe. They weren't in, but Mr William Risby, who was staying in the house, answered the door.

'Will you tell Mary's parents that she has gone away to Scotland for a week or a fortnight, please? I handed Mary's wages to her sister.'

'I'll tell them,' Risby said obligingly.

Ruxton, Mrs Anderson and the children arrived back at Dalton Square at about 7 p.m. Ruxton and the two older children, Elizabeth and Diane, went into the house to get the children's things. Just before the doctor came downstairs with the night clothes, Mr Hampshire arrived.

'Come into the waiting room,' Ruxton said to the Hampshires. 'The carpets and suit: if they're any use to you, you can have them. Mind you, the suit's badly stained and in a bad condition, but it's a good suit and you can always have it cleaned.'

The Hampshires accepted with pleasure, but when they gave the suit a good look they were taken aback by the amount of blood on it. 'I wore it this morning when I cut my hand,' Ruxton explained. And then he told Mrs Hampshire, 'If you want the carpets in the yard you can have them, too.' However, the Hampshires couldn't take them away that same evening because by then it was raining heavily and the carpets were soaking wet.

Whether it was generosity, a simple desire to get rid at all costs of the suit and carpets or plain stupidity, of all the mistakes Ruxton made – and he made a whole host of them – giving the Hampshires the carpets and particularly the blood-stained suit was the most crass and eventually the most damaging to him.

He left the keys of the house with the Hampshires, telling them to turn off the lights and lock up when they had finished cleaning. They worked on until 9.30 p.m. Ruxton, meanwhile, went off with Mrs Anderson and his children back to Morecambe. On the way back he stopped the car at a chemist's shop and asked Mrs Anderson to buy 2lb of cotton wool. There is a strong presumption that Ruxton wanted so much cotton wool late on a Sunday night to mop up the blood from the dismembered bodies. It follows that Ruxton got Mrs Anderson to make the purchase because he wanted there to be no trace of his buying it himself. It was a feeble attempt at covering his tracks, but not the only one Ruxton made after the murders.

Ruxton's busy day was still not yet over. He left the youngest child with Mr Anderson and took Mrs Anderson and the other two children for a drive to see the illuminations. Trying to be a cheerful companion must have strained his patience to the limit. Weighing heavily on his mind was the fact that there were still the remains of two bodies at Dalton Square to be disposed of. He left the Andersons' house at about 9.30 p.m. From then until 7.30 a.m. the next morning no one could say where he was and what he was doing.

It is almost exactly 100 miles from Lancaster to Moffat. There was time enough for him to take the first of his grisly parcels there and dump them in the Linn.

Next morning, Monday 16th September, the charwoman, Mrs Oxley, turned up as usual at about 7.10 a.m. She kept ringing for about half an hour without success. The postman called while she was trying to get in. Eventually Mrs Oxley got fed up and went home for a while. There can be no doubt that Ruxton had spent the night making his first trip to get rid of parts of the two bodies, and was still on his way back when Mrs Oxley and the postman called.

By now he realised what a mistake he had made in giving the suit and carpets to the Hampshires. At 9 a.m. he turned up at their home and walked straight in without knocking. His appearance shocked Mrs Hampshire. With disbelief she saw that the normally dapper doctor was unshaven, had no collar and tie and was wearing an old raincoat. He looked pale and haggard.

Mrs Hampshire remarked how ill he looked. Ruxton replied that he *was* ill: he had been up all night with the pain in his hand. There is no doubt that he deserved to look ill after the night he had spent. He must have driven two hundred miles, terrified every mile of it in case he had an accident and his bloody cargo was discovered. Now he had another well-founded fear. He was regretting the incriminating gifts he had made to Mrs Hampshire.

'What did you take away with you last night?' he asked Mrs Hampshire.

'The suit, the carpets and the stair pads that were in the waiting room.' It was the last thing Ruxton wanted to hear.

'Where's the suit now?' he asked urgently.

'On the table.'

Ruxton went to the table and picked up the suit.

'I didn't realise quite how dirty it was,' Ruxton said in one of his rare truthful statements. 'I'll take it away and have it cleaned.'

'Oh, no, doctor. As you've been good enough to give us the suit, the least I can do is pay for the cleaning,' Mrs Hampshire replied, taking possession of the suit again. Bloodstained or not, it was a valuable gift, and she wasn't going to lose it.

'Look inside the pocket,' Ruxton said.

Puzzled, Mrs Hampshire did so. Ruxton pointed out the maker's label with his own name on it.

'Get me a pair of scissors,' he ordered agitatedly. Mrs Hampshire found a pair for him, but Ruxton's hand was too badly cut for him to be able to use them.

'I'll cut it out after you've gone, doctor,' Mrs Hampshire promised him.

That wasn't good enough. 'No, do it now, do it now,'

he said. 'It's very undignified for a man to wear another
man's suit and for other people to know about it,' he
explained. Surprised, Mrs Hampshire cut out the label.
This didn't satisfy Ruxton either. 'Burn it, burn it now,'
he urged her. She threw it into the fire, and Ruxton
breathed a sigh of relief. If he thought that he would be
able to deny that the suit was his if ever the question
arose, once again he was being extraordinarily
ingenuous.

'Will you come to my house today?' Ruxton asked
next. 'My charwoman is ill and I need you to open the
door to my patients for me.'

'Where's Mrs Ruxton?' enquired Mrs Hampshire.

'She's in Edinburgh.'

'You ought to send for her to come back, as you're
that ill, doctor,' said Mrs Hampshire.

'Oh, I don't want to spoil her holiday.'

Doubtlessly glad to be able to earn some extra
money, Mrs Hampshire agreed to go to Dalton Square
a little later. In those days the poorer working classes
didn't question themselves too closely about the actions
of the professional classes. Nevertheless, the first
tentative suspicions should have begun to stir at the
back of Mrs Hampshire's mind. She had already seen
how badly the suit he had given her was stained: the
waistcoat was so stained with dried blood that Mrs
Hampshire had been unable to do anything with it.
Now she decided to have a look at the carpets.

Two of them weren't too bad: but the third . . .!

This third carpet was still damp with blood, although
it had not been out in the rain.

'I laid the third carpet in the back yard and threw
about twenty to thirty buckets of water on it to try to
wash the blood off, and the colour of the water that
came off was like blood,' she said later.

Mrs Hampshire put it on the clothesline to dry, and
on her washday she had another go at it with the yard

brush and water. Still she couldn't get the congealed blood off.

Despite all this blood, Ruxton's odd behaviour and the disappearance of Isabella Ruxton and Mary Rogerson, Mrs Hampshire had no suspicion of Ruxton until two days before he was actually arrested.

When Ruxton returned to his home, arriving at about 9.15 a.m., he found Mrs Oxley had come back and was waiting at the door. The first thing that struck her, as it had struck Mrs Hampshire, was how scruffy he looked. Then, as they entered the house together, she noticed that the hall light was burning although it was broad daylight.

Later this was to prove to be a crucial point. Ruxton said at his trial that he always left the light on in the hall when the house was empty, but he turned it off when someone was in the house. It was clear, then, that he had left the house the previous night, leaving the hall light on, and had not been back all night to turn it off.

Mrs Oxley asked him about his bandaged hand, and he replied, with typical extravagance, 'I cut it with a tin opener on Sunday. I lost gallons and gallons of blood, and I've drunk gallons and gallons of water.' She went into the surgery with him and helped him change the bandage on his hand.

She went upstairs and found that the doors to the doctor's bedroom, the dining room and drawing room were all locked, and the keys were nowhere to be seen. It was the first time that Mrs Oxley had ever known a room to be locked and the key not available. In the lounge was an untouched meal; in the circumstances it is not surprising that Ruxton didn't have much of an appetite. In the yard was a heap of burned material. Mrs Oxley left at about 12.10 p.m., closing the front door with its spring lock behind her.

Twenty minutes later Mrs Hampshire arrived as arranged and let herself in. The house was empty and the upstairs rooms were still locked. Ruxton returned at about an hour after this, 1.30 p.m.

Mrs Hampshire was in the waiting room. 'Why did you send for me, doctor?' she asked. 'There's nothing for me to do here.'

'I sent for you to give me courage,' came the extraordinary reply.

Ruxton ordered a meal to be sent from a restaurant, and while they were waiting for it to be delivered they went upstairs to the lounge. He looked awful, and once again Mrs Hampshire asked why he didn't send for his wife. This time he said she was *in London*.

Fifth contradiction.

'You're not telling the truth, doctor,' Mrs Hampshire said daringly. Just how much truth he wasn't telling she couldn't possibly have guessed.

'I'm the unhappiest man in the world. My wife has gone off with another man and left me with the three children. You make a friend of a man; you treat him as a friend and he eats at your table, and he makes love to your wife behind your back. It's terrible. I could forgive extravagance or anything else, but infidelity, never.' The overwrought doctor, whose hold on his sanity had been tenuous to the extreme, and whose nerves had been strained to screaming pitch, broke down and wept. Nevertheless, he soon recovered control of himself. He attended his surgery and saw several patients.

Monday was the day the dustmen called at Dalton Square. Ruxton asked the driver, who was in charge of four men, to come into the yard and clear it out, for which he would pay them. The bloodstained carpets, bloodstained shirt and partly-burnt shirt were still there, and more: a heap of burnt debris. Even more significant were small pieces of oilcloth, a hamper of straw and a part of a blue silk dress with glass buttons. Mary Rogerson used to wear a dress like that.

'What exactly do you want taken away?' the driver, Joseph Gardiner, asked him.

'Everything. If you clean up the yard thoroughly I'll pay you for it,' Ruxton promised.

The men set to work, but before they could take away the carpets Mrs Hampshire appeared and told them to leave them. Mrs Hampshire had her eye on them for herself, bloody or not.

That same day the restless Dr Ruxton took his Hillman car – registration number ATC 272 – to the County Garage in Morecambe for servicing. He asked the proprietor, Henry Hudson, for the loan of another car while his own was in the garage. Hudson offered him an 8 h.p. Ford, but that was too small. So Hudson took him along to the Grand Garage where he hired a big, four-seater 12 h.p. Austin, registration number CP 8415. Ruxton had some heavy delivering to do.

At 9.15 that evening Bobby Edmondson was driving home when the driver of a car he did not know signalled him to stop. To his surprise he found that the driver was Dr Ruxton. He was quite affable with Edmondson and asked him how he was getting on with his professional examinations. Then, in answer to Edmondson's questions Ruxton said that Mrs Ruxton had his Hillman (it was at the garage being serviced), and had gone to Scotland for a few days with Mary Rogerson *and the children*.

Sixth contradiction, plus another pointless lie.

Ruxton drove on to the Andersons' home in Morecambe and asked if the children could stay another night. The Andersons agreed. Mr Anderson looked at Ruxton's cut hand, which had a diagonal cut across three fingers, exposing the bone on one of them.

'Good heavens! I'd like to see the tin-opener that did *that*,' Anderson said.

'I've seen enough of it; I've thrown it away,' Ruxton replied.

He left for home at about 11.30 p.m. and went to bed at midnight.

The next day, Tuesday 17th September, Mrs Oxley called as usual just after seven o'clock and was let in by Dr Ruxton. She made breakfast and packed some clothes for the children. Ruxton left at 9 a.m., called back briefly with the children to get some more clothes, and then took them to school. Mary Holmes, daughter of a decorator Arthur Holmes, said that Ruxton called to see her father at about midday, but he was out.

According to her, Ruxton told her that her father should have come to Dalton Square to redecorate the staircase the previous day, Monday 16th. Although a provisional booking had been made for the middle of September for Holmes to do some work at the doctor's house, no firm date had been fixed. Ruxton, of course, was trying to establish that Holmes was expected on Monday 16th September to explain why he had stripped the staircase, but this ad hoc plan to cover his tracks, like so many of his others, misfired.

Ruxton insisted that he called on the Monday 16th; it seems highly unlikely that he called on Tuesday 17th at midday. Norman Birkett, Ruxton's counsel, pointed out to Miss Holmes that some thirty-five minutes after she said Ruxton was talking to her, Ruxton, driving the hired Austin, was involved in a motor accident with a cyclist, Bernard Beattie, in Kendal, twenty miles away, on his way back towards Lancaster. Mr Beattie was knocked off his cycle and was shaken up, but not badly injured; his cycle, however, was a write-off.

Ruxton didn't stop after the accident, probably hoping to get away with it. After all, he had weightier matters on his mind.

He was out of luck. Beattie managed to note the number of the car, CP 8415, and report it to the police. It is often said that you can never find a policeman when you want one. Ruxton found one when he didn't want to: at Milnthorpe, seven miles south of Kendal and thirteen miles north of Lancaster, PC James Lowther, a point-duty policeman, stopped him at about 1 p.m.

Ruxton admitted that he had been involved in an accident in Kendal, and when he was cautioned he became almost hysterical and incoherent. One thing that he did say clearly and repeatedly, however, was that he had been to Carlisle on business and was returning to Lancaster. It is 67 miles from Lancaster to Carlisle, and 54 miles back to Kendal: approximately 120 miles in all. Now, if Miss Holmes was correct in saying that Ruxton visited her in Lancaster at midday, even a flat-out Formula One racing driver could not have done the journey Ruxton said he had done in thirty-five minutes. Assuming that Ruxton did actually leave Lancaster at the time he claimed, between 10.45 a.m. and 11 a.m. he did 120 miles in a little more than an hour and a half – certainly less than two hours – without allowing for any time spent in conducting his 'business', in a 1935 12 h.p. car on 1935 roads. Quite impossible. Stating that he had been to Carlisle was pure Walter Mitty stuff. It was a typical example of Ruxton's bad habit of saying the first thing that came into his head. In fact this eventually proved to be a fatal habit.

Ruxton later changed his original story when the timing proved it to be false. He said that he had left Lancaster to go to Seatle,* not Carlisle. A Mrs Edith Holme (not to be confused with Miss Holmes, the decorator's daughter) had a cottage in the village where she let rooms during the summer. The Ruxton children and Mary had stayed there earlier in the year. Ruxton said he wanted to make arrangements for the youngest

* Contemporary reports spell this Seattle, but modern maps and the Post Office Directory use the spelling Seatle.

child, Billie, to stay with Mrs Holme.

He explained that he left Lancaster between 10.45 a.m. and 11 a.m., but he lost his way and returned via Windermere and Kendal. Seatle is a very small village off the A590 Grange-over-Sands to Windermere road and it is not unlikely that someone could lose his way. Ruxton, though, had visited the place seven or eight times previously. (He said that he *always* lost his way going there.)

Why he lied originally and told the foolish story of going to Carlisle is difficult to understand at first sight, but on closer consideration there is a possible reason, a rather sinister one. He did not want to admit where he had really been because he had made the trip to dump one or more of his parcels of human remains, and 'Carlisle' sprang to mind because he had passed through there on the Sunday night when he made his first trip to dispose of pieces of body. It is true that all the parcels of flesh and bones that turned up were found in Scotland, but there were many parts of the two bodies that were never accounted for. They could have been disposed of anywhere. What makes this theory so chilling is that he had his youngest child, Billie, in the car with him.

Another charwoman, Mrs Mabel Smith, now enters the story. She normally worked four afternoons a week, 2 p.m. to 7 p.m., Monday to Thursday. She hadn't reported for work on Monday 16th because of a dental appointment, but turned up on Tuesday afternoon at 2 p.m., while Ruxton was still on his way back from Milnthorpe and his encounter with the police. There were ten to 12 patients in the waiting room: Ruxton's claims to have a busy practice were not exaggerated.

When she prepared to do some cleaning she found that the door of Ruxton's bedroom was locked and there was no sign of the key. Soon afterwards Ruxton

arrived in the hired Austin. He told her to start
stripping the paper from the walls from the top of the
stairs down to the bathroom.

The third regular servant, Mrs Curwen, a cook-
general, had been unaware of all the enormous activity
that had been going on at the Ruxton home since the
murder late on Saturday night. This poor woman
normally worked every day of the week, starting at
8.30 a.m. and going on until any time between
7.45 p.m. and 11 p.m. – sometimes a 15-hour day.
Sundays she could take things easily: she didn't start
until 10 a.m.

On Friday 13th September she had turned up for
work as usual, but there was nothing for her to do, and
Ruxton told her not to come until the following
Monday. She wasn't feeling well on that day – which is
not surprising, considering the long hours she worked –
and she didn't go to the Ruxton home. On this Tuesday
17th Ruxton went to Mrs Curwen's home and asked her
to come and take Billie out as Mrs Ruxton and Mary
Rogerson were on holiday in Edinburgh.

She took Billie out, and then in the afternoon she
started a fire in the yard under Ruxton's supervision,
and both she and Mrs Smith kept the fire going. At
first, at least, only papers were burned, and neither
woman saw Ruxton add anything to the flames. Mrs
Curwen stayed in the house until 7.45 p.m. that
Tuesday evening.

Ruxton appeared to have a fixation on fires. Before
she left he told her to make a large fire in the waiting
room: he was going to stay up all night as he couldn't
sleep with Mrs Ruxton being away.

That night two sisters, Dorothy and Catherine
Mather, a domestic servant and a shop assistant
respectively, who lived near Ruxton, saw the reflection
of a fire on the wall of the County Cinema, which
formed one side of the yard of the Ruxton house. It was

blazing fiercely at eight o'clock, and when they came back from a visit to the cinema the fire was still burning brightly. At midnight it was burning brightly enough to read by, Catherine Mather asserted. It is extraordinary how Ruxton allowed attention to be drawn to himself by lighting what was virtually a beacon, at a time when he surely wanted to be unobserved and unnoticed.

Ruxton vainly denied that there had been a fire at all that night. He said that he had been at the Andersons' home that evening and he brought his children home at about 10.30 p.m. Mrs Anderson later testified that he was at their home in the morning, not the evening.

Next day, Wednesday 18th September, the Ruxton house was swarming with people and buzzing with activity. Mrs Oxley and Mrs Curwen turned up for work in the morning. Mrs Anderson telephoned, leaving a message for Ruxton to pick up his two younger children Diane and Billie to take them to the carnival in Morecambe for the day. And, of course, there were many patients who wanted to see the doctor.

Mrs Smith arrived in the afternoon and got on with her work of stripping the paper from the walls of the staircase. While she was doing this something on the casement curtains of the window below the top landing caught her eye. She looked closer. They had bloodstains on them. She called Mrs Oxley and Mrs Curwen, who also saw the stains. Mrs Curwen took down the curtains and put them in the linen basket.

Dr Ruxton saw the activity and asked what was going on. When Mrs Curwen told him where she had put the curtains he rescued them from the basket and tore off the bottom part that was bloodstained and burned it in the kitchen fire. He gave the rest to the two women to use as dusters. Jokingly he remarked that the police would be saying next that he had murdered Mrs Smalley, a woman who had been found dead at

Morecambe and whose death the police were investigating.

Blood . . . blood . . . Next Mrs Smith found two bloodstains on one of the bathroom walls. There seemed no end to it.

In the afternoon Ruxton went to Morecambe where he took Mrs Anderson and his two youngest children, Diane and Billie, to see the carnival. The eldest child, Elizabeth, took part in the procession. Later that day the active Dr Ruxton took back the hired Austin car and picked up his own Hillman.

He returned to the Anderson home with Elizabeth between five and six o'clock, then hurried back to Lancaster to take his evening surgery before coming back to the Andersons' at about eight o'clock. He was hardly lively company: he was so exhausted that he fell asleep in an armchair in the front room. He went home at last at a quarter to one in the morning. The children remained with the Andersons overnight.

The next day, Thursday 19th, Ruxton must have believed he was near the end of his mammoth task of getting rid of all the evidence of the murders. He started the day by asking Mrs Oxley to get his breakfast in a hurry, because he was going to see a specialist about his hand. She was working in the kitchen at half-past seven when he brought his car to the back door. He entered the house, and as he passed the kitchen, he closed the door. Out of her sight he made several trips between the upstairs rooms and his car. Once again, imagination does not have to be strained to guess that he was carrying down parcels of the remains of the two women. His final instructions to Mrs Oxley as he set off at eight o'clock were to take the key when she left at lunchtime and give it to Mrs Curwen, and to tell her to inform any patients who called that if he were not back by three o'clock he would be back at seven.

Eight o'clock to three – seven hours, time enough to

drive to Moffat and back in daylight. It was another drive that would have strained the strongest nerves. He had got away with the first trip without any incident that might have led to the discovery of what he had in the car with him. The tension of this last drive must have been almost unbearable, as he felt that it was all that stood between him and safety. But one small accident, one unforeseen incident could mean disaster.

His account of what he did on this day underlined one of the obsessions that had bedevilled him in the days before he murdered his wife. He said he decided to go to Blackburn to spy on his wife and Bobby Edmondson; he suspected them of meeting secretly at an office which Isabella Ruxton had rented to carry on a bookmaking business. The trips up and down stairs that morning were to fetch a camera and tripod so he could photograph Edmondson's car if it was outside Mrs Ruxton's office. He picked a Thursday to go because if his wife thought he might be following her she would expect it to be on a Wednesday or a Sunday, his off days, and so she would be off her guard on a Thursday.

After Ruxton left the house that morning Mrs Oxley found that all the doors in the house that had been locked were now unlocked. She noticed an unpleasant smell which came from Ruxton's room and the dining room. Mrs Curwen turned up earlier than expected, only half an hour after Ruxton's departure, and found Mrs Oxley alone in the house. She agreed with Mrs Oxley about the smell and where it came from, but later said that the doors were still locked on that Thursday, and the door to Ruxton's room was not unlocked until the following day.

Mrs Smith arrived in the house later that Thursday, and she remarked on the smell. She identified the source as on the first-floor landing near the drawing room and dining room. Despite the conflicts of evidence it is evident that there was definitely an unpleasant smell in the house, and at one day towards the end of that week doors which had been locked previously were now unlocked.

Dorothy Neild, the Andersons' maid, brought Ruxton's children back to Dalton Square at half-past two that afternoon and left them with Mrs Curwen. Half an hour or so later Ruxton drove up to his house, coming from the north. When Mrs Hampshire came into his surgery, this time as a patient, he immediately asked her if she'd had the suit cleaned. Mrs Hampshire said that she had. It wasn't true, but she didn't want to get into an argument about it.

It was at some time about this date that Mrs Curwen noticed some unusual material in the rubbish that was being burned every afternoon in the back yard. She saw a swab of cotton wool with blood on it, pieces of partly-burned blue and red material, and what looked like three handles from a travelling case, all partly burned. The blue material resembled a coat that Mary Rogerson owned, and the red material a dressing gown which she used to wear.

With the unerring perception of hindsight it is extraordinary that the women who were so often in the house and could see Ruxton at close quarters suspected nothing. Goodness knows the signs were there: Ruxton said that his wife and Mary Rogerson had left suddenly for a holiday, without a word to anyone else; everyone knew the Ruxtons had ferocious rows involving physical violence; he threatened her life on a number of occasions; the Ruxtons were notorious for their bitter public quarrels; there was all that blood, on the stairs, in the bathroom, on Ruxton's suit; the locked rooms, the straw on the stairs; Ruxton's odd behaviour; the fires; the burned clothes and bloodstained towels . . . and the smell.

Yet perhaps it is not so surprising after all. Ruxton

was a doctor, and so was held in great respect by domestic servants. In 1935 in the provinces you didn't suspect doctors of dreadful villainy. Doctors are respectable. There was, too, the fact that the women who worked for him didn't want to believe ill of him, subconsciously at least. He gave them work, and work at that time was hard to come by.

That evening of that same crucial Thursday a fire was seen in the yard at half-past eight, and it was still burning at eleven o'clock. One witness saw Ruxton stirring up the fire. While he was making efforts to burn what was obviously his wife's and Mary Rogerson's clothes, so he could say that the two women had taken all their things with them, he was interrupted by a phone call. At about 10.15 p.m. Miss Beryl Beckett, a midwife, was attending a case at Skerton, between Lancaster and Morecambe. There were serious problems and so she telephoned Ruxton, who was the patient's doctor. He said he couldn't go because he had hurt his hand *with his car* – another of his pointless, spur-of-the-moment lies which would help get him into so much trouble later.

Beryl Beckett saw Ruxton the next day in connection with another case and he repeated to her that he had hurt his hand on the car. Then, to her astonishment, he ran out of the room.

That next day, Friday 20th, Mrs Curwen prepared lunch for Dr Ruxton. While he was eating it she observed that there was a nasty, stuffy smell in the house. Ruxton agreed, and told her to buy a spray and some eau-de-Cologne. He also told her that the previous day he had been to Blackburn, and he had walked up and down the street in front of Mrs Ruxton's office to see if he could spot her.

Later that day Bobby Edmondson saw Ruxton outside the house in his own car, the Hillman. Ruxton again affably asked him how he was getting on with his examinations. Then he volunteered the information that his wife's betting business had collapsed, and she and her sister were going to London. Ruxton was guilty of a serious oversight here. Earlier, when Edmondson saw him in a hired car, he told him that Mrs Ruxton had taken the (Hillman) car to Edinburgh. (In fact, as we know and was easily proved, it was being serviced at a local garage.) Now, here it was back at Ruxton's home. Yet Ruxton said nothing of his wife having returned.

At about five o'clock Ruxton went to a Miss Bessie Philbrook, who was another of his patients and who knew Isabella Ruxton socially. From time to time she took the Ruxton children out for walks. He asked her to take the children out while Mrs Curwen did some shopping. Miss Philbrook agreed, so Ruxton took her back to his house in his car. During the journey he said that his wife and Mary Rogerson were in Scotland. By now he had thought up another reason for their being away. Quite inconsequentially Ruxton asked Miss Philbrook if she knew that Mary was pregnant. It was a suggestion he would make to other people during the course of the next few days, when he elaborated the story by saying he thought Mrs Ruxton had taken Mary away to have an illegal abortion.

In 1935 the attitude towards abortions was far less liberal than it is today: very few legal abortions were performed, and arranging one was something that was done with the utmost secrecy. Probably Ruxton thought that this would stop Mary's friends and relatives making enquiries about her. This shabby ruse failed completely.

Miss Philbrook took the children home at seven o'clock, when Ruxton asked her to put the children to bed. She did so and stayed with them until ten o'clock while Ruxton made some house calls. The obliging Miss Philbrook baby-sat for the Ruxton children again on Sunday night while the doctor went to Morecambe.

The unfortunate Ruxton children were being shuttled around, between friends, servants and patients like stateless refugees. While the doctor was out Peter Rogerson, Mary's brother, called and was told he would have to come another time. When Ruxton got home at ten o'clock and learned of the call he said rather unpleasantly that Mary's brother was after her wages.

After all the massive cleaning by three charwomen, a patient and her husband (the Hampshires), fires over several days, a clear-out of the yard by the council dustmen and a successful disposal of the human remains, Ruxton must have thought that he had finally managed to eliminate all traces of the murders. But his efforts were like one of the labours of Heracles: whenever he cut off one of the heads of the Hydra, more grew in its place.

On Monday 23rd – Mondays were washing days at 2 Dalton Square – Mrs Smith turned out the linen basket at the top floor of the house. A white silk nightgown fell out. It had a bloodstain as big as the palm of her hand on the shoulder. Mrs Smith washed the nightgown and got the stain out, but didn't wash away the memory of what she saw.

It was about this time that Ruxton came into the kitchen where Mrs Oxley and Mrs Curwen were having breakfast. Mrs Smith, who normally worked in the afternoons, entered. She said that she had been interviewed by the police.

Ruxton immediately started 'shouting and carrying on', to use Mrs Oxley's expression.

'You know that this has always been an open house and you can go in and out of every room when you like!' He had conveniently forgotten the locked rooms, and the three women didn't care to remind him. Mrs Smith tried to mollify the doctor by saying 'People must be daft.'

'Yes, that's the word for it. They're daft,' Ruxton said, and stalked out of the kitchen.

Peter Rogerson turned up again that evening. Ruxton invited him in and explained that Mrs Ruxton and Mary had gone on a week's or a fortnight's tour.

'It's not unusual for me not to hear from Mrs Ruxton when she's away, but have you heard anything from Mary?' Ruxton asked. He went on, 'Has Mary had any trouble at home? Do you know anything of her going with a laundry boy?'

Peter Rogerson firmly said 'No' to both questions.

Ruxton ended the discussion by telling Rogerson that Mary had drawn her wages for the previous week in advance, and gave him the fifteen shillings for the current week.

He rounded off the day by getting Miss Philbrook to babysit for him again while he went to the local cinema to see *Clive of India*. It took a special sort of character to be able to do that – not good, but special.

The next day, Tuesday 24th, Ruxton, his confidence growing, changed tactics and switched from defence to attack. He charged into the detective office at Lancaster Town Hall where John Cook, a municipal employee, was on duty. Ruxton loudly complained about his servants being questioned concerning the death of Mrs Smalley. 'People are actually accusing me of killing her!' This was all news to Cook, and he said so.

'Look at my hand,' Ruxton went on, and he started unwinding the bandage on his right hand.

'No, don't do that, please,' Cook asked, but Ruxton was determined. He took off the bandage, which was sticking to the wounds in his hand. There were wounds on the little finger and third finger near the second joint. The cut on the little finger was particularly severe, Cook said later. As we know, Ruxton's friend, Herbert Anderson the dentist, noticed that the bone was exposed on this finger.

Meanwhile an officer from Blackburn, Detective Inspector John Moffat, who was investigating the death of Mrs Smalley, interviewed Mrs Curwen at the Lancaster Police Office that same day. At some time between three and four o'clock in the afternoon Ruxton burst in on him. It was a strange coincidence that the detective's name was Moffat, the same as the place where Ruxton had dumped the parcels of human remains; but Ruxton was too wound up to think about that.

Ruxton overwhelmed the detective inspector with a torrent of words. Moffat admitted that he could not write down a quarter of all that Ruxton actually said, he spoke so fast. As best as Moffat could remember – and he made his notes immediately after the interview – Ruxton said, 'Look here, Inspector Moffat, what the hell do the police want inquiring about my private affairs for? I don't know Mrs Smalley. I have enough trouble on my mind.' That was no exaggeration. 'Come across and search my house and interview the whole damned lot of us. It is nothing but professional jealousy. I am the most progressive doctor in this town. I have over two thousand patients on my panel and every doctor is jealous of me. Why should you be making enquiries about a professional man's affairs?'

Inspector Moffat was not investigating the disappearance of the two women; in fact he had not even heard of the case. Ruxton, of course, could think of nothing else, and in his hysterical outburst he revealed one of the things that were worrying him most.

'I can have my house cleaned and decorated whenever I like, and I can help the paper-hangers to scrape the papers off the walls without you interfering . . . ' He was aware that the efforts suddenly to get rid of the staircarpets and to clean the staircase were highly suspicious. He put his hands to his head, grabbed hold of his hair and shook his head violently. 'I know nothing of Mrs Smalley,' he said, 'and I was never out of my house that Thursday night.' He also claimed that his wife had left a note for him before she disappeared, saying 'I am going away, don't worry . . . ' Of course, he was unable to produce this (non-existent) note.

The next day, Wednesday 25th, the restless Ruxton went out again. He called on John Cook again to complain of police activity that was giving rise to the gossip connecting his name with the death of Mrs Smalley. It was an inconclusive interview.

More importantly, in the morning he went to see Mrs Rogerson, Mary's stepmother, at her home in Thornton Road, Morecambe. There he reinforced the story he was trying to establish of Mary's friendship with a laundry boy and her pregnancy, and Mrs Ruxton's plan to take Mary away and have her pregnancy terminated. Mrs Rogerson, not unreasonably, said it was all news to her. He had better come back and see Mary's father.

That evening Ruxton returned to Thornton Road to see Mr James Rogerson. In the meantime he thought up one or two elaborations of his basic theme. He told Mr Rogerson that Mrs Anderson was at his house one day and remarked, 'Look at Mary. She's pregnant.' To which Ruxton replied, he said, 'My God, she is, and I as a doctor know she is.' It was another instance of saying too much, for Mrs Anderson later denied that the conversation ever took place. Ruxton was piling up lies, the combined weight of which would help to sink him. Had he not involved Mrs Anderson to add credibility to his slander he may have left some doubt in people's minds about Mary, even though there was no other evidence to support his allegation that she was pregnant. (In fact there was some evidence to suggest that she was not.)

Ruxton went on to say to Mrs Anderson, he told Mr

Rogerson, 'She could have gone away and had the baby and kept it all quiet, and then she could have come back to our house and nobody would have known.'

Not unreasonably Mr Rogerson had some difficulty in believing Ruxton's story. He pointed out that Ruxton hadn't mentioned this laundry boy's name or where he came from; and he had never heard in his life that she had a boy. In truth, it would have been extremely difficult for Mary to find time to have even a casual boyfriend. Whether or not he believed any part of Ruxton's account, Mr Rogerson's attitude to his daughter was unchanged: he wanted her back. 'That girl must come back whatever her condition,' he said stoutly.

Ruxton elaborated his story further. He said that his wife 'has some thirty or forty pounds with her, and they will be staying at some big hotel and having a good time.' Given Mary's character, nothing could be more unlikely.

Rogerson doggedly said that if Mary was not back by Saturday he would report Mary as a missing girl to the police. Ruxton reacted to this. The eternal optimist, he tried to buy some time, perhaps hoping to bolster the story of his innocence. 'Don't go to the police,' he asked, 'and I'll bring her back on Sunday.' It would have been quite a trick if he could have pulled it off.

Ruxton was now thrashing around wildly in his efforts to divert suspicion from himself, only to have precisely the opposite effect when all the stories were put together. The next day, Thursday 26th September, Ruxton went to the hairdresser's where he met a friend, James Jefferson, an insurance superintendent who lived in Morecambe and had known the Ruxtons for about six years. They went on to Dalton Square where Ruxton told Jefferson that he suspected his wife of having an affair with young Edmondson, and that she and Mary had left him. He went on to say that Mr

Rogerson had threatened to tell the police, adding the extraordinary comment, 'Of course you know the sort of man he is. He's a man who would go to the police about anything.' Perhaps Ruxton thought it unreasonable for anyone to be concerned about a missing daughter.

That same evening Miss Philbrook came to babysit for Ruxton while he went to the cinema. It is hardly surprising that he wanted to get his mind off reality.

There is a macabre irony about the next development in the case. Ruxton had promised Mr Rogerson that he would bring back Mary on the following Sunday. On that day, the 29th, the first remains of the dead girl and Mrs Ruxton were discovered in Moffat, although no one in Lancaster knew of it yet. Eventually the finding of the remains was reported in the press. Ruxton was reading the paper in bed when he saw a story which said that one of the bodies was that of a man. He was delighted, and called Mrs Oxley to the bedside.

'Sit down,' he said, and 'listen to this.' He read out a report of the Ravine Murder, as the case was called then, in the *Daily Express*. 'So you see, Mrs Oxley, it is a man and a woman. It's not our two.'

'I hope not,' Mrs Oxley replied, and Ruxton began to laugh.

On Tuesday 1st October Mary Rogerson's father and stepmother called at Dalton Square in the evening. Ruxton invited them in with every sign of concern. 'I can't get to know where they [Mrs Ruxton and Mary] are,' he apologised, and then elaborated his story of their disappearance, pushing it into near-fantasy. Of the thirty to forty pounds he mentioned to Mr Rogerson that they had taken he said, 'They broke into my safe and took thirty pounds out of it. But don't worry: they'll be back when the money's gone.' The Rogersons refused to be placated and said they would inform the police. That same day Mrs Rogerson went to the police station to report that Mary had been missing for some time.

By the following Friday, 4th October, Ruxton must have realised that it would look suspicious if he himself did not report his wife's absence, at least, to the police. So he returned to the police station where he told Detective Constable John Winstanley that his wife had left on 15th September and taken the maid with her. In an attempt to substantiate his story that his wife had gone off voluntarily he overwhelmed his listener with another of his non-stop tirades. Referring to his wife Ruxton said, 'She can't have any love for the children. Not even a postcard for Elizabeth.' He took out and read extracts from a letter which he said he had sent to his wife in Edinburgh and which had been returned to him. Nevertheless, he would take her back even now, he said.

From talking about his wife he switched to the subject of Mrs Smalley, complaining that his practice might suffer from his name being connected with the Mrs Smalley case, and he didn't even know the woman. Suddenly Ruxton, not the calmest of men at the best of times, became even more excited. He took a bunch of keys from his trouser pocket, slammed them on the table and said 'Go and search the house; I'll stop here.' Winstanley, who must have been bored to distraction, tried to quieten Ruxton, but without success. When the doctor was in one of his clamorous moods it would have taken a bucket of cold water to subdue him. The spectre of Isabella Ruxton's alleged affair with Bobby Edmondson suddenly arose before Ruxton once more. He said that Edmondson knew where his wife was, and he suggested that the police intercept letters addressed to Edmondson to see if they contained any reference to Mrs Ruxton. Winstanley told him, of course, that the police had no authority to do any such thing.

Ruxton next said that his telephone bills had been

excessive and he had asked the postal authorities (this was long before British Telecom) to keep a record of the calls from his house, and these authorities had told him that silly love talk had been overheard on the phone and that repeated calls were being made to the town hall. His excitement mounted, and he banged on the table saying, with an expression that was pure Bulldog Drummond or Greyfriars School, 'The blighter, I could murder him.' His creative imagination was working furiously, and he recounted an occasion when, he said, he had to look for a pair of trousers which he kept under a mattress, and found two photographs: one of Mrs Ruxton and the other of Bobby Edmondson, face to face. Ruxton tore them up and demanded that all relations between his wife and Edmondson end at once.

This last story is ludicrously improbable. Why would Mrs Ruxton keep photographs of herself and her 'lover' under *Ruxton*'s mattress, for she and her husband had separate rooms?

Before the murders Ruxton's overheated imagination often made him talk and act extravagantly; after them his grip on reality became tenuous at best. So many of the stories he told were either childishly easy to disprove – like the one concerning the overheard 'silly love talk' telephone conversations – or plain incredible like the photographs under the mattress one; but they were told with seemingly emphatic sincerity. The question arises whether he had lost that grip on reality to the point that he actually came to believe his repeated assertions that Mrs Ruxton and Mary had gone to Edinburgh.

Mrs Rogerson, meanwhile, was making her own enquiries about Mary's disappearance. The next day, Saturday 5th October, she left Morecambe and went to Ruxton's house to ask for the address of Mrs Curwen, the housekeeper. Her reason for this was that she had heard that Mrs Ruxton and Mary had gone away to open a bookmaker's office and Mrs Curwen had been clearing it out, so perhaps Mrs Curwen might be able to tell her where her stepdaughter was. Ruxton gave Mrs Rogerson the address, and after she had seen Mrs Curwen she returned to Ruxton.

'I feel so upset about it all,' Ruxton told her. 'When Mrs Curwen goes home at night and all is quiet I look at the photograph of my wife in the drawing room. Mary has been working in conjunction with my wife, deceiving me, and sometimes I feel as if I could choke them both.'

'I hope you wouldn't choke Mary,' the unknowing Mrs Rogerson said, alarmed – but much too late.

'Oh, no, Mrs Rogerson, I don't mean that. I'm frantic. I don't know what I'm saying. I feel as if I could gas myself, and would do, only for my poor children.'

Mrs Rogerson went home, seemingly still uncertain whether Ruxton was telling the truth.

That same day Ruxton went to see Robert Edmondson Sr., a cabinet maker, and asked where his son Bobby was. 'In Edinburgh, with some friends,' Edmondson replied.

'What's their address?' Ruxton asked. Edmondson found that Ruxton's general manner was extremely odd; and the sly way he asked the question made him think that there was something behind it all, and he asked Ruxton why he wanted to know. Ruxton immediately burst into tears.

'Pull yourself together and tell me what's wrong,' Edmondson told him.

'I'm sorry for you,' Ruxton said unexpectedly. 'I think a lot about your Bobby, but my wife was going to Edinburgh and Bobby is in Edinburgh and I know there have been telephone messages.'

Edmondson didn't ask Ruxton what messages, and how he knew, but he told Ruxton they could easily be explained as Bobby would be back that day.

'I know that Bobby and Barbara [his sister], and also my wife, stayed at the Adelphi Hotel,' Ruxton said and talked incessantly about that trip of 7th September. When he got wound up and started talking he became wearing and difficult to stop. Edmondson managed to get a word in, however, and to stop Ruxton going on talking he explained the details: Mrs Ruxton drove Barbara, while Bobby drove his parents. Nevertheless Ruxton said he would like to talk to Bobby. At that moment Mrs Edmondson and Barbara came into the room and Ruxton signalled to Edmondson not to say anything about the subject while they were within hearing.

When Bobby got back from Edinburgh he and his father discussed Ruxton's visit and decided they had better go to see Ruxton. Bobby Edmondson must have been rather mystified by the whole story, for Ruxton had been friendly and not mentioned Mrs Ruxton at all whenever they met.

The next day they called on Ruxton at Dalton Square, and Bobby Edmondson confirmed everything that his father had said the previous day. Ruxton then unstopped one of his relentless torrents of words. He went on about his wife's gambling, her untruthfulness and extravagance and many other irrelevancies. The Edmondsons remarked that he appeared overwrought and he controlled himself with difficulty, which was probably something of an understatement.

Rambling as Ruxton's relentless monologue was, one implication came through to Edmondson loud and clear. He demanded of Ruxton, 'Are you saying that my son has anything to do with Mrs Ruxton going away?'

'Oh, no, no,' Ruxton assured him.

'There'll be trouble if I hear you or anyone else mentioning my son's name in connection with Mrs Ruxton going away,' Edmondson warned flatly.

Despite these spirited exchanges they shook hands

and parted on friendly terms – or at least, not hostile ones. But Ruxton couldn't leave well alone. His final words to Bobby Edmondson were that he really wanted his wife back – there may have been more truth in this than either of the Edmondsons realised – and that he was sure she'd return some day. He asked Bobby to do what he could to get her to come back – if he ever heard from her, Ruxton added, or heard of her.

Notwithstanding this amicable goodbye, Ruxton soon afterwards went round to the house of an acquaintance, Thomas Harrison, and asked him if he had seen Mrs Ruxton. He added, 'Tell Bobby Edmondson not to interfere in my affairs and to keep away from my wife.'

On Monday 7th October, Isabella Ruxton's sister Mrs Nelson received a letter from Ruxton. The doctor was clearly as prolix in his letter-writing as he was in his speech.

> My dear Sister,
> I am heartbroken and half-mad. Isobel has again left me. She has done this trick again after about ten months. Do you remember she left me bag and baggage last November, when I came to your house. She told me she was going to Edin. to take sole agency for Lancashire from Mr Wm Murphy for his football pools.

Ruxton goes on to talk about his wife's betting habits and the bills she has run up. He continues:

> . . . She has bought clothes and things to the tune of over £100 from various shops in Lancaster. She has evidently been backing horses, and a prominent bookie in Lancaster is demanding £21.15 from her. The most important thing is that she is trying to help our maid who is in a certain condition. I hope she does not involve herself into

any trouble with the law, because she will be liable for helping her for such affairs.

The children are asking for her daily and I really cannot sleep without her. Mine is only the temper, but in my heart she is my all in all. She has taken my £30 and two gold coins – half-sovereign and a whole one. She has been telling me for the past so many months that she would like to go in business of her own. Do you think she needs to do all that? I am afraid I cannot knock sense into her. She is highly impulsive and thinks she can be a millionaire overnight. According to the latest information she is somewhere in Birmingham, but I cannot keep running after her. I have got a very bad hand and it is my right hand. It is all painful and swollen. I am intending to come over to Edin. on Wednesday to talk things over with you.

Ruxton next asks about any relations Mrs Nelson and his wife may have in Canada and suggests that she may have gone there.

My life is impossible without her presence in the house. I do admit I have a temper, but your sister gives me strong cause of provocation now and again. In spite of all that I am terribly fond of my Belle. How could she be so heartless to leave me like that? Could you do me a favour?

Ruxton then asks his sister-in-law to give him the addresses of some people where his wife might have gone. He continues:

Has she been to your place or not? I want you to tell me the honest truth. Please do not help Isobel to keep away from me. I want you to help me keep my home together. I am simply distracted. I cannot even keep my mind on the practice. You must ask her on your own to come back to me. I

am surely coming to see you on Wednesday about
four. Till then, yours affectionately,
Bonnie. [Ruxton's nickname]

At this time, of course, Ruxton was desperately trying
to cover his tracks and was fighting for his life. Even so,
there is a rich hypocrisy about this letter that is
breathtaking. 'How could she be so heartless to leave
me like that?' There is a recurring note which points to
a preoccupation that even the fear of discovery can't
make him entirely forget: money – the clothes bills,
bookie's demands, 'my' £30 and the gold coins.

So far there had been no *direct* evidence to connect
the 'Ravine Murders' at Moffat, as the *Daily Express*
called the case, with the disappearance of Isabella
Ruxton and Mary Rogerson. On Wednesday 9th
October, however, pieces of concrete evidence pointed
unerringly from Moffat to the Lancaster area. It was
discovered that a *Daily Graphic* used to wrap some of
the remains was one of a special 'slip' edition. These
'slip' editions were so called because during the print
run of newspapers one or more of the plates used to
print the pages were slipped off the machine and other
plates with purely local stories were slipped on in their
place. Some 3,000-odd copies of this particular 'slip'
edition of the *Daily Graphic* were printed, carrying a
story about a beauty queen contest at Morecambe, and
were circulated only in the Morecambe–Lancaster
area.

Fate designed a further coincidence to accelerate the
drawing of police attention to Ruxton. On the very day
that the Chief Constable of Dumfries called the
Lancaster Borough Police with the information about
the Lancaster edition of a newspaper with the remains,
he was told of an article in the Glasgow *Daily Record*
reporting the disappearance of a young Lancaster
woman, Mary Rogerson, who worked in the house of a

Dr Buck Ruxton. The material for the article had been given to the paper by Mrs Rogerson.

Subsequently the police arranged for photographs of some clothing found with the remains to be published in North of England newspapers. Mrs Rogerson saw the photographs and identified a blouse as one she had personally repaired and given to Mary.

Meanwhile Ruxton was blissfully unaware that the hunt was closing in on him. The morning of that same Wednesday 9th October he was due to go to Edinburgh, he ordered Mrs Curwen to take his wife's clothes from the wardrobe in her bedroom because he intended to take the best of them to her (Mrs Ruxton's) sister. He chose some clothes and Mrs Curwen packed them in a suitcase. A pile of Mrs Ruxton's and Mary's clothes were left on the floor. Ruxton told Mrs Curwen to divide them up between herself and the other charwomen. As he was about to set off for Scotland Mrs Curwen reminded him that he'd forgotten the suitcase containing his wife's clothes.

'I can't be bothered with them today,' Ruxton said, and he left without the case.

The fact that he gave away some of Mary's clothes and then couldn't trouble to take his wife's clothes to where he supposedly believed her to be supported the prosecution case that Ruxton knew very well that he would see neither his wife nor Mary again. When it came to it, Ruxton had a fairly plausible excuse for not taking the case. He said that he intended to take his wife's clothes to Edinburgh to teach her a lesson, but changed his mind and decided not to do so in case it caused a permanent breach between them.

However, this whole episode was at odds with what he had already told Mrs Nelson in another letter which she received on the same day: that his wife had taken practically all her clothes away with her. This letter was as long as the previous one.

Dear Sister Jean,
. . . You say you cannot help me and do not wish
me to come to Bothwell Street. Perhaps Belle has
told you something which might have put you
against me . . .

Ruxton continues with more enquiries about any
relatives in Canada. Then he makes the crucial error of
writing:

She has taken practically everything with her. On
top of that she has purchased wearing apparel of
the value of over £100 . . .

And to make sure there is no possible misunderstand-
ing Ruxton adds 'One hundred pounds' in words. After
complaining about his wife's extravagance, Ruxton
writes:

. . . Please if you know where she is I appeal to
you to let me know. I will not even speak a wrong
word to her if she would just come back. I can't
understand her sudden change of attitude . . .

Ruxton arrived in Edinburgh at about four o'clock and
met Mrs Nelson at the home of her sister, Mrs Trench.
Mrs Nelson was beginning to have her suspicions about
Ruxton. She knew that Mary Rogerson was missing,
too, and she had heard of the discovery of the bodies at
Moffat. By now the pathologists had positively
identified the remains as both being of women. When
Ruxton, again relying on attack as the best form of
defence, asked Mrs Nelson if she was hiding his wife,
she replied, 'Don't you know where she is?'
'What do you mean?' Ruxton said quickly.
'Have you done anything to her?'
'I wouldn't harm a hair of her head,' Ruxton
declared. 'I love her too much.' Then, money never

being far from his thoughts he added, 'I don't stand to make a penny by her death.'

He became hyper-excited and spoke almost continuously for several hours. Mrs Nelson couldn't remember everything he said – she very likely didn't understand some of it anyway, for when he became excited Ruxton became almost incomprehensible. However, she clearly remembered that Ruxton repeated he believed that Mary Rogerson was pregnant, and he stressed what he had said in the letter that his wife had taken all her clothes with her except an old leather coat. Finally he said that he would be forced to publish her photograph in the papers and advertise for her.

Mrs Nelson told him that would be all right because Mary Rogerson's father had written to her and the police would be looking for her anyway. (In fact, while Mrs Nelson was talking, Mrs Rogerson was with the Lancaster police giving a description of Mary as a result of the call from the Chief Constable of Dumfries.) When he heard this Ruxton became angry at Mr Rogerson. He said that Mrs Rogerson was a nice woman but the father was unreasonable and didn't believe what Ruxton told him. Rogerson showed good judgement.

When Ruxton finally left the house he said quietly to Mrs Trench, 'If anybody comes asking questions, don't answer them.'

Ruxton arrived back at Lancaster at 3.50 a.m. the following morning, Thursday 10th October. Most people's spirits are at a low ebb at that time of the morning, and Ruxton, far from being the most stable of men, had been under unimaginable strain for nearly four weeks. When he was met by Inspector Thomas Clark of the Lancaster Borough Police Force on the bleak Castle Station, at that sombre hour, he was particularly vulnerable and cracked badly. Although

Ruxton almost certainly didn't know it, the regular practice was for a police officer to meet all trains in and out of Lancaster at that time of the morning. He must have feared that the detective had come especially to arrest him, and he said some stupid things and told at least one pointless lie that could easily be disproved.

Ruxton told Inspector Clark that he had been to Edinburgh to try to find his wife, but her sister knew nothing of her whereabouts. The inspector drove Ruxton back to his home and on the way Ruxton said, 'Inspector, Edmondson knows where my wife and maid are.' He went on to recount the story of when he followed his wife on her trip to Edinburgh when she and Bobby Edmondson stayed at the Adelphi Hotel in Liverpool – but he left out the significant fact that they were accompanied by Bobby Edmondson's father, mother and sister.

Ruxton then said rashly, 'I visited the hotel the next day and found that my wife and Edmondson had stayed at the hotel in the names of Mr and Mrs Edmondson' – a statement which could so easily be disproved. As he got out of the car he added, 'You enquire of Mr Edmondson at the Town Hall, and he will be able to tell you where my wife and maid are.'

Later that morning the signs that Ruxton was becoming unstitched became more pronounced and his statements were more unguarded. He rushed round to Mrs Hampshire, who was struck by the doctor's appearance. 'He was in a terrible way,' she said.

Ruxton told her that he had come because the police had been questioning him about Mary Rogerson. Immediately afterwards he asked her, 'What did you do about the suit?' He repeated the question four times.

'It's upstairs,' she replied.

'Burn it,' he said urgently. How he must have regretted the impulse which made him give it to her in the first place. 'Burn it!'

And that was not all. 'Have you had the carpets cleaned?'

'You're standing on one.'

Ruxton looked at it. 'You've got it fairly clean,' he admitted. 'What about the other?'

'It's awful, and I can't get it clean.'

'Burn it,' Ruxton said with increasing agitation. He paused. 'Mrs Hampshire, will you stand by me? I haven't got a friend in the place.' This, coming from the hitherto grand Dr Ruxton, must have disconcerted her. 'I'll do what I can,' she promised.

But there was nothing anyone could do for Ruxton now.

He prepared to leave, telling the startled Mrs Hampshire that he was going to the police to make a statement. 'Wait till I've given my statement before you give yours,' he asked.

By ten o'clock that night Ruxton had mustered enough courage to go over to the attack again. He called at the police station where Detective Constable Winstanley was on duty. Ruxton made a bravado entrance, saying as he walked in, 'Winstanley, all this damned nonsense is ruining my practice. Can nothing be done to stop this talk?' As if the very idea was preposterous he said that he actually thought that his name was being connected with the finding of the human remains at Moffat.

Winstanley simply answered that the police had no authority over the press, and although they were making enquiries, they had no authority to make any statement.

At that point Detective Sergeant Walter Stainton came into the office. Stainton, too, knew Ruxton well, of course. He was one of the officers who interviewed Ruxton some eighteen months earlier when Mrs Ruxton came to the police because she was afraid of her husband; and a year later – some five months

before this present interview – Stainton called at the
Ruxton home in answer to a telephone call when
Ruxton offered more threats of murder. When
Sergeant Stainton walked into the office to find Ruxton
babbling on to Winstanley he made himself scarce and
left the detective constable to deal with him. Ruxton
made a statement which Winstanley took down and
gave Ruxton to sign:

> Buck Ruxton states:
> I am a medical practitioner and I reside at 2
> Dalton Square, Lancaster. The following is a
> description of my wife. Name: Isabella Ruxton, 35
> years, about five feet six or seven inches, well
> built, fair hair, bridge of nose is uneven, three
> false teeth in upper jaw, gold clip shows when
> smiling, fair complexion, blue eyes, dressed in
> cream silk blouse, light brown small check coat
> and skirt, suede shoes dark brown colour, and had
> a v-shaped ring on forefinger of left hand. Speaks
> with a strong Scotch (*sic*) accent. I would like
> discreet enquiries made by the police with a view
> to finding my wife. She left home on Sunday 15th
> September, 1935, and I have not seen her since.
> (Sgd) B. Ruxton.
> Statement taken by John Winstanley, DC 11 on
> Thursday 10th October 1935.

As soon as this was done Ruxton went with Winstanley
to Dalton Square where he gave the detective a
photograph of Mrs Ruxton.

The next day Ruxton was hyperactive again. He
began to write out a document 'My Movements' which
he subsequently gave to the police. He made several
calls at the police station, starting at 10 a.m., when he
brandished a copy of the *Daily Express* at the
long-suffering Detective Sergeant Stainton. 'Look at
this, ruining my practice. Why don't they accuse me of
the Moffat murder? Someone will be putting a dead

baby on my doorstep and I will be accused of killing it.'
Next, Ruxton drew attention to his cut hand and
launched into the same long explanation of how he had
injured it.

Stainton then put a question to Ruxton that cut
through the fog of obfuscation and wild statements:
'Have you given away any carpets?'

Ruxton must have suddenly felt the net closing round
him. With a thin echo of his previous grandiloquence he
replied that the carpets on the stairs and landings were so
worn that he had given his servants the privilege of
taking them.

Detective Inspector William Green, who was investigating Mary Rogerson's disappearance was in the office
at the time. He asked Ruxton how he knew Mary was
pregnant.

'I haven't examined her, but it doesn't take a doctor's
examination to tell when a girl is pregnant. One day we
had some friends for tea and she was passing me to serve
at the other side of the table, and she was holding herself
in such a position, that there flashed through my mind
that there was something wrong with the girl. I looked
again and I noticed that her face was pinched, but, of
course, a woman can conceal her condition until she is
six or eight months pregnant. I just noticed a slight
swelling. I should say she was two or three months
pregnant.'

At noon Ruxton returned to the police station and
gave Captain Henry Vann authority to publish his wife's
photograph. At 9.30 p.m. Ruxton went once more to
the police station, carrying another copy of the *Daily
Express* with him. He took Capt. Vann's hand and
pointed out a paragraph in the paper. 'My dear Vann,
can't you do something about these newspaper reports?
Look at this: this newspaper says that this woman has a
full set of teeth in her lower jaw, and I know, of my own
knowledge, that Mary Rogerson has at least four teeth

missing in this jaw.'

Ruxton waved his arms about and became increasingly wound up to the point of hysteria and virtual incoherence. Once again he complained about the publicity ruining his practice and he made further accusations about Bobby Edmondson.

'This damned Bobby Edmondson is ruining my home. One day I tapped a telephone conversation when she spoke to this man. The conversation was in lovers' terms . . . ' On the subject of Bobby Edmondson, Ruxton had a number of mental cogs slipping badly.

Captain Vann tried to calm Ruxton, but Canute had better luck with the tide. Ruxton was inconsolably distraught and wept. With breathtaking chutzpah he asked Vann if it wasn't possible to publish a statement to the effect that there was no connection between the bodies at Moffat and his wife and maid. Vann phlegmatically replied that he would do so when he was satisfied that this was the case.

Saturday 12th October, 1935, was to be Ruxton's last day of liberty. By now the shadow of arrest was hanging low over him. He spent the day scurrying around Lancaster and Morecambe trying to persuade different people to agree to his version of various happenings in the period since the disappearance of the two women. Panic drove him into making some incautious remarks which were badly damaging to him.

He began by calling at the Andersons' home at about ten o'clock, when he asked Dorothy Neild, the maid, whether she could say that he had been at the Andersons' house every day since his wife went away. Miss Neild said on reflection that she could. That should have been enough for Ruxton, but he couldn't leave things there. He returned to the house about an hour later and asked her if she could say that he had been there on the Thursday following the Morecambe carnival, which was Thursday 19th September. Once again Miss Neild said that she could, but Ruxton simply couldn't leave well alone: he asked her if she could be sure of the day. 'Yes,' she told him.

In fact Thursday 19th September was the day Ruxton made several journeys between the bedroom of his house down to his car in the morning, past the door of the kitchen he had closed so that Mrs Oxley couldn't see what he was doing.

If Ruxton could have had the self-control and sang-froid to keep his questioning low-key and apparently nonchalant Dorothy Neild might well have sworn mistakenly that he was at the Andersons' house every day, including the crucial 19th September. But his persistence made her think more carefully, and she became certain that he hadn't called on that day.

A visit to Frank Eason, a decorator, was equally damaging to Ruxton's case. Eason had done some decorating for Ruxton in May of that year and again in September. When he called for payment Ruxton engaged him to decorate the staircase, which Eason began on the 2nd October.

On that last day of liberty Ruxton asked Eason whether he remembered him mentioning in May having his staircase decorated.

'No. You said "interior decorating",' Eason said flatly.

'Not the staircase?' Ruxton demanded anxiously. 'Don't you see they're saying I got you to decorate my staircase to cover up the bloodstains, as I have done a murder?'

Ruxton was even more rash with Arthur Howson, a hairdresser. During a conversation with him Ruxton declared that his wife had gone away and he didn't know where she was but he had proof that she had gone off with Bobby Edmondson – that old obsession again. As he left the hairdresser's shop Ruxton said that 'they'

were after him for the murder of Mrs Ruxton, Mary
Rogerson and Mrs Smalley.

Ruxton's desperation was exemplified by his visit to
Mary Rogerson's father, James Rogerson. Ruxton
must have known that Rogerson strongly suspected him
of having murdered Mary (despite Rogerson's later
denial), yet he summed up enough brazenness to call
on him and put painful questions to him.

Ruxton asked Rogerson how many teeth Mary had
had out, and where she had them extracted, but didn't
say why he wanted the information. He carefully noted
down what he was told. Mr Priestly at Lancaster had
done some extractions, Rogerson said, although he
didn't know how many. He remembered that she told
him that the bill was 12s 6d (62p).

Finally Ruxton asked if the police were connecting
Mary's disappearance with the Moffat murders, and
whether Rogerson did himself.

'Not at all,' was the reply, which was probably a
bigger lie than any Ruxton himself told that day. Very
likely all Rogerson wanted was to get Ruxton out of his
house as quickly as possible, a sentiment which Ruxton
shared. As Rogerson told the court at Ruxton's trial,
'He was in a great hurry to get out of the house.'

Later that day Ruxton asked Ernest Hall, a cinema
projectionist who had done a number of odd jobs at the
Dalton Square house, to visit him at his surgery.
Unaccountably Ruxton tried to get Hall to agree to
swear in any court that Mary Rogerson had opened the
door to him when he called on Saturday 14th
September, which was the night before the double
murder, but Hall refused, saying he was home in bed ill
on that night. What Ruxton hoped to achieve by
proving Mary was alive on the Saturday is baffling.

Ruxton had one more meeting about this time, a
highly significant one, but it was not mentioned in court
or referred to until after his execution. Shortly before

he was arrested Ruxton was visited in his surgery by a representative of the *News of the World*, who saw Ruxton again after he was in custody. At this second meeting Ruxton gave the *News of the World* man a sealed envelope.

'Take great care of this,' he said earnestly. 'They have charged me with murder, and I, in turn, charge you to place this envelope in safety and security. On no account is it to be opened before my death, if to die I am. If I am acquitted – and I think I must be acquitted – you will give it back to me.'

Ruxton met the newspaperman once more, towards the end of his trial. He repeated his command that the envelope was not to be opened before his death. He added that in the event of his death the envelope should be handed unopened to the editor.

To return to that fateful Saturday 12th October, at seven o'clock that evening after an exhausting, stressful day Ruxton telephoned Captain Vann (the Chief Constable) to say he was very pleased with the statement that Vann had issued to the press. Vann asked Ruxton to come to see him at his office. Ruxton arranged for the helpful Miss Philbrook to take care of the children and turned up at Vann's office at 9.30 p.m. It was his last moment as a free man.

Vann gave evidence at the Ruxton trial in a rather stilted and ingenuous-sounding police style. When Ruxton arrived 'there were a number of police officers from England and Scotland present. I told him that he could possibly give some useful help in finding his wife and maid. In addition I proposed to ask him to account for his movements between the 14th and 30th September, 1935. He then said, "I shall be pleased to tell you all I possibly can." I told him that I would take down in writing what he said, and I cautioned him.'

Ruxton produced an envelope from his pocket and handed over a ready-prepared statement entitled 'My

Movements', and then made a statement which was taken down and typed. He read it over, made some corrections which took him a little over an hour, and signed it.

By now it was 3.50 a.m. on Sunday 13th October. On a number of occasions Ruxton said he was tired and wanted to go home, but Captain Vann, in his own words 'persuaded him to stay'. Vann consulted with the Scottish police, and at long last, at 7.20 a.m. Ruxton was arrested and charged with the murder of Mary Rogerson. When he was cautioned he replied, 'Most emphatically not. Of course not. The furthest thing from my mind. What motive and why? What are you talking?'

Ruxton appeared before the magistrates at the Lancaster Police Court, as it was then called, and was remanded weekly until 5th November, when he was additionally charged with the murder of Mrs Ruxton. He was further regularly remanded and on 26th November evidence was given for the first time.

He was eventually committed for trial on both charges at Manchester Assizes, but only the case of Isabella Ruxton was proceeded with. When Ruxton was arrested, the police were more certain of the identity of one of the corpses as Mary Rogerson, but subsequent scientific tests made it certain that the other dismembered body was that of Isabella Ruxton.

Edward Slinger, Ruxton's solicitors, were able to brief Norman Birkett KC for the defence. He would be faced by formidable adversaries for the Crown: Mr J. C. Jackson KC led Mr Maxwell Fyfe KC (later Lord Kilmuir) and Mr Hartley Shawcross (later Lord Shawcross), who was to be a prosecutor at the Nuremberg War Trials and Attorney-General.

Birkett had a marvellous sense of professional objectivity. Late in his life he was asked in an interview if he had ever managed to win an acquittal for a defendant on a murder charge whom he believed in his heart to be guilty. He replied candidly that he had, and he had no regrets about it. The interviewer went on to ask Birkett if he had ever defended anyone on a murder charge whom he knew to be guilty. Birkett immediately pointed out the difference between believing and knowing.

'How can you defend a man you know to be guilty? The answer is you never do. You are not permitted to do so. You may think that he is guilty, and of course it is quite impossible for any man of sense to have a brief to defend some man, and read all about the facts without coming to some conclusion in his mind. But if he *thinks* [him to be guilty], that is quite irrelevant. He is not the judge.'

Birkett went on to cite the Ruxton case as a perfect example. 'No one could read, as I read, all the facts the prosecution were going to prove without feeling that, well, this is a very difficult case. But it didn't make me any the less eager to do everything I could for Dr Ruxton.'

Basically, the prosecution had to prove that the two dismembered bodies were those of Isabella Ruxton and Mary Rogerson, and that they were killed and dismembered at 2, Dalton Square. If they proved that, it was obvious that Ruxton had done the murders.

There really was no way in which Birkett could suggest that the two dismembered bodies were anyone other than Mrs Ruxton and Mary Rogerson. Apart from fingerprint evidence and identification of some of the clothing that was found with parts of the remains, there was the reconstruction carried out by Professor James Couper Brash, Professor of Anatomy at Edinburgh University. A photograph of Isabella Ruxton wearing a tiara was found, and the two skulls were photographed from the same angle as the studio portrait. The tiara in that portrait was found at the

Dalton Square house, which made it possible for the photographs of the skulls to be made on the same scale. Transparencies of the three sets of photographs were made.

The photograph of Skull No. 2 fitted exactly the photograph of Mrs Ruxton. Brash, like the other specialist medical witnesses, was extremely careful in his choice of words and was completely fair to Ruxton. He said that judging from the photographic evidence, Skull No. 2 could not be that of Mary Rogerson, but Skull No. 2 might be that of Mrs Ruxton. Those who have seen the photographs could have been in no doubt that it was definitely hers. This technique, new at the time, has since been used extensively in identification of bodies.

In his final speech Mr Jackson for the prosecution firmly alleged that if the bodies were indeed those of Mrs Ruxton and Mary Rogerson, it followed that Ruxton must have killed them, but Birkett even more firmly denied this. If the two women left Dalton Square on the morning of 16th September, 'it matters not what was found, so far as the guilt of the prisoner is concerned, as to where they went, why they went, how they went, or into whose hands they came.' This last phrase referred to the suggestion Ruxton had made that Mary Rogerson was pregnant, and Mrs Ruxton had taken her away to arrange for an illegal abortion.

It was clear from Norman Birkett's cross-examination of the scientific and medical witness that he had done an enormous amount of preparation for the case. Professor Glaister – who was also a barrister – was full of admiration for Birkett. Glaister particularly recalled an answer he gave in his own cross-examination which could have been a grave pitfall for a less alert counsel. Among the human remains was found a cyclops eye. Birkett was keen to establish that it was a human cyclops eye (a single eye in the middle of the forehead). If it *were* human, it would help tremendously to bolster the suggestion that Mary Rogerson had been pregnant and had gone for an abortion. The least Birkett hoped for was for Glaister to be unable to state positively that it was definitely animal, and not human.

The relevant question-and-answer exchanges were as follows:

> 'Was this cyclops eye put into formalin to preserve it?'
> 'It was put . . . into a one per cent formalin solution.'
> 'That would render it quite impossible now to apply any chemical tests to determine whether it be human or animal?'
> 'That depends on the degree of saturation of the tissue, and the method adopted in its removal.'

Birkett scented danger here. An unwary question could lead to Glaister saying that the eye had not been saturated enough to make classification of it impossible. Smoothly Birkett changed direction slightly without making it obvious:

> 'In the case of a cyclops eye being animal, it is usually a grazing animal, is it not?'
> 'A pig, very often.'
> 'There is always present what is called a tapetum which gives a metallic iridescence to the eye?'
> 'I believe so.'

The one question Birkett was *not* going to ask now was 'Did this eye have a metallic iridescence?'! Instead:

> 'It was, in any event, a most startling and remarkable thing to find?'
> 'It was very unexpected, but of course, in our

view after consideration, we could speculate as to
a cause of its being there – a reason.'

The pitfall yawned large before Birkett. In no way was
he going to ask Glaister to explain his speculation as to
a possible cause for the cyclops eye to be there. Again,
without the least sign of concern he smoothly changed
direction with few people actually being aware of it.

'Now, in Exhibit 136, photograph 25 shows the
left hand of what you have assigned as Body
No. 1 . . .'
'Yes, that is so . . . '

Birkett was now back on firm ground, and getting
Professor Glaister to agree with him. Thirty years later,
talking to me, Glaister recalled Birkett's unruffled,
polished performance at that moment with undi-
minished respect.

As we have said, Glaister had also carried out other
tests to establish the length of time between death and
the time when the remains were discovered by studying
which generation the maggots were which were found
in the parts of the bodies.

'When I explained this to the prosecution before the
case I was told "For God's sake don't mention that in
court. It'll thoroughly revolt the jury and put them off
listening to the evidence",' Glaister told me. 'So it
didn't come out in the trial.' There was enough horrific
detail without that as well.

Glaister was paid a handsome tribute by the judge.
'No one could sit in this court and listen to the evidence
of Professor Glaister . . . without feeling that there is a
man who is not only master of his profession, but who is
scrupulously fair and most anxious that his opinion,
however strongly he may hold it, shall not be put
unduly against the person on trial . . . '

There is a saying, 'You cannot play cards with a man

who holds all the trumps.' This was the prosecution's comfortable situation. The Crown proved conclusively time and again that the two bodies were those of Mrs Ruxton and Mary Rogerson, and although Birkett made no attempt to say otherwise, in an attempt to cloud the evidence he sometimes suggested that the experts had assigned some parts to the wrong bodies.

Also damning for Ruxton were the mutilations that had been carried out on the bodies in an attempt to prevent identification, for they drew attention to the very elements that he had tried to conceal. In addition to the mutilations already mentioned, there were others that removed parts of Mrs Ruxton's body which could have indicated that she died of asphyxiation – strangulation. Organs were removed from Mary Rogerson's body which could have established that she was not pregnant.

The second part of the prosecution's case, that the two women were killed at the Dalton Square house, was almost as conclusive as the identification evidence. Apart from the many witnesses to Ruxton's guilty behaviour and contradictory statements, there was the physical evidence of the blood still in the house – the stains in the bathroom and on the handrail of the stairs – despite all Ruxton's frantic efforts to get rid of it. There was protein under the eyelets of the stair rods, in drains and on one of those bloodstained carpets. Birkett got an admission from a prosecution witness that soap could have given the chemical reaction for protein in the scientific tests. And was it not perfectly reasonable for traces of blood and protein to be found in the drains of a doctor's house?

But there were the bloody carpets – and that suit.

The blood on the stair carpet? Birkett strove energetically to convince the jury that it was from Mrs Ruxton's miscarriage the previous year when she fell on the stairs, and from Ruxton's own hand which he cut, opening a tin of fruit, as he claimed.

The suit? Well, Ruxton often assisted dentists when they were doing extractions under anaesthetic. He could easily get bloodstains on his suit while holding the patient's head close to his chest. Ruxton, it appeared, never wore a white coat or overall when he was helping the dentists. And then there were the minor operations he performed at his surgery: circumcisions, Birkett mentioned, when the patient was held on Ruxton's knee. That would account for bloodstaining on his clothes. The imagination boggles – or recoils – from the picture this evokes.

Despite Birkett's determined and masterly defence, the evidence against Ruxton mounted remorselessly. There was the circumstantial evidence: Ruxton's unexplained absences and mysterious journeys, his several contradictory statements about the disappearance of the two women, the mysterious bonfires in his yard late at night, his desperate efforts just before he was arrested to persuade people to make false statements on his behalf.

There was all the physical evidence: including blood stains, protein traces, local newspaper, and irrefutable proof that the remains were of Isabella Ruxton and Mary Rogerson. One of the decapitated heads was wrapped in a pair of child's rompers identified as belonging to one of the Ruxton children, and other remains were in the blouse identified as Mary's by her mother who had mended it and given it to her. The judge made much of these two exhibits in his summing up. Yet there was one more item of physical evidence which could well have been enough to convict Ruxton on its own. Some of the remains were wrapped in pieces of torn bedsheet. These were compared with a single sheet that was taken from Mrs Ruxton's bed: the second sheet for the bed was missing.

Mr Fred Barwick, for twenty years the director of the

testing house of the Manchester Chamber of Com-
merce told the court:

> ' . . . in composition, weave, weight, thread per
> inch, counts of component yarns, direction of
> twist on yarn, turns per inch in yarn, and the class
> of cotton there are no differences. I took
> measurements of length and diameter of the
> cotton hairs and found no difference.'

This appears impressive at first sight, but that make of
sheet was produced in very great numbers. In respect of
all those particular measurements and tests made by Mr
Barwick, the four pieces of torn sheet with the bodies
would have matched many other sheets on beds in
Lancaster and surrounding districts.

But now fate played the ace of trumps against
Ruxton. The strengthening edge which runs down the
side of the sheet is called the selvedge. To quote Mr
Barwick again:

> 'In order to make the sheet stronger the threads
> [of the selvedge] are woven in a different order. In
> this particular sheet there are 26 threads working
> in pairs at the extreme edge . . . but only one
> selvedge is like that. Ordinarily they would be
> both alike, but in this sheet the other selvedge has
> three threads missing. Instead of having 26 double
> threads of 13 pairs of threads it has 23 threads, 22
> working in pairs, and one odd one.
>
> It is rather an unusual feature and the same
> feature was traced in the selvedges on the portions
> of sheeting [i.e., the pieces found with the human
> remains].'

This fault would be peculiar to the output of one single
loom. One particular warp – the lengthwise threads of
the material – would be made with these three selvedge
ends missing. The next time a warp was put into the

loom the fault would be corrected. It was the sort of fault that would be noticeable only under microscopic examination. In other words the single sheet from Ruxton's bed had a sort of 'fingerprint', and that same fingerprint was found on the four pieces of sheeting used to wrap parts of the bodies.

When the prosecution played that particular trump the distant sound of the gallows trap being sprung could almost be heard echoing through the court.

Ruxton was far from being a good witness on his own behalf. Even before he went into the witness box he was a trial – in a manner of speaking – to his own counsel. During the evidence of the prosecution witness he passed more than one hundred notes to Birkett calling attention to different points. Ruxton was examined for the best part of two days and his evidence was studded with outbursts of hysteria and tears. He denied everything. When his version of events differed from earlier witnesses he flatly declared that they weren't telling the truth.

Ruxton had no real answers to questions about his bloodstained suit. During his evidence Professor Glaister had remarked that no respectable doctor would ever wear a suit in that condition, and such a bloodstained suit would be a possible source of infection if worn by a doctor when attending confinements. Ruxton angrily retorted that he had never written a death certificate in 230 confinements. He insisted that the blood had accumulated on the suit for *two or three years*.

The prosecution had another trump to play. 'But surely,' Mr Jackson said, 'that suit was sent to the cleaners in August and returned on August 17th perfectly clean.'

Ruxton was clearly discomfited. 'My Belle does all the cleaning,' he said unconvincingly. 'I know nothing about it. I cannot say.'

Mr Jackson turned towards the back of the court and asked if there was a Mr Cherry there. A man came from the back of the court and stood near the witness box.

'Do you know this man, Mr Cherry, who is a cleaner?'

'I have never seen the gentleman before,' Ruxton replied.

In other words, the prosecution were saying that the enormous amount of blood on the suit had accumulated in the month before the disappearance of the two women. In fact, by now everyone was certain that it had accumulated in one night.

The judge summed up for several hours, and although he was fair, it had been obvious to everyone for some days what the verdict would be. The jury were out for a few minutes over two hours, and it is a fair bet that they spent some of that time getting the kinks out of their legs and having a long-delayed smoke.

When the Clerk of the Assize formally asked Ruxton if he had anything to say as to why sentence of death should not be passed according to law, Ruxton replied: 'Subject to the point that I be allowed to appeal, in the administration of justice. I submit that to Your Lordship and the jury. I want to thank everyone for the patience and fairness of my trial.'

Ruxton was irrepressible. Even the shadow of the noose could not diminish his self-esteem. 'I have never attempted to pass any special restrictions. I should like to hear whatever His Lordship has to say about it.'

'You will be hanged by the neck until you are dead' was the nub of what His Lordship had to say about it.

H. Montgomery Hyde reports in his book *Norman Birkett* that Ruxton sent a letter to his counsel the night before his execution. It is further example of Ruxton's extraordinary character.

Manchester Prison
7.20 p.m. Monday May 11 1936

Dear Mr Birkett,

This letter will be forwarded to you by my solicitor and trustee Mr C.F. Gardner of 31 Sun Street, Lancaster.

Thanks awfully, old man, for all you have done.

Please accept a trivial token of gratitude I have left you in my will. I am sure your wife will be delighted with it. Mr C.F. Gardner will send it on in due course.

May I beg a favour of you? If there should be any litigation re my estate, will you kindly give your services as a favour to a dying man?

I am leaving three bonny mites behind.

If you can, please be good to them. They are intelligent and goodlooking.

May you reach the highest pinnacle of the Legal Pedestal.

I'll bless you from above. Try your best to get in touch with Mr Gardner now and again and do your best for my children.

God bless you and yours,
Yours very sincerely,
Buck Ruxton.

Norman Birkett Esq., KC

Montgomery Hyde goes on to report that the 'trivial token of gratitude' was a set of silver forks with mother-of-pearl handles. Birkett felt unable to accept the bequest, but did go to considerable trouble afterwards to arrange for the care and education of the murderer's three orphaned children.

Even from beyond the grave Ruxton was able to cause another sensation. The Sunday after the execution, 17th May 1936, the *News of the World* reproduced his handwritten confession, dated the day after his arrest.

I killed Mrs Ruxton in a fit of temper because I
thought she had been with a man. I was Mad at
the time. Mary Rogerson was present at the time.
I had to kill her.
                    B. Ruxton.

DR THOMAS NEILL CREAM

All men possess in their bodies a poison
Pliny the Elder

Poison more deadly than a mad dog's tooth
Comedy of Errors

If you poison us, do we not die?
The Merchant of Venice

For the letter killeth . . .
Second Epistle of Paul
to the Corinthians

. . . see how large a letter I have written
Epistle of Paul to the Galatians

'I was Mad at the time,' Dr Ruxton wrote in his confession, and it is difficult to disagree with his own diagnosis. Some contemporary commentators of Dr Thomas Neill Cream considered that he was not mad, just plain very nasty, a judgement which depends on the individual's definition of madness. Ruxton's murders were committed in a wild *coup de folie*, and his desperate struggles to get out of trouble only dragged him down deeper into the quicksands.

Cream, on the other hand, was cold-blooded and bold to the point of recklessness in his early criminal career. Subsequently, although his murders were ruthlessly calculating, his actions were so extreme that it is tempting to explain them by saying he was insane. He was also an unusual criminal in that he was found guilty of murder twice, on different sides of the Atlantic. The judge at his London trial described the murder of which he was convicted as 'diabolical in its character, fraught with so much cold-blooded cruelty . . . with so much torture . . . '

While his early crimes had a clear motive – sexual or financial gain – there was no *apparent* motive for his South London murders, although inevitably it has been suggested that he was taking revenge on prostitutes because he had contracted a venereal disease from one. His behaviour gives some support to the theory that he could have been in the tertiary stage of syphilis, which can cause serious damage to the brain. Another, perhaps more popular theory, is that he was simply an over-sexed sadist with an ever-diminishing grip on sanity. This could well be because he took regular doses of morphia, opium and probably cocaine which sometimes left him looking quite stupefied.

One of the most extraordinary elements of the Cream case was the way he drew attention to the crime for which he was finally hanged. He would never have been suspected of the murder of Matilda Clover – in fact no one suspected that she *had* been murdered – had he not written one of his many bizarre letters. This one resulted in Clover being exhumed and Cream himself being the prime suspect for her killing of which he was undoubtedly guilty. It has been said that the one drawback of the perfect murder as far as the perpetrator is concerned is that no one knows that he did it and how clever he is. Perhaps a freakish desire for recognition was the explanation for Cream's otherwise inexplicable letters.

Cream was born in Glasgow on 27th May 1850, one of eight children of William and Mary Cream. Apparently his parents were honest and fairly prosperous, and there is no indication that anyone else of the family turned out to be a criminal, so there was nothing hereditary in his villainy. The family emigrated to Canada when Cream was five. William Cream became a manager of a shipbuilding firm in Quebec, and eventually Thomas was apprenticed to that trade in a different firm from his father's.

When Cream was twenty-two he abandoned the trade for a profession and enrolled at McGill University in Montreal. He was an ostentatious student. The fact that Cream ran the equivalent of a modern flashy car, a carriage and pair, testified to the generosity of the allowance his father made him. He dressed well, and wore jewelry; he had a reputation of being something of a ladies' man. In those days that could mean little more than heavy breathing and minimal erotic behaviour, but Cream's philandering was more serious than that, as we shall see.

Cream received the degree of MD in 1876. (A North American MD qualification is not the same as the rather more rare British MD). There are some reports that Cream wrote a first-class paper on the effects of chloroform.

In the autumn of 1874 Cream took out an insurance policy for $1,000 on his personal effects at his lodgings in Montreal. About a fortnight after he graduated from McGill there was a fire in his rooms. Cream was prudent enough not to claim the full $1,000, but put in a claim for $978.40. Perhaps he thought that this odd sum sounded convincing. In any case, it didn't convince the insurance company, who finally coughed up only $300 after going to arbitration.

About that time Cream met Flora Eliza Brooks, daughter of a hotel owner, who was on a visit to Montreal. They were soon engaged, and it is evident that the relationship matured quickly. On 6th September, when Flora had returned to her home in Waterloo, she was suddenly taken ill. The family doctor informed her father that she had been pregnant, and had been given an abortion. The ethics of divulging that information didn't seem to have bothered the doctor.

Mr Brooks immediately rushed to Montreal and confronted Cream at the Ottawa Hotel. He made an offer to Cream: marry Flora or be shot – a 19th century version of an offer he couldn't refuse.

Flora Brooks became Mrs Cream on the 11th September in a classic shotgun wedding. It was also one of the shortest marriages on record, for Cream left the house the following day 'to go to England to complete his medical training'. The unhappy Flora died less than a year later of tuberculosis, for which there was almost no chemotherapy available then. Cream had about as much sensibility as a shark. When news reached him of his wife's death, he claimed from the family $1,000 due

under the terms of the marriage contract. He settled for
$200.

The details of Cream's first stay in London are
sketchy, although there is one most curious story about
him. The celebrated lawyer Marshall Hall was briefed
to defend a man on a charge of bigamy. When he
walked into court he was taken aback to find a bevy of
young women, all of whom claimed to have gone
through a marriage ceremony with the accused.

Marshall Hall advised the bigamist to plead guilty,
but the man indignantly declared he was innocent.
'This is a clear case of mistaken identity. Communicate
with the jail at Sydney, Australia, and you will find that
I was there at the time I am supposed to have
committed these offences,' he said. A cable with the
name and full description of the accused was sent to the
prison. To the astonishment of everyone – except the
accused – a reply was sent confirming his story and
providing him with a perfect alibi.

Years later Marshall went to the Old Bailey to see
the trial of Thomas Neill Cream on a charge of murder.
He was astounded to see that Cream was the man he
had defended on the bigamy charge. The mystery was
never resolved, although Marshall Hall believed that
Cream had a double who was in the underworld, and
they used each other's terms of imprisonment as alibis.

To return to Cream's first visit to London: he
attended lectures at St. Thomas's Hospital from 1876 to
1878. In 1887 he failed the Royal College of Surgeons'
examinations in physiology and anatomy, but the
following year he passed examinations to gain the
double qualification of the Royal Colleges of Physicians
and Surgeons at Edinburgh. Armed with these
admirable qualifications, Cream returned to Canada
and set up practice in London, Ontario.

While he was practising there the body of a young
woman, Kate Gardener, a chambermaid in an hotel,

was found dead in the outside lavatory behind Cream's surgery, or 'office' as it is called in North America. At her side was a bottle of chloroform. Cream, it will be recalled, wrote a paper on the effects of chloroform at McGill University.

At the subsequent inquest it was revealed that the girl had been visiting Cream to get an abortion. Cream declared that Gardener named a local tradesman as the father of her unborn child, but the man concerned produced evidence that there had been an attempt to blackmail him. 'Blackmail' was a word that would be frequently associated with Cream's name and his aliases in the future.

Doctors testified at the inquest that it would have been impossible for the girl to have chloroformed herself as she was found. Professors Glaister and Rentoul report in their *Medical Jurisprudence and Toxicology* that chloroform is rarely taken in liquid form to commit suicide, although a few cases of murder by chloroform had been reported by the 1960s. The authors say that when a saturated pad has been applied with some degree of pressure to the region of the mouth and nostrils it tends to produce small, irregular areas of abrasion and excoriation.

Kate Gardener had such lesions on her face.

The verdict at the inquest was that 'the deceased died from chloroform, administered by some person unknown.' As far as the inhabitants of London, Ontario were concerned, the person most definitely *was* known, even if it could not be proved. Soon afterwards Cream left town for the United States.

He settled in Chicago and promptly went into business as an abortionist. In August, 1880 one of his patients died: Julia Faulkner, a Canadian woman. Cream was charged with murder, but the evidence against him was thin and he went free. Again.

Four months after this a Miss Stack, another of his

patients, died after taking a medicine he had prescribed. Cream tried to turn this tragedy to his advantage. He wrote blackmail letters to Frank Pyatt, who had made up the prescription Cream had given to Miss Stack.

Meanwhile, Cream was charged with sending scurrilous matter through the mail. He seems to have had an obsession for sending blackmailing letters: he sent even wilder ones in his final years in England. On this occasion his target was a Joseph Martin, a Chicago furrier. Cream had attended Martin's family and claimed that Martin owed him twenty dollars. Cream began his offensive with a couple of letters. According to contemporary reports, he first accused Martin of giving his wife and children certain diseases. Which particular diseases the reports were too delicate to mention, but it takes no great leap of the imagination to guess what they were.

Cream threatened Martin with exposure if he didn't pay his bill, and he added darkly that the proof of his allegations were certain prescriptions on file at the local pharmacy. He followed this with a second, similar letter with an addition of 'I will learn that damned vixen of a low wife of yours to speak ill of me.' Cream had medical qualifications, but obviously hadn't one in English.

Martin resolutely refused to pay the twenty dollars, so Cream followed up with a fusillade of three postcards. The second one read:

> You had better learn that low, vulgar wife of yours to keep her foul mouth shut, with her second-hand silk dohlmans and second-hand silk dresses, and not talk about others. Two can play at that game. I heard on very good authority that you had to leave England on account of a bastard child you left behind. T.N.C.

His final card ended:

> You had better learn that low, vulgar vixen
> woman of yours to keep a civil tongue in her head,
> and not talk about others. Two can play at that
> game. Remember the bastard child you left in
> England.

Cream's English was still deplorable.

Martin had had enough; he laid a complaint and
Cream was arrested. He was given bail of $1,200.

A newspaper of the period reacted with righteous
wrath and thundered:

> This thing of sending scurrilous postcards through
> the mails, and thereby attempting to blacken the
> reputation of people, has gone far enough. Cream
> has added the crowning infamy of attempting to
> blast that which every man holds dearest – the fair
> name of his wife and children – and the average
> husband and father will be pretty apt to conclude
> that even hanging would be too good for him
> should he be proved guilty.

At this time Cream was advertising a patent medicine
which was claimed to be a cure for epilepsy. Daniel
Stott, a station master on the North-Western Railway
who lived at the evocatively-named Grand Prairie,
Boone County, suffered from epilepsy. He sent his wife
Julia to see Cream in Chicago to buy some of his
miraculous cure.

It was a situation in real life and fiction as old as
mankind: Stott was sixty-one (and in those days the
average 61-year-old was like a poorly 75-year-old
today), while his wife was only thirty-three, slender,
and reportedly attractive. Julia soon became Cream's
mistress, and visited him regularly to procure supplies
of medicine for her ailing husband. At the same time
Cream started trying to insure Daniel Stott's life.

On 11 June 1881 Cream gave Julia Stott a prescription. She had it made up at a pharmacy and returned to Cream's surgery. There, she stated at the subsequent trial, she saw Cream put a white powder into the medicine and into some rhubarb pills. She would have been unbelievably naive not to suspect something, but she gave the medicine to her husband. Three days later he took some, and died in little more than a quarter of an hour.

There followed a series of events which were repeated with some embellishments in London ten years later with a different supporting cast but with Cream still playing the principal role.

Stott's death was not treated as suspicious, and the cause of death was given as an epileptic seizure. This was not surprising, given the symptoms of strychnine poisoning. To quote Glaister and Rentoul again:

> When a poisonous dose has been swallowed . . . An intensely bitter taste is perceived and soon afterwards there is a sensation of suffocation, accompanied by twitching of the muscles of the neck, body and limbs, followed by severe tetanic convulsions which involve all the muscles of the body. *During this state the muscles became stiff and rigid, so that the body is thrown into an arch, only the back of the head and heels touching the bed or ground.* [My italics.] . . . Breathing becomes difficult and imperfect, and the face in consequence becomes markedly cyanosed [blue]. As the result of the contraction of the muscles at the angles of the mouth *risus sardonicus* [sardonic smile] is produced. . . .The fingers are clenched in the palms of the hand, the feet arched inwards and the eyes staring and wild looking . . . during a spasm the patient is in complete possession of his senses, and experiences acute pain.

There is then a remission and the patient lies in a calm

but weakened condition, and may fall asleep.

> After a variable interval, depending on the severity of the toxic effects and often the result of some trivial cause . . . another attack similar to the first one comes on. In cases proceeding to a fatal issue the intervals of remission are short . . . Death usually supervenes either during a spasm from asphyxia induced by fixation of the chest wall, or from exhaustion due to the repetition of the attacks. Death, therefore, may follow very shortly after the spasms appear, or it may be delayed for some hours.

So Stott's death would have gone unremarked as anything other than a sad but natural passing. But Cream threw a great stone into the calm pool. He wrote to the coroner for Boone County, alleging that the pharmacist who had made up the last prescription made the fatal mistake of putting in too much strychnine. Cream demanded an exhumation. Coincidentally he persuaded Julia Stott to give him a power of attorney to sue the chemist's for heavy damages. The coroner treated Cream's letter as another crackpot communication, and ignored it.

Cream wasn't simply going to let go. He wrote to the District Attorney, who did act. Daniel Stott's body was exhumed. The stomach was found to contain four grains of strychnine. The smallest fatal dose that has been recorded is a quarter of a grain, and half a grain has also caused death.

Cream was still out on bail for sending scurrilous communications through the post. He jumped bail and fled to Canada, but he was caught near Windsor, Ontario. He returned voluntarily to Chicago without extradition proceedings being taken. He and Mrs Stott were jointly indicted for murder.

Mrs Stott not unexpectedly tried to put all the blame

on Cream and virtually turned State's Evidence against
him. The case against Cream was watertight. In
addition to Mrs Stott's evidence concerning Cream's
tampering with her husband's medicine, the state
actually gave a dose of Mr Stott's medicine to a dog,
which died within 15 minutes. Then there was the clear
evidence of premeditation with Cream's attempts to
take out an insurance on Stott's life.

Unaccountably Cream was found guilty only of
second-degree murder. Not that it did him much good:
he was sentenced to life imprisonment in November
1881. The widow escaped scot-free.

That, one would have thought, was that. Cream had
killed Miss Stack, Julia Faulkner, Katy Gardener and
Daniel Stott, not to mention performing illegal
abortions and a minor case of arson; now he had got his
comeuppance.

In 1887 Cream's father died, leaving him $16,000 – a
considerable sum in those days. Inexplicably a move
was set afoot to have Cream's sentence reduced. In
1890 Cream himself wrote to the celebrated and
sometimes less than savoury Pinkerton Detective
Agency asking them to try to find Mrs Stott. He hoped
that she might be persuaded to swear an affidavit in his
favour, but she had vanished without trace. Nevertheless the governor reduced Cream's sentence from life to
17 years, which meant that with remission for good
behaviour he was released on 31st July 1891.

Cream returned to Canada, where those close to him
began to suspect that he was insane. The executors of
his father's will gave him money to go to England for
the sake of his health – and coincidentally for the health
of Canadian citizens.

Cream set foot in England again on 1st October 1891
and travelled from Liverpool to London where he
stayed for a couple of days at an hotel in Fleet Street. It
is clear that Cream came to England already

determined to murder prostitutes, for he began looking for victims within two days of arriving in London.

Official descriptions of Cream and information given by some of his victims provide an accurate picture of the man. He was 5 feet 9 inches tall – above average for the period – solidly built, bald at the front of his head, with a prominent chin and wearing a thick moustache. He also had a ferocious squint.

Women were the principal and compulsive subject of conversation with him – unpleasant, sexual conversation. He always had pornographic photographs with him, and he was only too ready to show them to his companions. Significantly, poisons and money were other subjects that preoccupied him. He was always well-dressed and spoke with a soft voice and an American accent. He was overly fond of gin, cigars and chewing gum. Much more deadly was his addiction to pills compounded of strychnine, morphia and cocaine. He made the dubious claim that this deadly mixture was an aphrodisiac.

Although modern editions of Black's Medical Dictionary have largely deleted the entry, until comparatively recently the entry under 'Strychine' read:

> Strychnine in small doses is a widely used stimulating drug, although in larger amounts it is a dangerous poison.
> . . . The drug acts mainly on the nervous system. When taken in small doses over a considerable time it sharpens the mental powers and increases sensibility so that sight and hearing are improved, and the sense of touch becomes more acute. The heart beats more quickly and more strongly under its uses.
> . . . All the functions of the [spinal] cord are more quickly and more vigorously carried out, reflex action is increased, the muscles are kept in a state

of greater tone, and there is a general sense of
increased bodily well-being.

. . . Strychnine is used chiefly as a 'tonic',
combined with remedies during convalescence
from weakening diseases, in fatigue brought on by
overwork . . .

So maybe Cream had a point when he said that his
strychnine mixture was an aphrodisiac. But it also made
him as jumpy as a nervous gerbil. Cream rarely laughed
or smiled, and was always restive. He simply could not
keep still: even when he was seated he moved his legs
about and fidgeted with anything on the table in front
of him. He constantly moved his head to watch anyone
moving near him. He was not a great deal of fun to be
with.

On Wednesday 7th October he called at 103
Lambeth Palace Road and arranged to move into a
first-floor front room the following day. In the evening
of his first day in his new lodgings he began looking for
victims.

The district he had picked for his murderous
operations was a triangle bounded by Blackfriars Road,
Lambeth Road and the River Thames. At that period it
was a sordid, poverty-stricken, filthy slum infested with
petty criminals and young women who became
prostitutes out of sheer necessity, and then tried to
numb their sense of awful reality with cheap liquor.
Some idea of the quality of life of the 'unfortunates', as
they were euphemistically called, can be measured by
the fact that Cream boasted that he often had their
sexual favours for a shilling!

There was precious little sympathy for these poor
creatures, which only deepened their despair. Marshall
Hall, defending a prostitute on a murder charge about
this time, reminded the jury, 'Remember, that these
women are what men make them; even this woman was

at one time a beautiful and innocent child.' It was a minority view. A number of charitable organisations, some understanding and uncritical, others rather patronising, tried to help these 'fallen women' and 'unfortunates'. It was a daunting task.

Cream's first target was Elizabeth Masters, a prostitute. He picked her up at Ludgate Circus, had a drink with her at a pub and then went to her rooms at Orient Buildings, Hercules Road, a street off Lambeth Road. After going to bed with her Cream took her to Gatti's Music Hall in Westminster Bridge Road. At the bar they met Elizabeth May, another prostitute who had the room next to Masters' at Orient Buildings. The trio had a few drinks at the King Lud in Ludgate Circus, and before the party broke up Cream said he would write to Masters to arrange an appointment.

On Friday 9th October Cream ordered a pair of spectacles to help correct his squint, and arranged by letter to call on Elizabeth Masters between three and five o'clock. Apparently Masters became belligerent when she drank, for in the letter Cream told her not to be so cross as she was at their first meeting. He signed the letter 'Fred'. He also asked her not to destroy the letter but to keep it until he called. The point of that, it seems obvious, was so he could be sure to destroy it himself.

Masters showed the letter to her friend Elizabeth May and that afternoon they both waited at the window to see 'Fred' arrive. He came to Hercules street all right, but before he got to Orient Buildings he was attracted to a third prostitute, Matilda Clover, who smiled at him. Masters and May saw Cream follow Clover past their front door. The two girls rushed out, presumably furious at seeing someone poach their client. They followed Cream and Matilda Clover and saw him go into 27 Lambeth Road with her. They waited outside for half an hour, but Cream was still occupied inside and they finally went home disappointed.

About this time, and certainly before 12th October, Cream bought a quantity of 'nux vomica' from a chemist's in Parliament Street. Nux vomica is prepared from the seeds of *Strychna nux vomica*. The alkaloids strychnine and brucine can be obtained from these seeds. As it is a scheduled poison, Cream had to give a written order for the drug, which he signed 'Thomas Neill MD, 103 Lambeth Palace Road'. A couple of days after this he ordered some gelatine capsules. These were supplied, but Cream said that they were too large and they were subsequently changed for No. 5 capsules.

On Tuesday 13th October Ellen Donworth, a 19-year-old prostitute living at Duke Street, off Westminster Bridge Road, died after being poisoned by a liquid. Donworth was also known as Ellen Linnell; many of the women involved in the Cream case used more than one name.

Exactly a week later Matilda Clover died as the result of taking poison in capsules.

Donworth's death caused a furore in the area and was known as 'The Lambeth Mystery'. She had received a letter fixing an appointment with a man at the York Hotel in Waterloo Road. This was for between six and seven o'clock. At about a quarter to eight Donworth was seen leaning against a wall opposite The Wellington public house in Waterloo Road. She fell on her face and a man named James Style ran over to her, got her to her feet and helped her home. She was obviously in a bad way, staggering, trembling and with her face twitching. Her landlady assumed that she had been drinking, but realised she was ill when she was seized by terrible convulsions that were so severe that it took several people to hold her down.

An assistant of Dr Lowe, medical officer of the South Lambeth Medical Institute, was called in and found her suffering from tetanus-like convulsions. In periods of remission between attacks Donworth told both her landlady and the assistant that she had twice been given a drink out of a bottle of white stuff from a tall gentleman with cross eyes, a silk hat and bushy whiskers.

Donworth was immediately transferred to St Thomas's Hospital, but she was dead on arrival. An autopsy provided no clue to the cause of death, but an analysis of the stomach contents revealed that she had been killed by strychnine.

The inquest opened at the hospital on 15th October and ended on the 22nd. The jury returned a verdict of 'Poisoning by strychnine and morphia by a person or persons unknown.' While the inquest was being held Cream was busy. He wrote one of his extraordinary letters to Mr George Wyatt, the Deputy Coroner for East Surrey. This letter, like others, was later identified as Cream's work by the distinctive handwriting.

London, 19th October, 1891

To: G.P. Wyatt, Esq.,
Deputy Coroner,
East Surrey.

I am writing to say that if you and your satellites fail to bring the murderer of Ellen Donworth, *alias* Ellen Linnell, late of 8 Duke Street, Westminster Bridge Road, to justice, that I am willing to give you such assistance as will bring the murderer to justice, provided your Government is willing to pay me 300,000 L for my services. No pay if not successful.

A. O'BRIEN, Detective.

This was not the only letter Cream sent that day. He wrote to 27-year-old Matilda Clover, mother of a two-year-old boy, who lived in a second-floor front room at 27 Lambeth Road. The father of the child was a man known as Fred, who had left Clover a month or so before her death, following a quarrel. Living in the house were the landlady, Mrs Phillips, more usually known as Mrs Vowles; Mr Vowles, a cab-driver; a 21-year-old servant named Lucy Rose; Matilda Clover and her child; and Mrs Phillips's grandson Edgar.

Lucy Rose was in Clover's room the day before her death on the 20th October. She noticed an open letter on the table. Lucy read the letter, and was able to recall the contents of the letter in some detail. It was a most evocative letter that gives a hint of the world Cream was living in. It said in effect, 'Miss Clover, Meet me outside the Canterbury at 7.30 if you can come clean and sober. Do you remember the night I bought you your boots? You were so drunk you could not speak to me. Please bring this paper and envelope with you. Yours, Fred.'

The letter was not found when Clover's room was searched after she died, and it is clear that she obeyed the instruction to take the letter with her to the rendezvous and Cream destroyed it. In the absence of the letter it was not mentioned at Cream's trial, although its existence and content are not in doubt.

On the 20th Clover went out in the early evening and came back some time later. Lucy let her into the house accompanied by a man, whom Lucy described as being tall and broad, with a heavy moustache, aged about forty, and wearing a large coat with a cape and a tall silk hat. However, at the inquest she was unable to recognise the man as Cream.

Soon after her arrival Clover went out again to get some beer, leaving the man alone in her room. He left finally, and as Clover saw him out she said 'Good night, Fred.'

An hour or so after that Clover went out again,

asking Lucy Rose to look after her child. The servant went to bed at about ten o'clock in her room on the first floor, under Clover's. What time Clover returned to her room is uncertain.

At three o'clock in the morning Lucy Rose and the landlady Mrs Vowles were woken by screams of agony coming from Clover's room. Lucy was awake first and she ran into Mrs Vowles's room. The two women then rushed into Clover's bedroom.

Matilda Clover was undressed, lying on her back on her bed, with her head jammed between the bedstead and the wall. She was screaming with agony. 'I'm glad you've come; I've been calling a long time,' she said. According to Lucy Rose's statement at the coroner's inquest Clover said, 'That wretch Fred has given me some pills and they have made me ill.' At Cream's trial Lucy changed her statement slightly and said Clover told her that she had been poisoned by some pills given to her by Cream. Unfortunately both Lucy's and Mrs Vowles's impression was that Matilda Clover was suffering from alcoholic poisoning: she was an extremely heavy drinker and had been receiving treatment for the condition from a Dr Graham.

There were moments of remission from the spasms; and with the perfect vision of hindsight we can see that Clover's sufferings were the classic symptoms of strychnine poisoning. She was given a cup of tea and some soda and milk, which she could not keep down. Mrs Vowles decided that she needed medical attention. She called at Dr Graham's address at about half-past four, but he was out on a case. Clover's condition was worsening, and Mrs Vowles called at the doctor's home again at half-past six. This time Dr Graham was concerned with a case of childbirth and he sent her on to Dr McCarthy.

At seven o'clock McCarthy's unqualified but experienced assistant Francis Coppin came to see

Clover. (Dr McCarthy had purchased the practice from
Coppin's father.) Coppin had some fourteen years'
experience in that area of London, and consequently
'had a good deal of experience of drink in its various
forms'. When he examined Clover she had a rapid
pulse, was bathed in perspiration and was trembling.
She suffered another convulsion while he was with her.
When Mrs Vowles told Coppin of Clover's excessive
drinking, he decided that she was suffering from what
he described as 'epileptic fits, convulsions due to
alcoholic poisoning . . . There was nothing to point out
to me that she died from anything other than delirium
tremens.'

Coppin stayed with Clover for about ten minutees
and then left. He prescribed some medicine for her
which Mrs Vowles's grandson went to collect. Lucy
Rose said, 'The first drop I gave her she turned all
black.' Just before nine o'clock that morning Mrs
Vowles rushed round to see Coppin again and he gave
her some more medicine. When he learned that Clover
had died he told Mrs Vowles that he was not qualified
to give a death certificate and said she should see Dr
Graham.

That doctor provided a death certificate with the cause
of death given as 'to the best of my knowledge and belief
the cause of her death was, primarily, delirium tremens,
secondly syncope,' which today merely means fainting,
although Dr Graham described it as 'failing of the
heart's action'. He explained that he already knew that
Clover was a heavy drinker and he based the cause of
death as given in the certificate on the information that
Mrs Vowles gave Francis Coppin. At Cream's trial the
Attorney General told Graham that he had been guilty
of a very grave dereliction of duty.

There is a pathetic little coda to the story of Matilda
Clover's death. Lucy Rose said that just before Clover
died she was wearing new boots, purchased at Lilley's

in Westminster Bridge Road. ('Do you remember when I bought you your boots?' Cream had written.) 'The day after she died the boots were pawned,' Lucy said.

Shortly after Clover's death, Cream asked Emily Sleaper, his landlady's daughter, to take a letter round to a house in Lambeth Road.

'What's the letter for?' Sleaper asked.

'I know a girl there and I think she's been poisoned. I want to find out whether she's dead or not.'

'You'd better go yourself,' the woman told him. 'I don't like to go under the circumstances.'

'I'll enquire myself, then,' Cream said, and added, 'I think I know who poisoned her.'

'Who do you think it was?'

'Lord Russell.'

It seems that Cream had plucked this name out of the air, for at that moment Sleaper was reading a report in the *Daily Telegraph* of the sensational Russell divorce case.

The connection between Cream and Clover, and his knowledge that she had been poisoned, was beginning to be established. Cream was starting to leave a trail behind him like a man walking across wet concrete. A couple of nights after having poisoned Clover, Cream picked up another prostitute, this one a Mrs Louisa Harris, who was known as Lou Harvey because she was living with a young man, Charles Harvey, a former bus employee but then out of work. Cream and Harvey met just after midnight at St James Hall in Regent Street, and went to an hotel in Berwick Street, off Oxford Street, where they passed the night together, leaving at about eight o'clock the next morning. Before they parted Cream said he was a doctor and mentioned that Harvey had some spots on her forehead.

Cream made an arrangement with Harvey to meet at 7.30 p.m. that evening by Charing Cross Underground

Station (now Embankment Station) and said he would bring some pills to cure her spots and then take her to a music hall. Harvey clearly had her doubts about Cream, for she told her live-in lover Charles Harvey – who seemed at the very least to accept complacently her activities as a prostitute – of the pills or medicine Cream had promised.

They went together to the Embankment, but they parted in Northumberland Avenue: Lou Harvey walked on while he followed her on the other side of the road to the meeting place. Cream was waiting for Lou Harvey at the station.

'Have you brought the pills?' Harvey asked.

'Yes. I had them made in Westminster Bridge Road. Would you like a glass of wine?'

'Shall I take the pills first?'

'No, take them afterwards.'

They walked to the nearby Northumberland public house where they had a glass of wine. A flower-seller came into the pub and Cream bought some roses for Harvey. It was an odd gesture, in view of what he had in mind. He was giving her funeral flowers before she was dead.

After a while they returned to the Embankment. 'I can't come with you to the music hall tonight,' Cream said, 'because I have an appointment at St Thomas's Hospital at nine o'clock, and I'll be kept there till ten-thirty. Get a cab and go to the music hall on your own and meet me outside at eleven. Then we'll go and spend the night at that same hotel.'

He gave Harvey some figs and told her to eat them after she had taken the pills, or capsules. He took the capsules, wrapped in tissue paper, from his waistcoat pocket and put them into her right hand.

'Put them in your mouth right away, one by one. Don't bite them, swallow them.'

They were both very wary of each other. Harvey put

her hand to her mouth and pretended to swallow the capsules, but she slipped them into her left hand.

'Show me your hand,' Cream ordered her. Harvey held out her empty right hand.

'Now the other one.'

The capsules were still in her left hand, but Harvey managed to throw them away behind her. She held out her empty hand to Cream, who was satisfied. He gave her five shillings (25p) for a seat at the music hall. She refused his offer to get her a cab, saying she could get one herself.

'Meet me at eleven,' were Cream's final words to her.

Lou met Charles Harvey at the corner of the street and told him everything that had happened. After that she cheerfully went off to the music hall, unaware of how near to an agonising death she had been. At eleven o'clock Harvey went outside the music hall and waited until 11.30 p.m., but Cream failed to put in an appearance. He didn't expect Harvey to keep her part of the rendezvous.

Matilda Clover was given a pauper's funeral on 27th October at Tooting Cemetery. In everyone's mind at that time it was a case of death from drink and the truth of her murder seemed to have been buried with her. On 5th November Cream wrote another of his letters for his own incomprehensible reasons. Were it not for the fact that he wrote some letters leading directly to his own downfall one might think that some of the others were prompted by nothing more than a badly twisted sense of practical joking. This latest letter was to Mr F.W.D. Smith of W.H. Smith & Co.

Mr F.W.D. Smith   London, 5th November, 1891.
c/o William H. Smith & Son,
186 Strand

Sir,
On Tuesday night, 13th October (last month) a

girl named Ellen Donworth, but sometimes calling herself Ellen Linnell, who lived at 8 Duke Street, Westminster Bridge road, was poisoned with strychnine. After her death, among her effects were found two letters incriminating you, which, if they ever become public property, will surely convict you of the crime. I enclose a copy of one of the letters which the girl received on the morning of the 13th October (the day on which she died). Just read it, and then judge for yourself what hope of escape you have if the law officers ever get hold of these letters. Think of the shame and disgrace it will bring on your family if you are arrested and put in prison for this crime. My object in writing to you is to ask if you will retain me at once as your counsellor and legal adviser. If you employ me at once to act for you in this matter, I will save you from all exposure and shame in the matter; but if you wait till arrested before retaining me, then I cannot act for you, as no lawyer can save you after the authorities get hold of these two letters. If you wish to retain me, just write a few lines on paper saying 'Mr Fred Smith wishes to see Mr Bayne, the barrister, at once.' Paste this on one of your shop windows at 186 Strand next Tuesday morning, and when I see it I can drop in and have a private interview with you. I can save you if you retain me in time, but not otherwise.

Yours truly,

H. Bayne.

The copy of the letter referred to read:

Miss Ellen Linnell,

I wrote and warned you once before that Frederick Smith, of W.H. Smith & Son, was going to poison you, and I am writing now to say that if you take any of the medicine he gave you for the purpose of bringing on your courses you will die. I saw Frederick Smith prepare the medicine he gave you, and I saw him put enough strychnine in the medicine he gave you for to kill a horse. If you take any of it you will die.

(Signed) H.M.B.

The police were immediately informed of these letters, and at their request, the paper inviting Mr Bayne to call was stuck in one of the shop windows. Not surprisingly, 'Mr H. Bayne, Barrister', did not turn up. Again, it is difficult to understand Cream's motive for sending this and subsequent letters.

On the 28th November he wrote another letter which completely reopened the Matilda Clover case. As we have said, there had been no suspicion of any foul play, even less that strychnine had been the cause of her death. This latest letter, signed with the fictitious name of M. Malone, was to Dr William Henry Broadbent, a distinguished physician.

London, 28th November, 1891.

Dr W.H. Broadbent,

Sir,

Miss Clover, who, until a short time ago, lived at 27 Lambeth Road, S.E., died at the above address on 20th October (last month) through being poisoned with strychnine. After her death a search of her effects was made, and evidence was found which showed that you not only gave her the medicine which caused her death, but you had been hired for the purpose of poisoning her. This evidence is in the hands of one of our detectives, who will give the evidence either to you or to the police authorities for the sum of 2500 L (two thousand five hundred pounds sterling). You can have the evidence for 2500 L, and in that way save yourself from ruin. If the matter is disposed of to the police it will, of course, be made public by being placed in the papers, and ruin you for ever. Now, sir, if you want the evidence for 2500 L just

put a personal in the *Daily Chronicle*, saying you
will pay Malone 2500 L for his services, and I will
send a party to settle this matter. If you do not
want the evidence, of course, it will be turned over
to the police at once and published, and your ruin
will surely follow. Think well before you decide on
this matter. It is just this – 2500 L sterling on the
one hand, and ruin, shame and disgrace on the
other. Answer by personal on the first page of the
Daily Chronicle any time next week. I am not
humbugging you. I have evidence strong enough
to ruin you for ever.
                          M MALONE

It is an unbelievable letter in more than one sense. If
there was anyone in the world who knew that Dr
Broadbent had not poisoned Matilda Clover it was
Cream himself; and he knew there could not possibly
be anything that could be made to look like proof
against Broadbent. There simply was no possibility that
the doctor would be taken in and cough up the £2500.

Dr Broadbent at once handed the letter to the police.
An advertisement was placed in the Personal column of
the *Daily Chronicle* inviting 'Malone' to call. Police
officers kept watch on Dr Broadbent's house from the
Friday when the advertisement appeared until one
o'clock the next day, but 'M. Malone' failed to appear.
Broadbent and the police took the letter to be the work
of a lunatic – perhaps they weren't all that far from the
truth – and took the matter no further. Nothing was
done about investigating Matilda Clover's death.

In addition to letter-writing and associating with
prostitutes Cream found time to meet a Laura
Sabbatini, who lived in Berkhamstead. Both Laura and
her mother took 'Dr Neill' to be a perfectly respectable
doctor. After a relatively short acquaintanceship,
Cream and Laura Sabbatini became engaged.

On 5th January 1892 Cream left Lambeth Palace

Road, saying that he was going on a visit to America. (In fact he went to Canada.) He spent the next day with the Sabbatinis at Berkhamstead where he made out a holograph will leaving everything to Miss Sabbatini. This document was one used at Cream's trial to identify the handwriting on some of the bizarre letters that he wrote.

Cream left for Canada the following day, 7th January, 1892. While staying at Blanchard's Hotel in Quebec Cream met a John Wilson McCulloch, a commercial traveller in coffee, spices and extracts. The two men met several times a day for nine days, and although they were apparently on good terms, McCulloch had reservations about Cream.

On one occasion McCulloch told Cream he was not feeling well. Cream accompanied him to his room and gave him a couple of pills. Another time Cream took McCulloch to his room and showed him a score of bottles of samples of pills and patent medicines he had received from the United States. Then he opened his tin trunk and took out a cash box, from which he took out a bottle of whitish crystals. 'That is poison,' Cream told McCulloch. 'I give that to the women to get them out of the family way.'

'How do you do that?'

'I give it to them in these,' Cream explained, and showed him a box of capsules. Next he produced a set of false whiskers, which he wore 'to prevent identification when operating', which McCulloch knew from what Cream had told him before meant when he was performing abortions.

Cream's main topic of conversation was his adventures with women. He boasted that he had 'a lot of fun' with women and had had intercourse with three women in one night, between 10 p.m. and 3 a.m. This was when he mentioned that he paid them a shilling each and showed him some indecent photographs. 'He always had a loose tongue about women,' McCulloch added. Cream confided to him that he suffered from headaches and insomnia and he took morphia for relief. It appears that in Quebec, at least, Cream sometimes appeared to be in a complete daze from taking morphia, and probably opium.

McCulloch finally became completely disenchanted with Cream's company. They had a conversation about an American who had come to Canada with a lot of money.

'I should have had that man's money,' Cream said.

'How's that?'

'I could give that man a pill and put him to sleep and his money would have been mine.'

'You'd kill a man for $2,000, would you?'

'I ought to have done it. I regret I didn't do it . . . '

That permanently put McCulloch off Cream. When he read in the papers that Dr Neill of London had been identified as Dr Cream of Canada he got into touch with the police and was subpoenaed to come to England and give evidence at Cream's trial.

While Cream was in Quebec he had one of his more inexplicable rushes of blood to the head. He had printed 500 leaflets:

ELLEN DONWORTH'S DEATH

To the Guests of the Metropole Hotel

Ladies and Gentlemen
I hereby notify you that the person who poisoned Ellen Donworth on the 13th last October is today in the employ of the Metropole Hotel and that your lives are in danger as long as you remain in this hotel.

Yours respectfully
W.H. MURRAY

London April 1892

Another contact Cream made in Quebec was a Mr M.A. Kingman, who was an agent for a manufacturing chemist, the G.F. Harvey Manufacturing Company, of Saratoga Springs, New York. He arranged for an order of 500 1/16 strychnine pills among other drugs to be sent to him. Later he wrote to the company offering his services as their London agent, which they declined, but they supplied him with some more pills. He visited the company and bought a case of medicines, and although the company still refused to give him an official agency, they agreed to pay him a commission on any orders he sent. Cream was confident that he would do well out of this arrangement and he secured some $1,400 from his father's estate to finance his business venture.

On 23rd March Cream sailed from New York, and arrived in Liverpool on the 1st April. Next day he was in London, and after a visit to the Sabbatinis in Berkhamstead he returned to his old lodgings at 103 Lambeth Palace Road on the 9th April. He was there for only two days before London was shocked by two more awful deaths.

Three weeks earlier two prostitutes had come to London from Brighton, Alice Marsh, aged twenty-one, and Emma Shrivell, aged only eighteen, and taken adjoining rooms at 118 Stamford Street, which runs from Waterloo Road to Blackfriars Road. It was a dreary place. These two young women, according to a statement made by Shrivell shortly before she died, had a man friend they knew as Fred, who said he was a doctor. He was about 5 feet 8 inches to 5 feet 9 inches tall, of stoutish build, dark, bald on top of his head and wearing glasses. He generally wore a black overcoat and a tall silk hat.

On the night of the 11th April Shrivell and Alice Marsh had a meal of tinned salmon and bottled beer. After they had eaten Fred gave them each three capsules. Charlotte Vogt, the girls' landlady, went to bed at about eleven o'clock, when the house was quiet.

At about a quarter to two in the morning (now 12th April) PC George Cumley of L Division saw a man being let out of 118 Stamford Street by a young woman, whom he later identified as being Emma Shrivell. The man he described as being about 5 feet 9 inches to 5 feet 10 inches tall, about forty to forty-five years of age, wearing a moustache, dressed in a dark overcoat with a tall silk hat and wearing glasses. The constable thought nothing of the incident: it was an all too frequent occurrence on this part of his beat.

At half-past two Mrs Vogt was woken by screaming and shrieking. Alarmed, she got up quickly and ran into the corridor where Alice Marsh, wearing only a nightdress, was crying out in agony. Immediately she sent her husband for a cab and a policeman. Almost at once she heard Emma Shrivell upstairs screaming 'Alice!' Vogt rushed upstairs where she found the 18-year-old, also in agony, on the floor leaning against the foot of a sofa. Now Marsh, downstairs, began screaming again and Vogt ran back down. Marsh was lying on her stomach in the passage, her body racked with what Vogt called 'twitching'. Between bouts of this 'twitching' Marsh was quite conscious and was able to talk to Vogt. The landlady tried to give the girls an emetic, mustard and water, but without effect.

Mr Vogt returned with a cab and PC William Eversfield of L Division. By now there was a fairly general commotion. PC Cumley, the officer who had seen Shrivell at the door of the house earlier that morning, had been sent for and he arrived at number 118 just as Eversfield was carrying Shrivell into the cab. Marsh was still in the house, lying over the seat of a chair, face downwards, in the passage, and Cumley carried her into the cab. She was dead on arrival at hospital.

Shrivell was able to answer questions put to her by the constables, but her statement was not admissable in court because it was not considered to be a dying declaration. To be admitted as a dying declaration the person must be in such a condition that immediate death is probable, and the person believe that the condition will be the cause of immediate death. Shrivell, it was considered, was not aware that she was dying. In any case, although Cream was eventually charged with the murders of Marsh, Shrivell, Donworth and Clover, only the case of Matilda Clover was proceeded with.

Cumley reported to his senior officers his sighting of the man coming out of number 118 on that morning, and from then on he kept an eye open for him in the area.

The tin which had contained the salmon the girls had eaten was examined, but was shown to be uncontaminated and as contemporary reports had it, the theory of 'ptomaine' poisoning was abandoned. Ptomaines are a product of decomposition of protein by bacteria, or in other words, of putrefaction. Although ptomaines are poisonous and were once thought to be a main cause of food poisoning, in fact it is the bacteria and not the ptomaines which cause the trouble. In any case ptomaines have such an evil smell that any food so badly contaminated as to contain a dangerous amount of ptomaines would be quite uneatable anyway.

The tempo of the Cream case now increased, and events came crowding one on the other.

Cream borrowed from Mrs Sleaper a copy of *Lloyd's Weekly Newspaper* which had a report of the inquests on Shrivell and Marsh. 'It was a cold-blooded murder,' he commented. The next day, Easter Monday, 18th April 1892, Cream went into the rooms of a young medical student who was lodging in the house, Walter Harper, while Mrs Sleaper was there. Harper was the son of Dr Joseph Harper, who had a practice in Barnstaple.

Cream asked Mrs Sleaper a number of questions about Harper and his background, and he looked at his medical books. Sleaper answered his questions, which seemed harmless enough to her. She told Cream where Harper's home was, and that he was a very quiet young man.

'It was Mr Harper who poisoned those girls in Stamford Street,' he said.

'He's the last man in the world to do such a thing,' the shocked Mrs Sleaper replied. 'You must be mad.' She was nearer the truth than she knew.

'Don't tell anyone,' Cream continued, unabashed. 'The police have proof.'

'How do you know?'

'I have a detective friend from America. Each of the women had a letter before her death warning them not to take the stuff that Mr Harper would give them. The police have the letters.'

On the following Wednesday Cream went to Berkhamstead to visit his fiancée Laura Sabbatini and her mother. Cream played the pious gentleman and took Laura to church. Whenever he visited the Sabbatinis he asked to have a Bible in his room.

The next week, the 26th April, Dr Joseph Harper received a letter dated the previous day.

Dr Harper, Barnstaple.

Dear Sir,

I am writing to inform you that one of my operators has indisputable evidence that your son, W.J. Harper, a medical student at St Thomas's [sic] Hospital, poisoned two girls named Alice Marsh and Emma Shrivell on the 12th inst., and that I am willing to give you the said evidence (so that you can suppress it) for the sum of 1500 L sterling. The evidence in my hands is strong

enough to convict and hang your son, but I shall
give it to you for 1500 L sterling, or sell it to the
police for the same amount. The publication of this
evidence will ruin you and your family for ever, and
you know that as well as I do.

To show you what I am writing is true, I am
willing to send you a copy of the evidence against
your son, so that when you read it you will need no
one to tell you that it will convict your son. Answer
my letter at once through the columns of the
London *Daily Chronicle* as follows: 'W.H.M. – Will
pay you for your services – Dr. H.' After I see this
in paper I will communicate with you again. As I
said before, I am perfectly willing to satisfy you that
I have strong evidence against your son by giving
you a copy of it before you pay me a penny. If you
do not answer it at once I am going to give the
evidence to the Coroner at once.

Yours respectfully,
W.H. MURRAY.

Although there was a certain sameness about Cream's
letters, his price had plummeted drastically from his
first demand for £300,000.

Cream made three visits to the Sabbatinis in April.
On the third, from the 30th April to the 3rd May, he
got Laura Sabbatini to write some letters for him. Not
unnaturally, considering the contents of the letters, she
asked Cream why he wanted her to write them, but he
refused to give her any reason.

London, 2nd May, 1892.

To Coroner Wyatt
  St. Thomas's Hospital,
    London.

Dear Sir,
    Will you please give the enclosed letter to the
Foreman of the Coroner's jury, at the inquest on

Alice Marsh and Emma Shrivell, and oblige,
                    Yours respectfully,
                    Wm. H. Murray.

                                London, 2nd May, 1892.
To the Foreman of the Coroner's Jury
in the cases of Alice Marsh and Emma Shrivell.

Dear Sir,

I beg to inform you that one of my operators has positive proof that Walter Harper, a medical student at St. Thomas's Hospital, and a son of Dr Harper, of Bear Street, Barnstaple, is responsible for the deaths of Alice Marsh and Emma Shrivell, he having poisoned those girls with strychnine. That proof you can have on paying my bill for services to George Clarke, detective, 20 Cockspur Street, Charing Cross, to whom I will give the proof on his paying my bill.
                    Yours respectfully,
                    Wm. H. Murray.

To George Clarke, Esq., Detective,
    20 Cockspur Street, Charing Cross,
        London, 4th May, 1892.

Dear Sir,

If Mr Wyatt, Coroner, calls on you in regard to the murders of Alice Marsh and Emma Shrivell, you can tell him that you will give him proof positive to him that W. Harper, student, of St Thomas's Hospital, son of Dr Harper, Bear Street, Barnstaple, poisoned those girls with strychnine, provided the Coroner will pay you for your services. Proof of this will be forthcoming. I will write you again in a few days.
                    Yours respectfully,
                    Wm. H. Murray.

From the initial demand for £300,000, Cream had now come right down to mentioning no price at all.

There was a Henry John Clark (no 'e'), who had a private detective's office at the Cockspur Street address, but it goes without saying that he knew nothing of this affair and had never heard of 'Wm. H. Murray, Detective'.

The incredible naivety of Laura Sabbatini as displayed by her willingness to write these letters goes some way to explaining how she could become engaged to a man like Cream, although there is no doubt that he did have a strong animal magnetism for some women. She did ask him if he did have the evidence referred to in the letters.

'A friend of mine, a detective, has it.'

'Why do you want me to sign the name Murray?'

'That's the name of my friend.'

'How do you come to know him?'

'I'll tell you one day.'

Meanwhile, the deaths of Donworth, Marsh and Shrivell had galvanised the police into action. Inspector George Harvey of L Division, stationed at Lambeth, sent his officers to all parts of London to question prostitutes. One of these detectives, Sergeant Alfred Ward, went to see Lucy Rose, the servant in Matilda Clover's lodgings, in the course of his general enquiries about prostitutes, and she mentioned Matilda's strange death. He reported back to Inspector Harvey. The consequence was that Harvey applied for an exhumation order for Matilda Clover; she was exhumed on the 6th May and Dr Sir Thomas Stevenson found strychnine in the body.

Ever since PC Cumley had seen Cream leaving 118 Stamford Street he had kept an eye open for him. On the 12th May he was alone on duty in Westminster Bridge Road when he recognised Cream as he walked up and down outside the Canterbury Music Hall. The

Canterbury was a well-known rendezvous for prostitutes and punters. Cumley sent word to Sergeant Ward.

Later that same night Cumley and Ward saw Cream again outside a public house in Westminster Bridge Road with a woman. The two policemen followed them to her home at Elliott's Row, St George's Road, close to the Elephant and Castle. They waited until Cream came out, and followed him in turn to 103 Lambeth Palace Road. It seems that at the trial Ward tried to take the credit for spotting Cream, but the probability is that Cumley saw him first. In any case, after they discovered where he lived Cream was put under police surveillance.

Another important character in the drama now put in an appearance, a man named John Haynes, who said that he was an engineer but also played another part. He admitted that he had worked as a detective for the government. Haynes had gone to lodge at 129 Westminster Bridge Road, the home of a William Armitage, a photographer, and his wife Margaret. At that house Haynes met Cream. One day Armitage, while Haynes was there, said that his house was being watched, and asked Cream if he was the one who was being shadowed. Cream denied it: 'No, certainly not,' he declared.

Cream had arranged to go out that evening with Haynes, but Haynes had second thoughts when he heard that the house was under surveillance. 'I can't go to the music hall with you tonight without making inquiry,' he said. Subsequently, at Cream's trial, somewhat enigmatically he told the court, 'That night I went to make enquiries.' His inquiry or enquiries were obviously successful, for the following day he remonstrated with Cream. 'You ought to have told me that you've been followed for some time.' Cream confessed that he was being watched, but it was in mistake for a man who lived in the same house as himself: Walter Harper. He made a long, rambling statement during which Haynes took notes, and when Haynes revealed that he had been working for the British Government Cream became very confidential.

Even at a century's distance there seems to be something *louche* about the Armitage household. Armitage introduced Cream to the sometime government agent Haynes, who was living there, and then introduced him to Sergeant Patrick McIntyre of the CID. In one of his fits of rash confidentiality Cream made a fatal mistake with McIntyre. He first complained to him that a 'rip' (a prostitute) he met in Westminster Bridge Road told him she had been sent after him to find out who he was as they suspected him of having a connection with the Stamford Street poisoning cases. At this McIntyre pricked up his ears, for until now Cream had not mentioned the murders. Next Cream showed McIntyre a letter addressed to Marsh and Shrivell which had been through the post. He said that a detective named Murray had given him the letter in the street – as likely a story as the explanation of a man found wearing a stolen gold watch saying he bought it from a man in a pub. This letter warned the young women to be wary of Dr (*sic*) Harper as he would serve them as he had served Matilda Clover and Lou Harvey. This really set a couple of cats among the pigeons.

This was the first time that McIntyre had heard the name Clover, and certainly he was unaware that she had been poisoned. [Although the fact that Clover had been poisoned was mentioned in the blackmailing letter to Dr Broadbent from 'M. Malone' the previous November, it will be remembered that the police made no enquiries about her death at the time.]

It was also the first time the name Lou Harvey had come to the notice of the police. When Harvey's name was linked with Clover's they immediately started

hunting for information about the death of this Lou
Harvey.

Cream was beginning to thrash around like a fish in a
closing net, but he had only himself to blame for it. On
26th May Cream got his solicitors to write to the Chief
Commissioner of Police, complaining that he was being
followed by detectives, including Sergeant McIntyre.
Cream complained that this was damaging his business
of selling drugs to doctors and pharmacists.

An Inspector John Tunbridge was assigned to
investigate the South Lambeth poisoning cases. He had
an inconclusive interview with Cream at his lodgings,
and on 1st June he travelled to Braunton in Devonshire
to see young Dr Harper, who had now qualified, and
was in practice. Harper and the inspector travelled over
to Barnstaple to see Dr Harper Sr. He produced the
letter from 'M. Malone', and when Tunbridge read it
he must have given an inward whoop of joy, for it was
an extremely valuable piece of evidence. It was in
Cream's handwriting, and it referred to Matilda Clover
being poisoned – long before anyone had ever
suspected it. More: it provided the perfect pretext for
arresting Cream, on a charge of blackmail, and keeping
him locked up while the police sought more evidence to
support a charge of murder.

Cream booked a passage to America, but before he
could flee he was arrested in the evening of 3rd June at
Lambeth Palace Road and charged with attempted
blackmail. He was still remanded in custody on this
charge when the inquest was held on Matilda Clover. It
opened on 22nd June at Tooting Vestry Hall.

A major witness was the elusive Lou Harvey, now
living in Brighton, who gave evidence in her real name
of Louisa Harris. She had seen her name in the
newspapers, and wrote to the Coroner and the Chief
Commissioner of Police.

After all the witnesses had been heard the coroner

said that in order to satisfy himself and the jury, Cream
must be sworn. At that point the inquest turned into an
undignified farce which recalls American trials and
enquiries when witnesses 'take the Fifth' – invoke the
Fifth Amendment to the Constitution under which no
one is obliged to incriminate himself. 'I refuse to
answer on the grounds that it may tend to incriminate
me' is the cry that has become one of the great clichés
of our time. Cream anticipated it.

The Coroner said he must be sworn.

> **Neill:** My instructions are not to open my mouth.
> **Coroner:** You must be sworn. All I wish to ask you
> is your name and occupation.
> **Mr Waters** (Cream's solicitor): He declines,
> through me, to give evidence.
> **Coroner:** I must know it from his own lips, and he
> must be sworn.
> **Mr Waters:** Under these circumstances, he will
> consent to be sworn.

Oh, no he won't, was Cream's attitude.

> **Cream:** I decline to say anything whatever. I have
> received my instructions. I shall not open my
> mouth. I may do so later, but I will not do so now.
> **Mr Waters:** I submit that this is a technical farce
> but Neill* can be sworn and then he will decline to
> give evidence.

Cream took the oath. Not that it did any good.

> **Coroner:** What is your name?
> **Cream:** I decline to answer any question in regard
> to that.
> **Coroner:** But you must tell me that.

* Cream was using the name Dr Thomas Neill in England, and he was
charged under that name.

Even now the coroner's plaintive, exasperated tone echoes across the years.

> **Cream:** No, sir. I have got my instructions what to do, and I shall abide by them whatever the consequences are.
> **Coroner:** Is your name Thomas Neill Cream?
> **Cream:** I decline to answer that question.
> **Coroner:** Are you a qualified medical man?
> **Cream:** [No answer.]

Cream's obduracy was pointless, and probably even counter-productive. The jury consulted for no more than twenty minutes before bringing in a verdict which could not have been plainer: 'We are unanimously agreed that Matilda Clover died by strychnine poisoning, and that the poison was administered by Thomas Neill with intent to destroy life. We therefore find him guilty of wilful murder.'

A contemporary account quaintly comments: 'An excited mob gave Neill an unkindly welcome on his leaving the Vestry Hall.'

This was on the 7th July, but Cream was not charged with murder until the 18th July: the authorities were in no hurry because they had him in custody, remanded on the blackmailing charge. He appeared at Bow Street Police Court (now Magistrates' Court) on 21st July, and the hearing continued until the 22nd August.

During this time Cream wrote a sheaf of letters – in a disguised hand – to his fiancée Laura Sabbatini. They reflect a fluctuating relationship. First he attacked her for having testified that the letter and the will he made out to her were in his writing and then went on to tell her that she must swear that she never saw him write anything. If the police asked her anything about him, she was to say she didn't know and couldn't remember, and she was to burn anything with his writing on.

Astonishingly this failed to make her suspicious of

him, for she wrote back saying she would stick to him to the end, much to Cream's delight. He wrote again, proclaiming his innocence of murder and insisting that the authorities had no real evidence against him. In fact he was not far from the truth here: the case against him for the murder of Matilda Clover, the one count that was proceeded with, was pretty feeble.

By now we begin to learn something of Laura Sabbatini's character. We do not have her letters to Cream, but his replies to her reflect an extraordinary lack of judgement that borders on foolishness. After thanking her for the loan of £10 and wishing they could be married, 'then you could not testify against me; for a man's wife is never allowed to testify against him', Cream writes:

> Why did you not let me know you were so fond of me when I was with you? Your letters are a revelation to me. I know now that you love me, but I never felt sure of it before . . . If I had known . . . that you are so fond of me, how much happier I should have been.

Cream admits a 'fondness' for Laura Sabbatini, but he can never bring himself to write of *loving* her, except in his last letter during the Bow Street hearing, and even then perfunctorily. Once more he strongly argues his innocence of killing Donworth, Clover, Marsh and Shrivell and the authorities' lack of evidence against him. He concludes this letter:

> Love to you now, my dear little girl, from
> Yours affectionately,
> NEILL.

Although she was not listed among Cream's victims, in a way Laura Sabbatini was one, too.

The trial of Thomas Neill Cream, charged as Thomas

Neill, opened at the Old Bailey on Monday, 17th
October 1892 before Mr Justice Hawkins (later Sir
Henry Hawkins). It was held at the former Old Bailey,
before the present Central Criminal Court was built. It
was a deplorable place, small, cramped and almost
unbearably stuffy. It was a tradition that the dais of
each court was strewn with dried herbs, and the judges
and aldermen given small bouquets of flowers each day
of a trial. The judges sniffed the bouquets to overcome
the foetid smell of the court. Originally it was believed
that the flowers and herbs warded off any infection of
deadly jail fever from the prison next door. Be that as it
may, the Old Bailey where Cream was tried had its own
characteristic smell of sweat, smoke and unwashed
bodies.

He was indicted for a number of offences: the
murders of Alice Marsh, Ellen Donworth, Emma
Shrivell and Matilda Clover; demanding money with
menaces from Joseph Harper and William Henry
Broadbent; and for attempting to administer strychnine
to Louisa Harris with intent to murder her – to all of
which Cream pleaded 'Not guilty'.

The Crown fielded a team of four counsel: the
Attorney-General, Sir Charles Russell QC, MP (later
Lord Russell of Killowen); the Hon. Bernard Coleridge
QC, MP; Mr Henry Sutton and Mr Charles Gill.
Russell was originally a fairly uninhibited advocate,
and once was vigorously criticised for a cross-
examination that overstepped the bounds of propriety.
He took the criticism to heart, and by the time he
became Attorney General he was more moderate.

Cream's defence was led by Mr Geoghegan, assisted
by Messrs H. Warburton, Clifford Luxmoore Drew and
W. Howel Scratton. Geoghegan, who had a strong Irish
accent, was an extremely eloquent advocate and one
who was difficult to stop once he was launched on one
of his floods of oratory.

[There was a celebrated case when Geoghegan appeared before the Privy Council as leader to Marshall Hall, another powerful and almost irrepressible orator. They were representing Frederick Deeming, whose life of crime had elements in common with those of Cream, Jack the Ripper and John Christie. Deeming, a plausible confidence trickster, murdered a number of women and cemented their bodies under kitchen, scullery or bedroom floors in three continents. He was eventually arrested, tried and sentenced to death in Melbourne. From there he cabled an appeal to the Privy Council. Normally the Council intervene only when there has been a flagrant miscarriage of justice, but they sat to hear Deeming's appeal.

Geoghegan was in full flight when an important telegram arrived which Marshall Hall felt he should see. He tugged on Geoghegan's gown several times, but the Irishman continued speaking. At last Geoghegan lost his patience. In a stage whisper which could be heard at the back of the court he told Marshall: 'Don't dare to interrupt me when I am addressing this court!' he roared. Marshall kept silent until the end of his leader's speech and the court adjourned.

'Why did you keep interrupting me like that?' Geoghegan demanded.

Marshall Hall handed him the telegram. It was from the prison chaplain in Australia: 'Deeming hanged this morning.']

Although Cream was charged with four murders and one attempted murder, only the Matilda Clover case was proceeded with. The evidence against him in this case was fairly thin, as it was in the other cases. It was clear to both the prosecution and defence counsel that the main hope of convicting Cream was if the evidence against him in the other cases were admitted. This was the only legal point of any interest in the case, and after a powerful argument by the Attorney General and an equally forceful counter-argument by Mr Geoghegan, Mr Justice Hawkins ruled, without hesitation, that the evidence was admissable. Although Cream himself did not seem to realise it, that ruling effectively annihilated his chances of an acquittal.

There was a similar point of law in the celebrated 'Brides in the Bath' case some twenty years later, when evidence of the deaths in the bath of two of George Joseph Smith's previous wives was admitted, and led to his conviction.

At the time of Cream's trial the accused was not allowed to give evidence on his own behalf, a law which probably saved more prisoners than it convicted. [After the passing of the Criminal Evidence Act in 1898 the fact that a prisoner did not go into the witness box in his own defence usually made a bad impression on the jury, although the prosecution and the judge were not allowed to comment on the accused's silence.] So Mr Geoghegan relied on his own cross-examination of the prosecution witnesses and his eloquence in his address to the jury.

He had one severe handicap: he did not have the right of reply. Since the defence called no witnesses normally the prosecution would have summed up their case first, but the prosecution was led by the Attorney General, who always had the last word. In today's courts Geoghegan's speech would be considered impossibly extravagant and emotional, but by the standards of a hundred years ago it was superb. He concluded:

> I say between you and the prisoner at the bar, between the Crown and the prisoner, there stands a figure, and that figure is the Genius of the Law of England. It is the best protector a man can have in his hour of need. It demands that the guilt of

the accused shall be brought home to him as clear as the light of Heaven now streaming into this court, and it is under the protection of that figure I leave my client, Thomas Neill.

When Cream returned to Holloway Prison after Geoghegan's speech on his behalf he sang and danced in his cell, so confident was he of a 'Not guilty' verdict. The next day thoroughly disabused him of this idea. The judge's summing-up was deadly. The jury were out for only ten minutes before returning with a verdict of 'Guilty'. Mr Justice Hawkins pronounced sentence of death.

Cream was relatively unimpressed, and as he left the dock he was heard to say, 'They shall never hang me.'

He was wrong.

DR EDWARD WILLIAM PRITCHARD

*When a doctor does go wrong, he
is the first of criminals*
                              Conan Doyle

*The Doctor said that Death was but
A scientific fact*
                              Oscar Wilde

*When a man knows he is to be hanged . . . it
concentrates his mind wonderfully.*
                              Dr Johnson

*I think we ought to let him hang there.
Let him twist slowly, slowly in the wind.*
                              John D. Erlichman

Of all the deadly doctors dealt with in this book, merciless and totally without any redeeming feature as most of them were, none was as sickeningly hypocritical and sanctimonious as the odious Dr Edward William Pritchard. He condemned his mother-in-law and wife to agonising deaths, much more lingering than those suffered by Cream's victims, and as his wife lay dying in bed he 'comforted' her with loving words on his lips and with poison in his hand. Just after she died he cried out, 'Come back, come back my dear Mary Jane! Don't leave your Edward!' When his wife lay in her coffin at the home of her father, Pritchard insisted that the coffin be opened and in the presence of her relatives he kissed his dead victim on the lips.

Pritchard had very probably already committed one murder before he started his campaign to murder his wife and her mother. He escaped punishment, but not obloquy, for this first murder because there was not enough proof against him to stand up in court. In the last two cases, because of middle-class morality – the 'don't want to get involved . . . it's not my business' syndrome – and because of doctors' professional solidarity, no one did anything to stop his long drawn-out murders until it was too late.

One mystery remains: *why* Pritchard killed his wife and mother-in-law. There simply is no obvious motive. What was almost certainly his first murder was another matter. Although we cannot be certain of the details, it is easy to imagine why he would have wanted to kill the young Elizabeth McGirn and try to hide the fact that it was murder. We can easily see that McGirn might have caused him all sorts of problems.

On the other hand, there are absolutely no indications or grounds for speculation why he killed either of his next two victims. He did not murder his mother-in-law for financial reasons; he gained nothing by her death. Nor was she a handicap to him in any way; she idolised him. The death of Pritchard's wife, had it gone undetected, would have brought him no advantages. Mrs Pritchard knew he had affairs with other women, including an under-age servant girl in his own house, but did nothing about it, so he didn't have to get rid of her for sexual motives. And it is absolutely certain that she was not unfaithful, so there could be no question of his seeking revenge. What drove him to kill them, then?

The only hint of a possible physical or material motive is that Pritchard promised to marry the servant girl Mary McLeod if his wife died before he did, but there is no evidence and no suggestion that McLeod put any pressure on him to marry her. In fact all the indications are that McLeod didn't care for Pritchard and had sexual intercourse with him only under duress. At least, at first.

Some of the claims Pritchard made about himself clearly indicate that he frequently had only a tenuous grasp of reality. This strengthens the hypothesis that Pritchard's motive was purely psychological and not material. Contemporary observers suggested that he did it out of sheer arrogance from a desire to prove to himself how clever he was in getting away with murder. In fact he wasn't clever at all. Pritchard, like some other medical murderers who seem to have suffered from exalted opinions of their own intelligence, left as many traces behind him as a hare in a paperchase. Today we have a greater understanding of psychopathic behaviour, and we can envisage another, even more sickening motive. Simply, that Dr Pritchard was a sadist and actually enjoyed studying the almost indescribable sufferings of two helpless women while pretending to care for them. Across more than a century, the thought still chills the blood.

Edward William Pritchard was born at Southsea, Hampshire, in December 1825. The family had a strong naval and medical tradition. His father was a captain in the Royal Navy; two of his uncles were said to have been admirals, a brother was a naval surgeon and another was secretary to the Royal Navy Commander-in-Chief, Plymouth.

Before his fifteenth birthday he was apprenticed to two surgeons with a large practice in Portsmouth. Although a contemporary report declares that his knowledge of medicine was of the shallowest, he appeared before the Court of Examiners of the College of Surgeons when he was twenty years old and was admitted a member. He also underwent an examination by the Navy Board, was gazetted as an assistant surgeon and joined *HMS Victory* a month before his twenty-first birthday. He saw a considerable amount of sea duty and while serving on *HMS Hecate* at home station he met Miss Mary Jane Taylor, who was to become his wife.

Mary Taylor was the daughter of a prosperous silk merchant in Edinburgh. She was staying in Portsmouth with an uncle, Dr David Cowan, a retired naval surgeon, when *Hecate* came into port. She was introduced to Pritchard at a ball; the relationship flourished and they were married in 1850 not long after they met.

They were not together for long because Pritchard didn't have enough money to leave the navy and set up a home for his wife, so he continued to serve in the *Hecate* while the new Mrs Pritchard returned to her parents' home in Edinburgh. The Taylors, meanwhile, were actively looking for a practice for their son-in-law.

They found one in Hunmanby, a couple of miles from
Filey and midway between Scarborough and Bridling-
ton. Pritchard resigned from the navy and set up home
there with his wife in March 1851. Soon after that he
opened a branch surgery in Filey. While living at
Hunmanby he contributed articles to medical and other
magazines, and wrote a number of books on matters of
local interest.

He became a freemason and made the most of his
membership to publicise himself. It is indicative of his
attitude that he had the insignia of the order printed on
his visiting cards. After his trial a Yorkshire paper
published an article about him with the clear vision of
hindsight and not blinkered by any concern of libel
actions – which is not to say that the article was
inaccurate. In the opening sentence he is described as
'fluent, plausible, amorous, politely impudent and
singularly untruthful'. The writer then warms to his
work and adds depth and colour to this sketch. There is
one choice sentence: 'His amativeness led him into
some amours that did not increase public confidence in
him as a professional man . . . '

In effect, the article takes a long time to say that he
was a compulsive liar, a spendthrift and a highly sexed
megalomaniac. All that, as we now know, was not the
worst of him, by far.

In 1857 Pritchard purchased the diploma of a Doctor
of Medicine *in absentia* from the University of
Erlangen, which is some ten miles north of Nuremburg.
The bare report suggests that diploma mills are not a
modern invention. Pritchard also became a Licentiate
of the Society of Apothecaries in London on the
suggestive date of April the first. After some six years
in Yorkshire he sold his practice, leaving a mass of
unpaid bills for people to remember him by.

Next Pritchard became medical attendant to a man
travelling abroad. In 1859 he visited Egypt and the

Holy Land while his wife went back to her parents' home in Edinburgh.

He returned to Scotland in June of the following year and went to live with his wife at 11 Berkeley Terrace. Nineteenth-century Scottish doctors were hardly likely to be outgoing and responsive to any strangers, let alone to a dubious Sassenach like Pritchard. He had letters of introduction but undermined their value by his extravagant claims about himself; and it appears that he was too unctuous by far. He tried to get into the Faculty of Physicians and Surgeons, but no one would propose him. He was rejected by other medical societies, which required no more qualifications than a diploma, of which he had two, and a respectable character, of which he clearly had none.

It is easy to say of Pritchard that he had a thick skin, but that facile cliché distracts attention from his real character defects. The man was massively egocentric, had no self-critical faculty and no ability to understand others. He had a wildly fertile creative imagination – as we shall see from some of the stories he told – but no perceptive insight into others' feelings, no empathy; and it is of this that torturers and brutal killers are made.

When applying (unsuccessfully) for a Chair of Surgery, he wrote that he had many opportunities, in almost every part of the world, of gaining practical experience, and promulgating the principles of modern surgery. Most applicants present their CVs in the best possible light and it is expected of them, but Pritchard added some highly suspect testimonials allegedly from well-known medical men in England.

Rejected by his medical colleagues, Pritchard sought a larger stage for his self-promotion. He joined the Glasgow Atheneum and became a director of the institution and an Examiner in Physiology at the Society of Arts. In his efforts to become a public personality – there is the irresistible feeling that today he would have done everything he could to get on to television – he gave a number of lectures. Most of the talks were concerned with his travels, which appear to be sponsored by Baron Munchausen. Part of one of his talks has survived: 'I have plucked the eaglets from their eyries in the deserts of Arabia and hunted the Nubian lion in the prairies of North America . . . '

Pritchard also claimed to be a friend of Garibaldi, and brandished a walking stick engraved 'Presented by General Garibaldi to Edward William Pritchard.' It is all too clear that if Garibaldi had been asked about 'his friend' Edward William Pritchard he would have replied 'Who?'

In his indefatigable search for a sort of fame Pritchard had a large number of copies of his photograph printed which he sold to stationers at below cost; he also handed them out liberally to chance acquaintances. He was hardly a nineteenth-century pin-up. He was tall and well-built, and had not unpleasing features, true; but he was bald, and in carefully arranging hair from the side of his head and plastering it across his scalp he emphasised his baldness rather than disguised it. His most striking feature was his beard: spade-shaped, heavy and full, reaching down nearly to the top button of his waistcoat, looking as formidable as a camel-thorn hedge.

Nevertheless, he built up a large practice, which gave him opportunities to make sexual advances to his women patients. He narrowly escaped prosecution for one incident in which a married woman, in the terminology of the period, was grossly insulted.

So far his anti-social behaviour had been confined to sexual impropriety, financial dishonesty and obnoxious obsequiousness. On the night of 4th–5th May 1863 there is almost irresistible evidence that Pritchard's actions took a sinister turn. That night a fire broke out in his home in the room of a young servant girl, Elizabeth McGirn. Pritchard subsequently said that he had been woken by his two sons calling out to him from the room adjoining his own on the second floor. He got up, found smoke in the corridor and realised that the house was on fire. He went to the boys' room and led them down into the front hall then rushed back upstairs to the attic. He pushed open the door of the room which was so full of smoke he could not enter. He called out 'Elizabeth!' but, not unexpectedly, there was no reply.

Pritchard was going back downstairs to raise the alarm when the front doorbell rang. It was a policeman who had seen the glare of flames from the attic. In the words of a contemporary report, 'The alarm was immediately conveyed to the Anderson Police Office, and then to the central engine section by telegraph, and the brigade was speedily in attendance.'

When at last the fire was out, McGirn was found dead in bed, badly burned. The body was on its back, with the left arm by its side and the right arm bent. The tissues of this arm and the chest were burnt away and the head was badly charred. The rest of the body, covered with bedclothes, was comparatively untouched, except for the feet, which were outside the blankets and were charred.

The theory advanced for the tragedy was that the girl, who often read in bed by the light of a gas jet, had fallen asleep and the gas had set fire to the bed hangings. She was suffocated by the smoke and then burnt. This theory was given weight at the time because McGirn had not tried to escape the fire and was lying in a normal position for sleeping.

However, there were a few uncomfortable coincidences and minor mysteries about the whole affair. Mrs Pritchard and the household's other servant girl were away that evening. When Pritchard himself returned home at about 11 p.m. that Monday night he noticed, he said, that the light was still burning in the attic room. Oddly enough he diverted from his usual custom of speaking to the servant to see if there had been any calls for him, and did not go up to her room.

It was later remarked that there was an unexplained time lapse between the policeman ringing at the front door and Pritchard answering it, although he said that he had been out of bed for some time before that. As far as McGirn is concerned, it is true that people killed in fires often die of asphyxiation rather than burning, but it is almost inconceivable that the girl would not have made some voluntary or involuntary movement as soon as she started inhaling smoke. 'The only presumption . . . ' a contemporary writer declares, 'is that the girl was dead, or under the influence of a soporific, before the fire was kindled.' It seems a reasonable assumption.

Then there is the matter of the book that McGirn was supposed to have been reading. Not the least trace of it was discovered, and it strains credulity to snapping point to say that the fire could have left not the slightest vestige of charred paper or ash. The fact the body's right arm was bent at the elbow does not necessarily suggest that the girl had been holding a book. The classic 'pugilistic attitude' of fatal burns victims is well-known.

At the time there was no apparent motive for any crime. However, it is probably not without significance that Elizabeth McGirn's successor as a servant was fifteen-year-old Mary McLeod, who was seduced by Pritchard while Mrs Pritchard was away in the summer of 1863. Sexual intimacy continued for some 18 months – until just before Mrs Pritchard's death – during which time McLeod became pregnant and Pritchard gave her an abortion. In those days of widespread sexual hypocrisy a servant girl had little option if the master of the house decided he wanted to go to bed with her. At the lower levels of working class life many would-be 'respectable' women were forced by sheer economic necessity into semi-prostitution. Pritchard gave the girl small presents, including a ring, a brooch and a locket that contained a photograph of himself. Mary McLeod took out the photograph and destroyed it.

Not long after the fire at the Berkeley Terrace house the Pritchards moved to 22 Royal Crescent, where the family were joined by the new servant girl. A year to the day later they again moved, this time to a house in Clarence Place, off Sauchiehall Street. It was near Madeleine Smith's former home. She was a 21-year-old architect's daughter, tried in 1857 for the murder of her lover, 30-year-old Émile L'Angelier. The verdict was Not Proven.

The purchase price of the house was £2,000, a considerable sum then. Pritchard borrowed £1,600 on the security of the house, and Mrs Taylor, his mother-in-law, lent him the balance, plus another £100 cash. When she sent the money she wrote:

> Once more let me express the hope that a very short time will relieve you from all trouble. I will do all I can to push the thing [purchase of the house] on. My love to Mary and the children.
> Ever, dear Edward, yours affecty.,
> Jane Taylor

Pritchard seems to have been strapped for cash at the time: he had overdrafts at two banks, despite his busy practice. Perhaps it is not too surprising, for the Pritchard household was large. There were Dr and Mrs Pritchard, four of their children (the eldest, a daughter, had been brought up by her grandparents and lived with them in Edinburgh), the cook Catherine Lattimer and Mary McLeod, who acted as housemaid and nurse to the children and covert mistress to the doctor. Towards the end of the year a couple of medical students, Thomas Connell and Richard King, came to stay at the house and presumably made some contribution to household expenses.

During the summer of 1864 Mrs Pritchard walked in on her husband kissing Mary McLeod in one of the bedrooms. Although Mrs Pritchard said nothing to the girl then and there, Mary later took the initiative and spoke to her. She said she wanted to leave the house, but Mrs Pritchard would not let her go. 'I'll speak to the doctor,' she said, adding, 'He's a nasty, dirty man.'

Whatever she said to the nasty, dirty man had no effect because he continued having sexual intercourse with the girl and, as we have seen, procured an abortion for her.

(Later, at Pritchard's trial Mary, not yet seventeen years old, gave evidence of Mrs Pritchard's sickness and the events leading up to her death with some degree of composure; but when the Solicitor-General questioned her about her relations with the doctor she became badly distressed. In the moral atmosphere of the place and period it must have been a terrible ordeal for a young girl: she couldn't bring herself to answer some of the questions until she was brought under great pressure by the Solicitor-General and the Lord Justice-Clerk. It was a harrowing scene; the effect on public opinion of the detestable Pritchard is not difficult to imagine. For all that, there is a nagging suspicion that there could be other reasons for McLeod's discomfiture.)

On the 19th September 1864 Pritchard made the first of many purchases of drugs at a branch of the Glasgow Apothecaries Company in Sauchiehall Street: ten grains of strychnine, although there was no suggestion of Mrs Pritchard's being poisoned with this particular drug. In fact, the servants and other members of the household did not notice a marked deterioration in Mrs Pritchard's health until nearly six weeks later, at the end of October. She was confined to bed with general sickness and vomiting, caused, as she thought, by a chill.

On the 16th November Pritchard made another visit to the chemists in Sauchiehall Street, when he purchased an ounce of laudanum and an ounce of tartar emetic. Laudanum, of course, is another name for opium; tartar emetic is antimony potassium tartrate. It was used for the treatment of fever and bronchitis in Pritchard's time; now antimony is given for treatment of Schistosomiasis or Bilharziasis, which is an infestation of blood flukes endemic in Egypt, many parts of tropical Africa and South America.

John Campbell, the manager, was taken aback by the amount of the tartar emetic: an ounce is 435.5 grains, and the usual dose given as an emetic was two grains. In fact, Campbell said later, the shop would sell only about two ounces in a year to the whole of the medical profession and the general public.

Glaister and Rentoul give the following symptoms of acute poisoning by antimony:

> An astringent metallic taste in the mouth, a sensation of heat and constriction of the throat; dysphagia [*difficulty in swallowing*] to some extent; gastric pain followed by vomiting of an incessant character and accompanied or succeeded by diarrhoea; faintness and profound prostration . . . cramps in the abdomen and limbs . . .

Eight days later Pritchard bought an ounce of tincture of aconite.* A tincture is an alcoholic solution, generally of a vegetable substance. Glaister and

---

* See pp 192–3. In the Pritchard case experts and non-experts alike used the name aconite almost exclusively in their testimony. To avoid possible confusion 'aconite' is employed throughout in this case.

Rentoul, again, describe the symptoms of aconite poisoning:

> Onset is from a few minutes to an hour after taking the poison: numbness, burning, and a tingling of the mouth and throat . . . severe pain and tenderness in the stomach; nausea and vomiting; numbness, loss of power and pain in the limbs; giddiness, singing in the ears, deafness and impairment of vision; indistinct articulation . . .

These are the poisons that Pritchard gave his wife and his mother-in-law, who doted on him.

Two days after Pritchard purchased the aconite, the 26th November, his wife went to stay with her relatives in Edinburgh, where her health improved rapidly. She was away for about a month. During her absence Pritchard made another of his massive purchases of aconite, this time in the form of an ounce of Fleming's Tincture of Aconite. This preparation is about six times stronger than the ordinary tincture, and the pharmacist John Campbell must have wondered what on earth was going on. He would not expect to sell more than an ounce or so of Fleming's Tincture in a whole year. However, firmly applying the principle of 'It's none of my business', he didn't ask 'Why do you need so much?' Further purchases by Pritchard failed to prod him into voicing his curiosity.

Mrs Pritchard returned home to Glasgow on the 22nd December to spend Christmas with her family. The improvement in her condition during her visit to her relations was maintained, and she remained in good health at home in Glasgow for a fortnight or so. Then there was a recurrence of her former illness: general sickness and vomiting, usually after meals, and particularly liquid ones. The unhappy woman spent most of her time in bed, coming downstairs to eat with her family only rarely. By this time Pritchard, of course, had laid in a heavy stock of antimony and aconite.

This chronic illness suddenly became acute on the 1st of February. Mrs Pritchard was in the dining room when she went into the pantry and began vomiting violently. She managed to get up to her bedroom unaided, but about half an hour later she rang her bedroom bell. Catherine Lattimer, who had been the Pritchards' cook for some ten years, went up to her and was shocked to see how ill Mrs Pritchard was. She was lying in bed with her clothes on.

'Catherine, I have lost my senses,' she said, speaking with some difficulty. 'I was never as bad as this before.' In addition to violent vomiting she also suffered from agonizing cramps in the hands and down one side, leaving her very exhausted. Lattimer noticed that Mrs Pritchard's fingers were straight out while the thumbs were twisted underneath them with the cramp. As we can see, Lattimer described in other words the symptoms of aconite poisoning. Mrs Pritchard didn't ask for her husband, but Lattimer fetched him upstairs from the consulting room. The doctor gave his wife a little spirits and water. Alcohol seems to have been a popular remedy at the time.

After this attack Pritchard wrote to a Dr James Cowan, a retired doctor living in Edinburgh who was Mrs Pritchard's second cousin, saying he was worried about his wife's condition, and asking him to come to visit her. Cowan arrived on the 7th February. Mrs Pritchard was able to come down from her bedroom to the drawing room unaided. Cowan found Mrs Pritchard rather better than he had expected from the tone of Pritchard's letter, but he thought she had been wrong to come downstairs to him. She described her symptoms, although Cowan later admitted that he did not ask her many questions: he went to see her more as a friend than as a doctor, he said. He prescribed a mustard poultice for her abdomen and champagne and ice to combat her exhaustion.

The fact that Dr Cowan apparently wasn't suspicious of anything perhaps encouraged Pritchard, for that same day he again went to his friendly neighbourhood poison supplier in Sauchiehall Street and bought an ounce of tartarised antimony and an ounce of tincture of aconite.

Dr Cowan returned to Edinburgh the next day, the 8th February, but maybe in the train he began to feel uneasy about Mrs Pritchard's case. When he arrived back in Edinburgh he went to see Mrs Pritchard's mother, Mrs Taylor. He urged her to go to Glasgow to nurse her daughter. The Pritchard household was a large one, and with only two servants in the house Mary Jane wasn't receiving all the attention she needed.

That same night Mrs Pritchard suffered another attack of severe spasms. When one pieces together testimonies given at Pritchard's trial a scenario is formed of a wild, hysterical and tragi-comic – much more tragic than comic – night.

Downstairs, three floors below, Catherine Lattimer heard Mrs Pritchard calling out. She rushed upstairs to find Mrs Pritchard in a hysterical condition. Dr Pritchard, as unemotional as an executioner, was at the bedside trying, Lattimer said, to calm her.

'I want to see another doctor,' she managed to say. 'Fetch Dr Gairdner.' Dr William Gairdner was Professor of Medicine at the University of Glasgow, and knew Pritchard. Mrs Pritchard asked for him because he had been a class-fellow of her brother at college.

Gairdner was at work on preparing a lecture for the next morning when Mary McLeod came with a message at some time between midnight and 1.30 a.m. on the night of 8th–9th February. He went to the Pritchard home immediately.

'My wife has been very sick and her stomach cannot bear food,' Pritchard told Gairdner. 'Dr Cowan has seen her and he prescribed stimulants. I've given her some champagne, and some chloroform.' He then took Gairdner to his wife's bedroom. Mrs Pritchard was in bed. 'She had a flushed face and was in a considerable state of excitement,' Gairdner said later. She explained that she was unwell because she had taken chloroform. 'I don't blame the doctor [Pritchard],' she went on. [But] . . . 'I never liked chloroform.' Gairdner examined her, and found nothing to cause him any immediate alarm.

She had been sick and was exhausted, but she had a good pulse. The most remarkable thing about her, as far as Gairdner was concerned, was her state of high excitement – she had a lot to say – and the spasms in her hands. Mrs Pritchard held them up above her head so Dr Gairdner could see that the wrists were turned in and the thumbs inverted towards the wrists.

'Catalepsy,' Pritchard said knowingly. Catalepsy, according to one authority, 'is a term applied to a nervous affliction characterized by the sudden suspension of sensation and volition, accompanied by a peculiar rigidity of the whole, or of certain muscles, of the body.'

Rather ungallantly, and probably contrary to some sexual discimination legislation, the author continues, 'The subjects of catalepsy are in most instances females of highly nervous or hysterical temperament.'

Gairdner was unimpressed by Pritchard's diagnosis of catalepsy. He thought it had nothing to do with Mrs Pritchard's illness. He'd already formed a pretty good idea of what was wrong with Mrs Pritchard: she was drunk. In fact Mrs Pritchard drank very little and no one had ever seen her drunk.

He went to the fire to warm his hands before making a further examination. Mrs Pritchard screamed out at the top of her voice, 'Oh, you cruel, cruel man! You unfeeling man, don't leave me!' Gairdner went back to the bed and tried to soothe her.

'I'm not going to leave you,' he told her. He returned to the fire to warm his hands. This provoked another screaming fit from Mrs Pritchard. Gairdner was unmoved: he put it all down to the drink, and it is far from impossible that Pritchard had given his wife a few slugs of champagne and a dose of chloroform to produce that effect. While Gairdner, smugly satisfied with his diagnosis of drunkenness, again warmed his hands at the fire, Pritchard remained at the bedside, standing over his wife, apparently affected by her illness.

'Don't cry,' Mrs Pritchard told him sharply. 'If you cry you are a hypocrite.'

Mary McLeod, who came into the room, said she actually saw Pritchard crying. This really was an Oscar-winning performance of indescribable hypocrisy by the cold-blooded murderer. McLeod also said that Mrs Pritchard's words were, 'Don't cry. If you cry it was you that did it.' However, this could have been a mishearing of 'If you cry, you are a hypocrite.' Mary McLeod had every reason not to give Pritchard the benefit of any doubt.

Pritchard probably realised it was pointless making any more effort to impress his wife and Gairdner. He went over to the fire to join the other doctor. Looking across at the two men Mrs Pritchard called out, 'You are all hypocrites together.'

Before he left, Gairdner gave Pritchard a stern warning and roundly admonished him for his 'impropriety' in giving his wife stimulants.

'It was ordered by Dr Cowan,' Pritchard said.

'Well, it's a very bad treatment,' Gairdner retorted.

Pritchard asked about giving his wife chloroform.

'No stimulants and no more medicine till I see her

again,' Gairdner said sternly. He called about midday the following morning. 'My wife is better and quite quiet,' Pritchard declared. Certainly she appeared to be in better health.

'No stimulants and no medicine,' Gairdner repeated to Mrs Pritchard. 'When you want food you should have a plain, boiled egg, and milk and bread. If your stomach has fair play it will digest the milk and simple food I've mentioned.'

Gairdner was not asked to return, and this was the last that he saw of Mrs Pritchard. Nevertheless, it is clear that he had his suspicions: at the very least he was troubled by the situation. So he wrote to her brother, Dr Michael Taylor of Penrith, about his feelings, and strongly urged that he have his sister come and stay with him. Dr Taylor contacted Pritchard, who said he was perfectly willing for her to go, but that she wasn't yet fit enough to travel. Of course, she never would be.

Meanwhile, following Dr Cowan's advice, Mrs Taylor informed her son-in-law that she was on her way to stay with her daughter and help look after her. Pritchard made his preparations to receive her: he went out and bought another ounce of tincture of aconite. Chemist John Campbell still kept to himself any misgivings about these astonishing quantities of poison Dr Pritchard was buying. Even the Borgias could not have been more blatant.

Mrs Taylor arrived at the Pritchard home on the 10th February. She was a hardy, vigorous woman despite her seventy years, although she had one weakness. She was addicted to a medicine with the unusual name Battley's Sedative Solution. This folksy-sounding remedy was nothing more than an opium preparation. She began taking it to alleviate what was then described as neuralgic headaches, but could well have been migraine. Opium is, of course, habit-forming and people who take the drug frequently develop a tolerance to it. Soon after Mrs Taylor arrived she gave Mary McLeod a bottle to take to the chemist's to have it filled with the solution. Mrs Taylor carried this bottle around with her. According to Pritchard she took a swig from time to time. However, no one ever saw Mrs Taylor the worse for opium and there were no signs of her over-dosing with opium until possibly – although not probably – the day of her death.

On Monday 13th February Mrs Pritchard was briefly well enough to decide she would like some tapioca, that unpleasant, gooey staple of British public school life. Kenneth, the middle of the three boys, went to get a bag from a local grocer's.

This seemingly innocuous bag of bland ground cassava was to assume some importance in Pritchard's eventual trial. The bag was briefly left on the hall table before being taken down to the kitchen, either by Mrs Taylor or the servant Mary McLeod. Catherine Lattimer cooked half a cupful and McLeod took it up to the dining room.

Mrs Taylor had some – whether Mrs Pritchard did too is uncertain – and immediately vomited. With grim but accurate unconscious insight she remarked, 'I must have the same complaint as my daughter.'

Later, after Pritchard had been arrested, the remains of the packet of tapioca was recovered from the kitchen. It was laced with antimony. He simply hadn't had the elementary nous to dispose of this physical evidence.

On the Thursday of that week Catherine Lattimer left the Pritchard's service to go to live with a friend, Margaret Graham, a dressmaker. Lattimer's place was taken by a Mary Patterson, but Lattimer didn't cut off all contact with the Pritchards. She returned to the house occasionally to take out the children.

Mary Patterson did not see Mrs Pritchard during her first days at the house, and would not do so until the dreadful night when Mrs Taylor died.

Two days after Patterson's arrival Dr Pritchard set out

for Sauchiehall Street to buy some more poison. This time he went to a different chemist's shop, owned by John Currie, where he had regularly bought drugs during the three years since he arrived in Glasgow.

In addition to two ounces of morphia solution he bought an ounce of the hyper-strength Fleming's Tincture of Aconite. The massive single purchase of a year's normal sale of this preparation of aconite provoked no overt reaction of surprise or curiosity from Currie, either at the time or later, which seems a masterful exercise of self-control. Currie would not be the only tight-lipped actor in this appalling story of double murder. Perhaps, if he had known of Pritchard's purchases from John Campbell's shop he may have raised an eyebrow. As it was, Pritchard was single-handedly creating a local shortage of aconite.

From the moment Mrs Taylor arrived in the Pritchard home she nursed her daughter day and night, spending almost all her time in the sickroom. Her presence was a major obstacle to Pritchard's plans to murder his wife, for Mrs Taylor prepared most of her daughter's meals herself, in the sickroom. If Pritchard were to poison his wife, his mother-in-law had to be got out of the way. While he was scheming to kill Mrs Taylor and his wife, Pritchard found time to carry on a weighty correspondence with Mrs Pritchard's brother Dr Michael Taylor, his daughter who was in Edinburgh with Mrs Taylor Sr., and his father-in-law.

To Dr Taylor Pritchard wrote detailed symptoms of Mrs Pritchard's illness and his own suggested treatment of her. His letters to his daughter and father-in-law were unbelievably, revoltingly hypocritical. One letter to his daughter read:

> Kiss dearest grandma for me – love her and help her all you can, and when the rolling years pass away you will remember my advice and be happier

by far by doing so than I can positively make you understand now. Pray to our Heavenly Father quietly and alone to spare her to us, to protect you from all harm, and make you a good girl – in due time a Christian woman and a blessing to us all. Never forget kind friends, and those who have an interest in your well-doing.

The sheer enormity of this sanctimonious hypocrisy really does take the breath away.

On the 24th February Catherine Lattimer called on the Pritchards. Mrs Taylor said she was very worried about her daughter – as well she might be – and she couldn't understand what was making her ill.

At seven o'clock that evening she left the sickroom to have tea with Dr Pritchard and the family. After the meal she began writing some letters and she sent McLeod to buy some sausages for her supper. They seem to have had odd hours for meals in the Pritchard ménage, and the servants were expected to be on call at all hours. (In addition, when Mary McLeod's backbreaking household chores were done she had to serve Pritchard's sexual needs as well.)

Mrs Taylor returned to the sickroom, the last time she would climb those stairs. A few minutes later she violently rang the bell. It heralded a living nightmare that Mary McLeod would never forget. She went upstairs to find Mrs Taylor sitting in a chair, trying to vomit. She told McLeod to get some hot water, but it didn't help her to vomit or to feel any better. Mrs Pritchard, sitting up in bed, ordered McLeod to fetch her husband.

McLeod returned to the sickroom twice more. The second time Mrs Taylor was still sitting in the chair, unconscious, her head hanging down on her breast. Mrs Pritchard had managed to drag herself out of what would soon be her own deathbed and was pleading agonisingly with her mother to speak to her.

Pritchard sent Thomas Connell, one of the lodgers, for Dr James Paterson. This doctor appeared on stage late in the drama. Paterson was one of the major characters in the long-drawn out tragedy. His incomprehensible apathy and 'don't make waves' attitude were nothing short of grossly criminal. If he'd had a grain of sensibility – or maybe it was simple courage he lacked – Mrs Pritchard's life would have been saved. Although, as we shall see, he was mercilessly excoriated in measured language at the trial, and generally savaged by the public afterwards, he got off lightly.

Dr Paterson arrived at the Pritchards' home just before a quarter to 11. Pritchard met Paterson in the hall and led him to the consulting room on the first floor before taking him up to the sickroom.

'My wife has been very poorly for some time,' Pritchard said. 'A few days ago I telegraphed her mother to come to look after her.' In fact the initiative for the visit was probably Mrs Taylor's, not Pritchard's.

He went on to say that Mrs Taylor had fallen from her chair while having a fit, and added that she 'was in the habit of taking a drop'. One writer subsequently commented that this was a deliberate and wicked lie. In view of Pritchard's other crimes this was like calling Jack the Ripper wicked for having used a dirty knife.

Dr Paterson went upstairs to encounter a scene probably unmatched in all his thirty years' experience as a general practitioner in Glasgow. For a start, the foetid atmosphere in that room must have been enough to unsettle the strongest stomach meeting it for the first time. Mrs Pritchard had been there for days, suffering continuously from sickness and diarrhoea.

Mrs Taylor, still alive but comatose, was lying fully clothed on top of the bed on the side nearer Dr Pritchard, where Mary McLeod and Pritchard had lifted her. She was wearing a cap with a pathetic little artificial flower in it. Beyond her Mrs Pritchard, wearing a nightdress, was under the bedclothes. Her hair was in wild disarray.

Paterson's first impression was that Mrs Taylor had previously been in good health, 'showing not the slightest sign of being addicted to the use of spirituous or intoxicating liquors. She was rather above the ordinary size, good-looking' and, he said with appalling snobbishness, 'altogether a superior-looking person for her station in life.'

Mrs Taylor's face was pale, her eyelids were partly closed, her face was covered with a clammy perspiration and her pulse was almost imperceptible. From these and other indications Paterson diagnosed that Mrs Taylor was under the influence of opium or some other powerful narcotic. He immediately announced he thought she was dying.

Pritchard led Paterson away from the bedside, out of Mrs Pritchard's earshot. Paterson said he thought that there was nothing they could do for the poor woman. Still, as a last resort they could try mustard poultices on the soles of the feet, the calves and the inside of the thighs. They should also give her a turpentine enema as quickly as possible. The imagination reels.

Pritchard prepared the enema, mentioning to Paterson that he had given her one a little earlier, in which he had added a glass of brandy. This obsession with alcohol was quite extraordinary.

Mrs Taylor seemed to regain some consciousness. Pritchard clapped his mother-in-law on the shoulder and said 'You are getting better, darling.' Paterson shook his head ominously to convey to Pritchard, 'Never in this world.' At that moment the poor poisoned, tortured and abused woman lost control of her bowels and bladder. Paterson reiterated that he thought the case was hopeless, but Pritchard gave her the enema nevertheless.

And all the time Mrs Pritchard, herself suffering grievously from poison, was there in the room, beside her mother, conscious of what was being done to her.

While Dr Paterson was examining and treating Mrs Taylor he constantly kept glancing at Mrs Pritchard – and no wonder. In addition to her scarecrow hair she was obviously weak and exhausted. Her thin, feverishly flushed, bony face, according to Paterson, had a semi-imbecilic expression; her voice was peculiarly weak – 'very much resembling a person verging into the collapsed state of cholera', he later said confusingly. At first Paterson attributed her condition to the effects of the recent gastric attack that Dr Pritchard said she had suffered, together with the aggravation of the symptoms 'by the consternation and grief caused by the alarming condition of her mother'. Then, Paterson said, he 'became convinced that Mrs Pritchard was under the depressing influence of antimony'.

And he said nothing; he did nothing.

He had a second chance to remedy matters and save Mrs Pritchard's life, but again he remained inactive and silent. There are the stories of five murderous doctors in this book, murderers by design. Perhaps there should be a sixth: Dr Paterson, murderer by default.

Without asking Dr Pritchard about his wife or making any comment about her condition, Paterson left the house some time between midnight and 1 a.m. Soon afterwards Pritchard again sent Mary McLeod the two hundred yards to fetch Dr Paterson. He was already in bed, and claimed that as he was 'very much fatigued with the previous day's work, I was unwilling to rise.' Nevertheless, he sent his compliments to Dr Pritchard saying that if Dr Pritchard really thought that he could be of any use he would rise and visit Mrs Taylor, although he considered – rightly – that her condition was hopeless. Pritchard left it at that, and Paterson was able to stay in bed.

At one o'clock in the morning of Saturday the 25th February Mary Patterson was standing at the top of the stairs when Dr Pritchard came out of the sickroom.

'Mrs Taylor has gone,' he said.

So ended Act I of the grim, three-act tragedy of the Pritchards.

Patterson entered the room and set eyes on Mrs Pritchard for the first time. She was kneeling up on the bed beside her mother, rubbing her right hand. When Mrs Pritchard realised that Dr Paterson was not coming back to see her mother she asked her husband, 'Edward, can you do nothing yourself?'

His answer was brutal. 'No. What can I do for a dead woman? Can I recall life?'

Pritchard told his wife she should go downstairs, but she asked to be left for a while longer for she believed that her mother was not quite dead. Patterson had no doubts that she was. She had touched Mrs Taylor's forehead and felt that she was already growing cold.

Another room was prepared on a lower floor for Mrs Pritchard; she made her way to it slowly and painfully. Pritchard offered to carry her, but she refused.

'I prefer to walk,' she said coldly.

At first sight it is reasonable to believe that by this time Mrs Pritchard strongly suspected her husband was poisoning her. However, because of her weakened physical condition and the depression caused by her mother's death it could be that her spirit was broken and she had come to accept fatalistically her own death at the hand of her husband. In her more lucid moments Mrs Pritchard never directly accused her husband of poisoning her, but she was sometimes equivocal when talking to friends and acquaintances about the cause of her illness. Perhaps that is as far as she dared to go.

Mary Patterson and a Mrs Jessie Nabb, who did washing for the family, laid out Mrs Taylor's body. While they were doing this they found the old lady's bottle of Battley's Sedative Solution in a pocket of her dress. When Dr Pritchard heard of this – Mary McLeod told him – he hurried up to them and demanded the bottle. Patterson took the bottle from under the chest of drawers where she had put it and handed it over. Pritchard put on one of his acts. He raised his hands and looked up towards heaven, saying, 'Good heavens! Has she taken this much since Tuesday?' It was a convincing performance – at the time.

'Don't say anything about this,' he went on. 'It could cause trouble and it wouldn't do for a man in my position to be spoken of.' He was right about it causing trouble.

Pritchard· walked off with the bottle half full of Battley's Sedative Solution – which was heavily laced with antimony and aconite. He had secured the vital physical evidence, but then he made a second unbelievably stupid mistake. For some inexplicable reason he didn't simply pour away the incriminating proof of poisoning. He left it in the house, just as he had left the poisoned tapioca. It was a blunder he would make yet again. In a written confession after his conviction Pritchard said he added the poison *after* Mrs Taylor's death, but like other parts of this particular statement, it was highly suspect – and illogical.

By now Mr Taylor had come to Glasgow. With an extraordinary lack of sensitivity Pritchard sent him along to Dr Paterson's house to ask for his wife's death certificate. This was Paterson's first knowledge that the old lady had died. Paterson quite rightly refused, and with equal insensitivity. He told Mr Taylor that he was surprised that Dr Pritchard had sent for the certificate. 'As a medical practitioner he should know that it is not given to friends, but to the District Registrar.'

On Wednesday the 1st March Dr Pritchard met Dr Paterson by chance in the street. The thought is irresistible that Paterson was caught off guard, for

Pritchard must have been in the top ten of people whom Paterson would not want to meet. Pritchard told Paterson that he was on his way to Edinburgh to bury his mother-in-law, and asked Paterson to call and see Mrs Pritchard the following day. Paterson could find no excuse for not going. So, on the morning of Thursday the 2nd March Dr Paterson visited Mrs Pritchard.

She was irritable, weak and bedridden, but her first thoughts were for her late mother, not herself. 'Do you really think my mother was dying when you saw her?'

'I did, most decidedly.'

Mrs Pritchard clasped her hands together and exclaimed feebly, 'Good God, is it possible?'

Paterson questioned her about her mother's use of Battley's Sedative Solution. She told him that her mother occasionally drank the solution, but was not an habitual user. Paterson now turned his attention to Mrs Pritchard herself.

She had a thickly coated tongue, a weak, rapid pulse and had a generally severely debilitated appearance. In answer to his questions she said she had suffered from sickness, vomiting, constant severe thirst and diarrhoea. For this condition Paterson prescribed small quantities of champagne and brandy – to help her get back her strength, he said – with occasional small pieces of ice to alleviate her thirst. He also recommended her to take at frequent intervals easily digested nutritious food such as beef tea, calf-foot jelly, chicken soup and arrowroot. He further wrote a prescription for a mixture of calomel, blue or grey powder (a mixture of mercury and chalk, once used to check diarrhoea) and ipecacuanha. This last medicine is the root of a Brazilian shrub which contains an alkaloid, emetine. In small quantities it acts as a gentle stimulant to the mucous membrane of the stomach; in larger doses it produces vomiting. Paterson gave the prescription to Mrs Pritchard and told her to hand it to her husband when he returned home later.

What is so extraordinary about Dr Paterson's behaviour is that he gave her this advice and medical prescriptions which were useless for her condition when all the time he was convinced that she was suffering from antimony poisoning, and there was only one person who could have been giving it to her. Why did he not simply say to Dr Pritchard, 'Your wife has all the symptoms of antimony poisoning'? Even Pritchard would have been forced to think twice about continuing to poison his wife.

There can be no doubt that Dr Paterson was aware that Pritchard was slowly murdering his wife, as was confirmed by his reaction to a form he received the next day from the registrar, James Struthers, who asked him to give details of the duration of Mrs Taylor's illness and what caused her death. Paterson refused to complete the form and sent a note explaining why. This feebly ineffectual gesture was the only overt action he could bring himself to make to draw attention to what was being done to Mrs Pritchard.

The note was as follows:

> 6 Windsor Place, 4th March 1865.
>
> Dear Sir,
>
> I am surprised that I am called on to certify *the cause of death* in this case. I only saw the person for a few minutes of a very short period before her death. She seemed to be under some narcotic, but Dr Pritchard, who was present from the first moment of her illness until death occurred, and which happened in his own house, may certify the cause. The death was certainly sudden, unexpected, and to me mysterious.
>
> I am, dear Sir, yours faithfully,
>
> James Paterson, M.D.
>
> To Mr James Struthers, registrar.

Paterson argued that this note had a three-fold motive. The first was to do what was in his power to save Mrs

Pritchard's life; the second to guard his professional reputation; the third to detect the poisoner. He had a strange idea of what was in his power to save the unfortunate woman.

Struthers destroyed the letter without showing it to the authorities, which left Paterson, as he said, at a loss to understand. It really was a most reprehensible act of stupidity and failure of duty. Struthers must take part of the blame for Pritchard not being stopped in his tracks. Just the same, there can be no excuse for Dr Paterson's not telling the authorities straight out that Mrs Pritchard was being poisoned. Even if the criminally short-sighted registrar could just about be forgiven for ignoring Paterson's oblique and heavily coded letter, there could be absolutely no excuse for a second, even more serious, failing.

Paterson's third motive for sending the letter, ' . . . if possible, to detect the poisoner . . . ' is sheer hypocritical evasion of basic human duty. But of course, Dr Paterson was concerned to safeguard his professional reputation, as we shall see later from his testimony at Pritchard's trial. Paterson gave a very liberal interpretation to this preservation of his reputation: 'Don't make waves and don't be beastly about fellow doctors.'

The fact that Dr Paterson refused to certify Mrs Taylor's death caused Dr Pritchard neither embarrassment nor difficulty. He simply signed Mrs Taylor's death certificate himself. It read: 'Primary cause, paralysis, duration 12 hours. Secondary cause, apoplexy, duration one hour.'

This singular document is revelatory in two respects. First, it establishes the quality of Dr Pritchard's medical knowledge; and second, it demonstrates how culpably cursory was the registrar's scrutiny of the certificate – particularly after the note from Dr Paterson declaring that he found the death mysterious.

Apoplexy is more commonly known as a stroke, and to state that paralysis *preceded* a stroke is like saying a bruise appeared *before* a blow from a hammer. This ludicrously improbable certificate passed unremarked. Pritchard could well have thought himself bombproof. There is more. Pritchard certified that Mrs Taylor was paralysed for twelve hours before her death: i.e., from 1.00 p.m. Friday to 1.00 a.m. Saturday, when she died. But at 7.00 p.m. she had tea with her family, wrote some letters and sent McLeod out to buy some sausages.

On Sunday the 5th March Pritchard called on Paterson. It must have been as welcome a visit as a 3 a.m. knock on the door by the Gestapo. But Pritchard was all sweetness and light. 'My wife has been much relieved by the medicines and treatment you have ordered,' Pritchard said brightly. 'She greatly relished the small quantities of champagne and brandy and felt refreshed by the cooling, effervescing draught and the ice.'

Pritchard, we know, could turn on the charm when he wanted to, and this visit could well have persuaded Dr Paterson that Pritchard had realised he was on to him and so he had given up the idea of poisoning his wife. Pritchard needn't have bothered, if that was his motive. Paterson would remain inert and irresolute to the end.

Apparently, Mrs Pritchard's condition did actually improve briefly at this time. The following Wednesday, when Janet Hamilton, her dressmaker, called she managed to come down to the drawing room. Hamilton thought she looked better than when she saw her last, shortly after her mother's death.

'I don't understand the retching which keeps troubling me,' Mrs Pritchard said. She added two significant remarks. 'The retching always comes on after food' and 'It's very strange that I'm always well in

Edinburgh and ill at home.' Janet Hilton suggested asininely that this might be because Edinburgh was her native air.

'I don't know about that,' Mrs Pritchard replied.

Mrs Pritchard's life was now running down to its last few days. On Monday the 13th March Dr Pritchard bought his last supply of Fleming's Tincture of Aconite, half an ounce of it, at John Currie's shop in Sauchiehall Street, and next day he bought a solution of two grains of atropine and followed it with another five grains on the Thursday.

It was the aconite which was the significant purchase. The same evening Pritchard sent Mary McLeod up to his wife with a piece of cheese she had asked to have for her supper. For some reason Mrs Pritchard told McLeod to taste the cheese. Perhaps it looked mouldy, or discoloured. More likely, if Mrs Pritchard hadn't previously suspected that her husband was trying to kill her, she did now. The servant tasted a piece 'about the size of a pea' and at once she felt a burning sensation in her throat and a powerful thirst.

'Take it away,' Mrs Pritchard told her, and the cheese was taken down to the pantry. At about seven o'clock the following morning, Tuesday, Mary Patterson found it there and she tried some. She, too, had a burning sensation in her throat coupled with a strong thirst. She had eaten more than McLeod and soon afterwards she vomited violently and had to go to bed for the rest of the morning.

Pritchard's next poisonous assault was on Wednesday evening, the 15th. He told Patterson to make an egg-flip for his wife. 'Beat it up very smooth,' he told her, 'otherwise Mrs Pritchard will not take it.'

While Patterson was beating an egg in the pantry he said he would get some sugar for it. No one then or later seemed to think it curious that Pritchard had to leave the pantry and the kitchen – where one would expect to find sugar – and go for it in the dining room.

He went to the dining room, then through the hall *into the consulting room* before returning to the pantry with two lumps of sugar which he dropped into the beaten egg. He would add the whisky when he took the egg-flip to Mrs Pritchard, he said.

A quarter of an hour later McLeod came to collect the egg-flip. Patterson added hot water. 'I hope it's warm enough,' she said to McLeod. 'The kettle has been off the boil for some time.'

'Taste it,' McLeod suggested.

Patterson took a teaspoonful. 'What a taste it has!' she exclaimed disgustedly. It was horrible, and bitter. She experienced the same sensations as when she ate the cheese the previous day: she felt sick and had a burning, bitter feeling in her throat.

Mary McLeod took the egg-flip up to Mrs Pritchard, who was in bed. Meanwhile, downstairs Patterson had begun to vomit; she continued to have further attacks throughout the night.

In the bedroom Mrs Pritchard took about a wineglassful of the notorious egg-flip, and she, too, was sick almost immediately afterwards. Mary McLeod said she stayed in the room until about four o'clock in the morning when she at last went down to the room she shared with Patterson.

What happened then was disputed by the two women at the trial. Patterson testified that she told McLeod how ill she had been: 'I thought I'd die without seeing the face of anyone alive, alone in that room.' Then she asked whether Mrs Pritchard was so ill that she needed both her husband and Mary McLeod with her. 'Mrs Pritchard wouldn't let me leave the room,' McLeod replied, according to Patterson.

McLeod's version was that when she returned to the room Patterson was asleep and said nothing about being ill until later that morning. McLeod also declared

that Patterson had made no reference either to the
egg-flip having made her feel ill or about the cheese
tasting horrible. When pressed hard by the Solicitor-
General and the Lord Justice-Clerk on both points she
claimed she couldn't remember.

It is now that a strong strain of ambivalence can be
seen in Mary McLeod's behaviour. As we know, at the
beginning of her service with the Pritchards she
complained to Mrs Pritchard of the doctor's forcing
himself on her. She wanted to leave the household but
stayed on only because Mrs Pritchard asked her to.

Two years of regular sex with Dr Pritchard –
reluctant though she may have been to begin the
relationship – could well have reversed completely her
attitude. In basic terms, she could have come to enjoy
it. To the vast majority of people the first glass of beer
tastes unpleasant, the first glass of whisky more so. It
hasn't kept the world teetotal. The clear change in
Mary McLeod's relationship with Dr Pritchard also
casts a new light on McLeod's absence from her own
bedroom until 4 a.m. on that occasion.

Pritchard, it is evident, trusted McLeod: he got her
to take up to Mrs Pritchard the food and drink he had
laced with poison. On the other hand, he specifically
ordered the cook, Mary Patterson, to stay away from
his wife's bedroom. When Patterson and Mrs Nabb
found the bottle of Battley's Sedative Solution in Mrs
Taylor's pocket and hid it under a chest of drawers, it
was McLeod who told Dr Pritchard. So, some elements
of McLeod's behaviour in those last weeks and at the
trial can be interpreted as attempts to cover for Dr
Pritchard and, at the same time, herself.

Then there was the significant incident on Friday, the
17th March, the day before Mrs Pritchard died.
Between midday and one o'clock the servants' bell
rang, and then rang again. Mary McLeod should have
answered it, but when it rang a third time Patterson

went to see who was ringing. The rooms each had different-sounding bells, and as she was not sure which one had rung, Patterson first went to the consulting room. The door was slightly ajar and Patterson could hear Dr Pritchard inside.

'Did you ring, doctor?' she asked. There was no reply. Patterson pushed the door to open it, but something, or somebody, was obstructing it.

Patterson didn't insist. She went upstairs towards Mrs Pritchard's room. After a few moments Dr Pritchard came out of the consulting room and followed Patterson upstairs. He was followed in turn by Mary McLeod. So while Mrs Pritchard was urgently ringing her bell for attention, her husband and Mary McLeod were in the consulting room, keeping quiet behind a door that would not open. In view of the now long-standing sexual relationship between Pritchard and McLeod it can safely be assumed that they weren't playing draughts.

Mrs Pritchard had rung only for someone to take away her chamber pot, which Patterson primly described at the trial as 'a certain vessel'. Some twenty minutes later Patterson returned to the bedroom to talk to Mrs Pritchard about the children's clothes. As Patterson entered, Mrs Pritchard finished a long drink and handed the glass to her husband, who was standing beside the bed. She was calm and coherent when she gave her instructions to Patterson.

At five o'clock that afternoon Mrs Pritchard's bell rang violently, signalling the last scene of Act II of this private drama. Mary McLeod went to answer the bell. A few moments later she called down to Patterson. 'Come upstairs,' she said agitatedly.

Patterson found McLeod leading Mrs Pritchard back from the landing into the bedroom and then into bed. As Patterson arranged the bedclothes Mrs Pritchard said, 'Never mind me. Attend to my mother. Rub her, and give her breath.' Mrs Pritchard asked for a pillow and began to rub it. The two servants realised that she was quite out of her mind, and believed the pillow to be her mother.

Mrs Pritchard turned to Patterson and asked her to rub her cold, cramped hands. Then she said unaccountably, 'I did not know anything about this until the boys came in dressed.' None of the boys had come in. Ailie, the youngest daughter came into the room. Mrs Pritchard did not know who she was, and Patterson had to tell her.

Just before 8 o'clock Pritchard called at Dr Paterson's house and asked him to go back with him to see Mrs Pritchard. Paterson was almost certainly loath to return to Pritchard's home after his previous experiences there, but he accompanied Pritchard nevertheless.

When Paterson went into the bedroom Mrs Pritchard was sitting up in bed, propped up with pillows. He was struck by her terribly altered appearance. He described her as having a peculiarly wild expression; her eyes were fiery red and sunken, her cheeks hollow and pinched-looking, and very flushed. However, she seemed to recognise Paterson and caught his hand. Mrs Pritchard muttered something about having vomited, but Pritchard said that she was only raving, she hadn't been vomiting.

When she complained of a severe thirst Pritchard poured out a glass of water from a carafe, saying, 'Here is some nice cold water, darling.' It is pointless to insist further on his hypocrisy and cruelty: it is simply beyond the comprehension of normal minds.

Mrs Pritchard became delirious, talking about a non-existent clock among other things. Pritchard told Paterson her condition was due to lack of sleep, so the doctor wrote out a prescription for a morphia-based sleeping draught. To Paterson's surprise Pritchard said he kept no drugs in the house, which was most unusual for a physician who did night work. After this ineffectual consultation Dr Paterson went home.

A little later Pritchard came down to the kitchen for some coal. He spoke to Mary Patterson. 'I've had my friend Dr Paterson to see Mrs Pritchard. He said she had taken too much wine.' There was evidence enough already to convict Pritchard a dozen times over even without these and all his other lies and contradictions which weighed heavily against Pritchard at his trial.

Pritchard went back upstairs, took off his trousers and got into bed with his wife, while McLeod lay on the sofa for a while.

Mrs Pritchard said, 'Don't sleep, Edward, I feel very faint.' At about 1.30 a.m. Pritchard told Mary McLeod to get a mustard poultice for his wife. 'Please hurry,' Mrs Pritchard urged her.

Memories of the exact sequence of events in this nightmarish situation understandably became confused. McLeod said that two mustard poultices were prepared; Patterson spoke only of one. For once McLeod's version seems the more likely. She went downstairs, woke Mary Patterson and told her to make the poultice. Patterson prepared it, handed it to McLeod who returned to the bedroom, where the poultice was applied to Mrs Pritchard. It had no effect, and Pritchard sent her for a second one.

Patterson made it up, and when she handed it over she asked if she should go up to the sickroom with her. 'I'll let you know if you're wanted,' McLeod replied as she went upstairs.

Almost immediately the bedroom bell rang and Patterson hurried upstairs. Pritchard was still in bed with his wife. Patterson looked at her, and touched her. She was cold; dead. The second poultice was lying near her. Pritchard pulled up Mrs Pritchard's nightdress and asked Patterson to put it on.

'There's no point in putting a poultice on a dead body,' Patterson said bluntly.

Pritchard launched into one of his over-the-top dramatic performances. 'Is she dead, Patterson?'

'Doctor, you should know better than I.'

'She cannot be dead, she has only fainted.' He turned to McLeod. 'Rush down and get some hot water.'

'It's no use putting hot water on a dead body,' the no-nonsense Patterson said.

After a pause, perhaps to get his second wind and more inspiration, Pritchard said, 'Come back, come back my darling Mary Jane. Do not leave your dear Edward.' He added, 'What a brute, what a heathen. To be so gentle, so mild. Patterson, kill me! Get Mrs King's rifle and shoot me!'

'Don't provoke the Almighty with such expressions. If God were to shut your mouth and mine, I don't know how we would be prepared to stand before a righteous God,' Patterson reprimanded him.

'True, Patterson. You are the wisest and kindest woman I ever saw.'

Few authors dare to write dialogue like that.

Eventually Pritchard left the bedroom so McLeod and Patterson could dress Mrs Pritchard's body. So, in the early hours of Saturday 18th March 1865 came the end of Act II of the Pritchard drama.

The doctor soon recovered his composure after that display of synthetic emotion. He sat down to write some letters, one of which was to the Clydesdale Bank and others to close friends of Mrs Pritchard. The bank letter had all the sincerity of the classic phrase 'the cheque is in the post'.

131 Sauchiehall Street, Glasgow.

Sir,

I am fully aware of the overdraft, and nothing short of the heavy affliction I have been visited with since the year commenced – in the loss of my mother, and this day of my wife, after long and severe illness – would have made me break my promise. If you will kindly tell Mr Readman, to whom I am well known, that immediately I can attend to business I will see him on the matter, please ask him if he can wait till after my dear wife's funeral on Thursday.

I am, sir, yours faithfully,

EDWARD W. PRITCHARD.

Alexr. Mathers, Esq.

Pritchard squeezed the last drop of pathos from the situation: he even called his mother-in-law Mrs Taylor his mother.

He went out to post the letters. When he returned he again played the slightly-deranged-by-grief husband. He called Mary Patterson from the kitchen. At the top of the stairs he said, 'My wife walked down the street with me. She told me to take care of Ailie and Fanny, but she never spoke about the boys. She kissed me on the cheek, then went away.'

He went to his consulting room. Very soon afterwards he had apparently recovered from this display of hallucinatory grief. He sent for Patterson and asked for his wife's ring and earrings which she had taken from the body.

On Monday the 20th Pritchard made out a death certificate for his wife. He gave the cause of death as gastric fever which lasted for two months. The same day he accompanied his wife's body to Edinburgh. It was taken to her father's house before being buried beside her mother in Grange Cemetery.

Since he started poisoning his wife Pritchard had put on some shows of hypocrisy that defy belief; now he achieved the almost impossible feat of surpassing his previous displays. At the Taylor home Pritchard insisted on having the coffin opened, and in front of an audience of Mrs Pritchard's relatives, he kissed the dead woman he had murdered on the lips, 'while displaying a great deal of emotion'.

The same day Pritchard returned to Glasgow – humming cheerfully to himself, one can easily imagine – planning to go back to Edinburgh for his wife's funeral on the Thursday. Time and luck had finally run out for Pritchard, however. The only pity, the enormous pity, was that it was too late to save his victims. While he was in Edinburgh things began to erupt in Glasgow. The detonator that set off the explosion of activity was an anonymous letter to the Procurator Fiscal. The consensus of public opinion was that Dr Paterson had sent it. He denied it, but few people believed him. The body of the letter read:

> Sir
>
> Dr Pritchard's Mother in law died suddenly and unexpectedly about three weeks ago in his house in Sauchiehall Street under circumstances at least very suspicious.
>
> His wife died today also suddenly and unexpectedly and under circumstances equally suspicious. We think it right to draw your attention to the above as the proper person to take action in the matter and see justice done.

There is a slightly familiar ring about this letter. The last sentence of the letter Paterson wrote to the registrar when he refused to sign a death certificate for Mrs Taylor (Page 153) read: 'The death was certainly sudden, unexpected, and to me mysterious.'

This second letter cranked the creaky legal machinery into life. Preliminary enquiries were enough to merit a warrant being issued for Dr Pritchard's arrest. As he got out of the Edinburgh train at Glasgow's Queen Street station he was arrested by Superintendent Alex McCall.

During the next few days the authorities' actions increased in tempo and volume. People close to the Pritchards were interviewed; visits to Glasgow chemists revealed that Dr Pritchard had bought inexplicably large amounts of poisons. The police descended on the Sauchiehall Street house and took away bottles and jars, clothes and bedlinen used by Mrs Pritchard, and – finally – the poisoned cheese, poisoned tapioca and the bottle of Battley's Sedative Solution.

When Mrs Nabb was interviewed she told the police of the sexual relationship between Pritchard and Mary McLeod, which must have caused them to prick up their ears. This suggested a strong possible motive for murder. McLeod was taken in and questioned closely at length in front of the Sheriff, but was finally released.

An autopsy was performed on Mrs Pritchard by Andrew Maclagen, Professor of Medical Jurisprudence at Edinburgh University, and Dr Henry Littlejohn. Their first finding was a positively negative one: they could discover nothing to suggest that Mrs Pritchard's death was due to natural causes. The authorities were hardly satisfied with that. Although Mrs Pritchard was buried next to her mother in Grange Cemetery on Wednesday the 22nd March, a day earlier than originally planned, before the burial several of Mrs Pritchard's internal organs were removed for later chemical analysis. That same day, before the analyses were made, Pritchard was formally charged with the murder of his wife.

While all this was going on the local press was in a lather of excitement. These days, of course, in Britain all media comment is strictly forbidden once someone has been arrested and charged: it would be considered contempt of court. Then, the newspapers were as unbridled and imaginative as, for example, American and French newspapers are today. Every step of the investigation was reported and full details given of the interrogation of witnesses. When the papers ran out of facts they turned to invention to produce theory, conjecture, hypothesis and supposition. It didn't advance the investigation, but it sold a lot of newspapers.

The coolest person in the whole affair was the man at its centre, Pritchard himself, unruffled in the calm of the eye of the hurricane that howled around him. He declared himself confident that his innocence would soon be established. He always was strong on fantasy.

The extraordinary thing – or at least, so it seems now – was that neither his own nor his wife's relations believed Pritchard to be guilty, even in the teeth of the fact that he had bought poison almost by the bucketload. The man was as practised a dissembler and as convincing as only a psychopath can be. Public opinion was also on Pritchard's side for the moment. There was no obvious or even obscure motive for him to have murdered his wife. When he was charged Pritchard proclaimed his innocence with sincerity and believability.

On Tuesday the 28th March Pritchard's balloon was punctured explosively. The lengthy medical report of the chemical analysis of Mrs Pritchard's viscera arrived at Police HQ in Glasgow. In essence it said that Mrs Pritchard had died of antimony poisoning. The unstable weathercock of public opinion, always sensitive to the least breeze, now swung violently against Pritchard. He was committed for trial.

So far there had been no suggestion that Mrs Taylor's death had been unnatural. Only Dr Paterson had his strong suspicions and as we know, he expressed them only obliquely to the registrar, who blundered criminally in simply throwing away the letter. It wasn't until much later – too late – that Paterson, or someone, wrote the anonymous letter to the Procurator-Fiscal. But the discovery of antimony in Mrs Pritchard's body prompted the authorities to issue an exhumation order for Mrs Taylor. Tests on her body, too, revealed the presence of antimony.

On Monday the 21st April Pritchard was additionally charged with the murder of his mother-in-law.

A contemporary newspaper report said that throughout all this Pritchard remained calm and self-possessed. The only thing that seemed to disconcert him was that when he was in Glasgow's North Prison he was not allowed a supply of pomade to dress his beard and hair. Apart from this minor vanity, he worked hard at making an excellent impression on everyone he came into contact with while he was in jail. He was successful. By all accounts it was difficult for people to believe that this cultured and refined man could be a particularly vicious murderer. It appears, too, that the effects of this image-building percolated through the prison walls to the general public outside.

On Monday 26th June Pritchard, now thirty-nine years old, was taken from the North Prison in Glasgow to the Calton Jail in Edinburgh, where he was kept until his trial, which began on Monday the 3rd July. He was charged with the murders of his wife and Mrs Taylor.

The Solicitor-General, 46-year-old George (later Lord) Young, led for the Crown, with 45-year-old Adam (later Lord) Gifford and 40-year-old James Arthur Crichton. Pritchard was represented by 37-year-old Andrew (later Lord) Rutherfurd Clark, 38-year-old William (later Lord) Watson and 28-year-old David Brand.

The judges were a pretty formidable trio: the Lord Justice-Clerk, 55-year-old Lord Glencorse, 50-year-old Lord Ardmillan and 51-year-old Lord Jerviswoode. No wonder that the unsophisticted Mary McLeod, still only sixteen years old, felt intimidated when she had to give evidence of her intimacy with Pritchard before that heavyweight battery of judges.

As soon as the indictment was read out Watson moved that the charges be heard separately, quoting a number of precedents. The Solicitor-General simply replied that the two murders were inseparable parts of the same story and ought to be tried together.

Rutherfurd Clark countered by saying that the danger to the prisoner was that though there might not be independent evidence sufficient to prove either of the charges, yet, taking the two together, the jury might hold that there was enough to prove both. Exactly. And that is why the prosecution wanted to take the two murders together. The motion for separate trials was refused.

A trial which lasts 5 days, with 151 exhibits and a possible 87 witnesses warned for the prosecution can scarcely be called a formality, yet after that ruling a formality is what Pritchard's trial became – in the sense that it foreshadowed a recurring line in early Western movies: 'We'll give him a fair trial before we hang him.'

The trial was a long-winded, prolix affair. The indictment alone ran to some 700-odd words, and must have taken a good seven minutes to read out. It began:

> Edward William Pritchard, now or lately a doctor of medicine and now or lately prisoner in the prison of Glasgow, you are indicted and accused, at the instance of James Moncrieff, Esquire, Her Majesty's Advocate, for Her Majesty's interest: That albeit, by the laws of this and every other well-governed realm, murder is a crime of an heinous nature, and severely punishable: Yet true it is and of verity, that you, the said Edward William Pritchard are guilty of the said crime, actor, or art and part . . .

And it concluded eventually:

> . . . All of which, or part thereof, being found

> proven by the verdict of an Assize, or admitted by
> the judicial confession of you, the said Edward
> William Pritchard, before the Lord Justice-
> General, Lord Justice-Clerk, and Lords Commis-
> sioners of Judiciary, you, the said Edward William
> Pritchard, ought to be punished with the pains of
> law, to deter others from committing the like
> crimes in all time coming . . .

Needless to say, Pritchard made no 'judicial confession' referred to in the indictment.

A contemporary observer described the trial as 'one of the most memorable of modern times'. It is true that the circumstances of the crime were extraordinary, and probably had few parallels in the following century and a quarter, even taking into account multiple crimes like the Yorkshire Ripper's and the Black Panther's. Only the Moors murders matched or surpassed Pritchard's in the combined elements of intimacy of the killers and the victims, and the pathological, cold-blooded heartlessness of the killings. For all that, Pritchard's trial itself was tedious for the most part. This may be an unfeeling way to describe a trial on a capital charge, but to wade through the transcript of the proceedings *post hoc* requires a certain determination and a high threshold of boredom. There were, nevertheless, two major points of interest: Mary McLeod's evidence and the slow, remorseless demolition of the pig-headed, stiff-necked Dr Paterson. By the time he had finished giving evidence about the cause of Mrs Taylor's death you wouldn't trust him to prescribe an aspirin for a headache.

Inevitably, the case caused enormous interest and entrance to the court had to be carefully controlled. The regulations for entry introduced at the trial of Madeleine Smith eight years earlier were applied again for the Pritchard case. If the public expected to see a Frankenstein's monster when Pritchard entered the dock, they were disappointed. One newspaper report described him as 'rather a good-looking fellow' and added he looked 'the most cool and unconcerned person in the court'.

Another journalist wrote of him: 'The impression conveyed is that of mildness, approaching perhaps to effeminacy. The expression on his face . . . was sad and thoughtful; he seemed cool and collected and watched the proceedings closely.'

Pritchard, the consummate actor and confidence man, put on a polished performance. 'He most always wept when, as a fond husband, it was proper that he should be moved – wept, or did something dexterous with his pocket handkerchief which might very well pass for weeping', it was reported. Clearly this journalist was not taken in by Pritchard.

The case against Pritchard was simple.

Pritchard bought large quantities of poison; both Mrs Pritchard and Mrs Taylor died of those poisons; only two people in the house could have given them the poison – Pritchard and Mary McLeod. Catherine Lattimer and Mary Patterson were also members of the household, but the poisoning of Mrs Pritchard began before Patterson joined the staff and continued after Lattimer had left.

The first turning point in the trial came with the appearance of Mary McLeod in the witness box. The early part of her lengthy testimony concerned food and drink given to the two women and the progress of their illness. When the Solicitor-General asked her, 'Had Mrs Pritchard ever seen the prisoner using any familiarity with you?' it pulled back a curtain from backstairs illicit sex that must have shocked the puritanical Scots of the period – not to mention the Victorian Sassenachs – and given them a thrill of secret pleasure as well.

Rutherfurd Clark for the defence vainly tried to keep

out her testimony concerning her intimacy with Pritchard. As McLeod told of her seduction, pregnancy and abortion, and this was followed by deadly medical evidence, one observer perceived a transformation in Pritchard:

> With the anxiety that had now evidently taken hold of him, a certain vulpine look might be detected, as he keenly fixed his eye on the girl's [McLeod's] countenance . . .
>
> Throughout the greater part of her protracted examination a change came over the seducer's features. The mild, gentlemanly expression which these had hitherto worn, had now in some degree disappeared; and at times one could almost fancy that traces of malignity could be seen . . .

'Could almost fancy' seems to be about right.

Doctors Douglas Maclagan, Arthur Gamgee, Henry Littlejohn and Frederick Penny gave evidence at great length with mind-numbing details of the postmortem examinations of the two women and the complicated chemical tests for poison carried out on their remains. The court was also given details of experiments on rabbits which were injected with pure Battley's Sedative Solution, which made them unconscious; and then with the Solution with aconite added, which killed them very unpleasantly. Injection of some of the contents of Mrs Taylor's bottle of Battley's Sedative Solution killed them in the same way.

In brief, the experts' conclusions were straightforward: Mrs Pritchard died from antimony poisoning administered over a considerable period; Mrs Taylor died of antimony poisoning administered over a shorter period and its effects were aggravated by the presence of aconite.

The evidence was overwhelming, and Rutherfurd Clark, whose chances of saving Pritchard from the

gallows were slightly less than General Custer's of
getting away from Sitting Bull, was unable to produce a
single medical witness to challenge the findings of the
Crown's experts.

There remains the testimony of Dr James Paterson.
From the outset he showed a strong dislike of Pritchard –
naturally enough – and his antagonism was so marked
that the Lord Justice-Clerk referred to it in his summing
up. But that was the least of the highly critical remarks
made about him by the Lord Justice-Clerk.

The initial attack on Paterson for not doing anything
about Mrs Pritchard's symptoms of antimony poisoning
came not from the Crown counsel as might be expected,
but from the defence. Just a few of the exchanges
between Paterson and Rutherfurd Clark are illu-
minating.

> **Paterson:** My impression was that she [Mrs Pritchard]
> was being poisoned by antimony.
> **Rutherfurd Clark:** As you thought that Mrs Pritchard
> was suffering in that way from antimony, did you ever
> go back to see her again?
> **Paterson:** I did not, and I believe that I would never
> have been called back again if I had not met Pritchard
> accidentally in the street.
> **Rutherfurd Clark:** Why did you not go back?
> **Paterson:** Because she was not my patient. I had
> nothing to do with her.
> **Rutherfurd Clark:** Then, though you saw a person
> suffering from what you believed to be poisoning by
> antimony, you did not think it worth your while to go
> near her again?
> **Paterson:** It was not my duty. I had no right to interfere
> in any family without being invited . . .
> **Rutherfurd Clark:** . . . you stood upon your dignity and
> did not go back to see what you believed to be a case of
> poisoning?
> **Paterson:** I had no right.
> **Rutherfurd Clark:** No right?

> **Paterson**: I had no power to do it.
> **Rutherfurd Clark**: No power?
> **Paterson**: *I was under no obligation.*

Rutherfurd Clark went on hammering at Paterson but was unable seriously to dent the man's armour-plated self-assurance and absolute certainty that he was completely right in his interpretation of acting ethically. It was breathtaking.

The Lord Justice-Clerk put two questions to Paterson that left him no place to hide.

> **Lord Justice-Clerk**: . . . I think you stated that your impression when you first saw Mrs Pritchard, on the 24th February, and afterwards when you saw her again on the 2nd March, that she was being poisoned by antimony?
> **Paterson**: That is what I said.
> **Lord Justice-Clerk**: Do you mean that you believed some person was engaged in administering poison to her for the purpose of procuring her death?
> **Paterson**: Yes, that was my meaning.

Perhaps something got through to Paterson after all.

His ordeal was not over. After the expert witnesses gave their evidence he was recalled to testify concerning Mrs Taylor's death. Despite the undeniable presence of aconite in Mrs Taylor's bottle of Battley's Sedative Solution and antimony in her body, Paterson stoutly maintained on several occasions that she died from the effects of opium.

> **Lord Justice-Clerk**: I would like to know now, before you go, what your opinion is now, after hearing the whole evidence, as to the cause of Mrs Taylor's death?

Paterson: It strikes me that she died from the effects of the narcotic.
Lord Justice-Clerk: You mean the opium?
Paterson: Yes, that is my own impression.

Pressed, Paterson agreed that Mrs Taylor's body did contain antimony and finally conceded grudgingly that he believed her death was caused by a combination of opium and antimony. More than a century later, even in the bare trial record can be seen the image of a stupidly stubborn man jutting his jaw as he argued an untenable opinion. One of the factors that made him dig in his heels was a Glaswegian's antipathy to Edinburghians. After Pritchard's execution Paterson wrote a long letter to the *Glasgow Herald* in his own defence. One passage reads:

> . . . But I see it all now; and from your editorial today, coupled with what I actually observed on in Court, it is abundantly evident that there was a most decided bias against everything professional connected with Glasgow, and an apparent feeling that it would never do to promulgate to the world that a Glasgow medical man knew his profession better than the three Edinburgh graduates . . .

Another part of the letter:

> I am thankful to Almighty God that I was so seldom in that wretched house. Had I gone back, as the Lord Justice-Clerk and Mr Andrew Rutherfurd Clark thought I was in duty bound to do, and could Mr Clark have proved that I had done so, there might have been got up some *sensational statement* [Paterson's italics], to allege that I was the one who had administered the antimony, when I was so sure, so positive, that it would be found in Mrs Pritchard's body!

Paterson's paranoia and thrashing around to exculpate himself are all too evident. He justifiably criticised Struthers, the registrar, for his incomprehensible failure to act on Paterson's letter of refusal to sign Mrs Taylor's death certificate. But there was no getting away from the fact of Paterson's own much more serious inaction. The public didn't forgive him.

Rutherfurd Clark had to rely on the seeming improbability of two such inhuman murders being committed by a man of Pritchard's education and background: there were few witnesses who could testify for the defence. He was reduced to calling two of the Pritchard children, Charles and Jane.

> **Charles Edward Pritchard**, aged eleven (not sworn): I am Dr Pritchard's eldest son. I lived with him in Glasgow. I was there when mamma died. My papa and mamma lived happily together. Papa and mamma were very fond of one another.

> **Jane Frances Pritchard**: I am the daughter of the prisoner, and am fourteen years of age. I lived a great deal with my grandmother in Lauder Road. Papa was often there with my grandmother. Grandmama and papa were very fond of each other. I have often heard her speaking very kindly of him, and him of her.

It was a bad tactical error to call them. The appearance of the two pathetic children in court only hardened the feeling against Pritchard. Rutherfurd Clark was also criticised for trying to suggest that Mary McLeod committed the murders, but he really had no choice. It had been firmly established that only she or Pritchard could have poisoned the two women, so in defending Pritchard, Rutherfurd Clark simply had to attack McLeod.

The Lord Justice-Clerk's summing-up was detailed

and long. Very long: it went to some fifteen thousand words and took most of the last day of the trial. He went over the evidence meticulously, and made the point that the absence of an apparent motive was no reason for finding Pritchard not guilty if the evidence against him was satisfactory. In fact it was overwhelming.

As far as Paterson was concerned, the Lord Justice-Clerk did not let him off lightly:

> He [Dr Paterson] said, in answer to a question I put to him, that his meaning was – what he intended to state in the box was – that he was under the decided impression, when he saw Mrs Pritchard on these occasions, that somebody was practising on her with poison. He thought it consistent with his duty as a citizen, to keep that opinion to himself. In that I cannot say I concur, and I should be very sorry to lead you to think so. I care not for professional etiquette or professional rule. There is a rule of life and a consideration that is far higher than these – and that is, the duty that every right-minded man owes to his neighbour, to prevent the destruction of human life in this world, and in that duty I cannot but say that Dr Paterson failed.

(In passing, under French law it is possible that Dr Paterson would have been guilty of a crime for voluntarily failing to help Mrs Pritchard who was in peril of her life.)

The jury, all-male of course, retired for only fifty-five minutes before returning to deliver a verdict of guilty of both murders.

It was neither the sort of trial nor the sort of occasion when the judge was going to be brief and keep the passing of the sentence of death to a minimum. After referring to the verdict, the Lord Justice-Clerk said to Pritchard:

You are aware that upon such a verdict one sentence only can be pronounced. [Pritchard bowed.] You must be condemned to suffer the last penalty of the law. [Pritchard bowed again.] It is neither my duty nor my inclination to say one word which shall have the effect of aggravating the horror of your position [*in fact he went on to say a great number of words*] and I leave it to the ministers of religion to address to you exhortations to repentance, which, by God's blessing, I hope may be attended by good result. Let me only remind you that you have but a short time on this earth . . .

The Lord Justice-Clerk put on the black cap and read out the sentence. It was nothing like the relatively short, sharp formula used in the last years of capital punishment:

In respect of the verdict before recorded, the Lord Justice-Clerk and Lords Commissioners of Justiciary decern and adjudge the panel, Edward William Pritchard, to be carried from the bar back to the prison of Edinburgh, and from thence forthwith to be transmitted under a sure guard till brought to and incarcerated in the prison of Glasgow, therein to be detained, and fed on bread and water only, till the 28th day of July current; and upon that day between the hours of eight and ten o'clock forenoon, ordain the said Edward William Pritchard to be taken forth of said prison to the common place of execution of the burgh of Glasgow, or to such place as the magistrates of Glasgow shall appoint as a place of execution, and there, by the hands of the common executioner, be hanged by the neck upon a gibbet till he be dead, and ordain that his body thereafter be buried within the precincts of the prison of Glasgow; and further ordain his whole moveable

goods and gear be escheat and inbrought to Her
Majesty's use.

The Lord Justice-Clerk removed the black cap and
added: 'Which is pronounced for your doom, and may
God Almighty have mercy on your soul.'

On Thursday the 27th July a crowd of men, women
and children – some with their parents – began to
gather on Glasgow Green, twenty-four hours before
the execution. Many slept out on the green overnight.
At 2 a.m. on Friday, the day of the execution, Calcraft
supervised the erection of the scaffold, which was
minutely described with macabre relish in the press.
Calcraft arrived to the accompaniment of cheers and a
few hisses.

At five o'clock a number of people arrived on the site
with large boards carrying Biblical texts, while several
religious speakers addressed the crowd at different
points.

Pritchard was woken at about 5.30 a.m. There was to
be no humane, quick-as-possible progress to the
gallows for him. Before he was hanged he had to
appear before another court of bailies and two other
officials to be asked if there was any reason why
sentence of death should not be carried out.

Pritchard was taken into court with an entourage
made up of the governor of the jail, three clergymen,
the jailer, three policemen and the hangman. The
phrase 'wanted to get into the act' springs irresistibly to
mind. There is the feeling that these days they would
have been surreptitiously glancing to see where the TV
cameras were. Among the spectators in the overcrowded courtroom were members of the Edinburgh
Phrenological Society, who would take a cast of
Pritchard's head after he had been hanged and shaved.

Pritchard was asked if he had anything to say. He bowed
and replied, 'I acknowledge the justice of the sentence.'

There followed a scene of black comedy which opened with some discussion as to the best way to the scaffold. Pritchard, one supposes, would have preferred to take the long, pretty way. This not unimportant matter settled, the prisoner and escort formed up and set off. As soon as they had exited from the courtroom there was a mad, undignified scramble for the door. The captain of police shouted that the magistrates should leave first, followed by the press and then the general public. The exit was jammed with struggling figures and by the time the last one was out he nearly missed the show. Pritchard was already on the scaffold with the blindfold over his head and the rope around his neck.

Calcraft, who had the execrable taste to wear a rose in his buttonhole – a faded one at that – was roundly booed as he mounted the scaffold. According to all reports, some of them frankly cold-bloodedly grisly, he did a sloppy job of the execution, which was not instantaneous.

That, it would appear, was that. Pritchard, however, was as determined as an ageing American singer to stay in the spotlight and make one more farewell appearance. From the grave he bounded back on to the stage again – in spirit, at least. While he was in jail awaiting execution he made three confessions, which were not to be published until after his death.

The first one implicated Mary McLeod. He said he murdered his wife with chloroform with McLeod present. She knew Mrs Pritchard was being poisoned and that the food she took to her contained poison. However, the authorities were convinced that Pritchard was lying about McLeod and this first confession was kept from the public.

Pritchard's second confession, of the 11th July, said that Mrs Taylor had caught him with Mary McLeod. He believed that his mother-in-law's death was due to an overdose of opium, and, he claimed, he put aconite into her bottle of Battley's Sedative solution *after* her death. As for his wife, she was so exhausted by the reaction to her mother's death that 'at her earnest request' he gave her chloroform.

> It was about midnight, Mary McLeod being in the room, and in an evil moment (besides being somewhat excited by whisky) I yielded to the temptation to give her sufficient to cause death, *which I did*. [Pritchard's italics.]
>
> I therefore declare, before God, as a dying man and in the presence of my spiritual adviser, that I am innocent of the crime of murder as far as Mrs Taylor is concerned, but acknowledge myself guilty of the adultery with Mary McLeod, and I declare my solemn repentance of my crime, earnestly praying that I may obtain Divine forgiveness before I suffer the penalty of the law.
> [*Signed*]   Edward William Pritchard.

If this formal, grave-sounding confession were true, there would have been serious doubts about Mary McLeod's total innocence of the murders. Pritchard was in a situation where he could be expected to tell the truth, at last. But even that wasn't his last word. Eight days later he made a final statement in which he confessed that he murdered *both* women, exculpated Mary McLeod and admitted that the principal points brought out at his trial were accurate:

> . . . I hereby confess that I alone, not Mary McLeod, poisoned my wife in the way brought out in the evidence at my trial. Mrs Taylor's death was caused according to the wording in the indictment. [*This accused Pritchard of administering tartarised antimony and aconite and opium, or one or more of them, or some other poison or poisons . . .*] I further state to be true the main facts brought out

at my trial. I hereby fully acknowledge, and now
plead wholly and solely 'Guilty' thereto – and may
God have mercy on my soul . . .

The last part of this final confession was as wildly
extraordinary as anything in this whole bizarre affair: 'I
have now to record my humble thanks to have taken
part, in any way, for my interest . . . ' Pritchard wrote.

At Oscar and other awards ceremonies it is the
tedious custom of the recipient to say, 'I have to thank'
and then he or she – usually she – gives a whole list of
people from the producer, through the director, writer,
cameraman, agent, mother and father down to the
gopher who put sugar in the coffee. These spuriously
humble winners pale into insignificance compared with
Pritchard. He began by thanking the judges at his trial,
then went on to mention more than *forty* people by
name 'and many others'. Understandably, the hangman, Calcraft, did not get a mention, but nor did any of
his defending counsel. He concluded:

> May each and all accept the thanks of a deeply
> penitent sinner, and may Heaven be their reward
> is the last prayer of
>   Edward William Pritchard.

DR GEORGE HENRY LAMSON

. . . A drug which it's the fashion to abuse
W.S. Gilbert

*. . . A drug which takes away grief and passion
and brings forgetfulness . . .*
Homer

But what are pity, conscience or fear . . .
Boris Pasternak

What drugs . . . what conjuration
Othello

On the surface, the case of Dr George Henry Lamson, accused of the murder of his 18-year-old brother-in-law Percy Malcolm John, was a simple case of murder for financial gain. Dr Lamson badly needed money, and killing Percy John was the simplest way of getting it. But there was far more to it than that.

Lamson became a drug addict with a massive habit – far heavier even than Cream's – which he acquired after being given treatment for war wounds suffered in the Russo-Turkish War. He served as a military surgeon with the Serbian forces, who were Russia's allies, and was wounded again in the Turko-Romanian war the following year. He was decorated a number of times for his work. One of his orders was the quaint-sounding Fifth Class of the Medjidieh.

The Lamson of that period was cultivated and scholarly, and he spoke a number of Continental languages; he enjoyed an excellent reputation and was received in Romanian society. By the time he neared the end of his stay in Romania Lamson was in charge of a hospital in Bucharest, which was sponsored by the London Red Cross. Dr Charles Vonklein, an American, served in the same hospital. Vonklein was startled by Lamson's obsession for prescribing aconitine for practically every illness or injury. He frequently warned Lamson of the danger he was subjecting his patients to. Lamson was usually incoherent, and just laughed at Vonklein's fears. In fact, Vonklein said, Lamson used aconitine on himself to the point that he was of unsound mind and totally irresponsible.

In 1881 Lamson was back in England, and often out

of his mind for long periods. During his visits to America some of his behaviour while under the influence of drugs was pure black farce. But when it came to the murder of Percy John, Lamson was clear-minded, cool, and above all inventive. Like Pritchard before him and Cream after him, Lamson left a signposted trail when he set out to buy poison. Yet the way he administered it had extreme subtlety and the applied psychological expertise of a master magician. In fact his ingenuity left the prosecution totally unable to solve satisfactorily the mystery of how Lamson managed to kill his young victim.

Even after Lamson's trial and conviction there were more sensations to come. The President of the United States, no less, Chester Alan Arthur of Vermont – as Vice-President he succeeded James Garfield, who was assassinated – cabled the British Home Secretary asking him to delay Lamson's execution to allow time for further evidence to be produced.

To return to the beginning of Lamson's story, he first returned to England after his military service in 1878. He met a Miss Kate George John, one of a family of two girls and two boys, who had become wards of court on the death of their parents. Kate had an elder married sister, Mrs Chapman; her brothers were Herbert and Percy John. This younger brother was a paraplegic. He suffered from double curvature of the spine, which caused the paralysis of his legs. He lived at Blenheim House, a boarding school at Wimbledon, where he seemed to be a cheerful young man, despite his handicap, and popular with the other boys. Since he couldn't walk, he had two wheelchairs, one which was kept on the second floor where he slept, the other in the basement where he spent the days. Every day one of the three boys with whom he shared a bedroom carried him down to the basement and then up to his bedroom at night.

When Kate John married Lamson that same year she became entitled to a share of the money left by her parents. At that time a married woman had no money of her own, so effectively the money went directly to Lamson. To be fair, it is quite clear that Kate was perfectly happy to hand over the money to him. She seems to have been devoted to her husband and was as submissive as a feudal Japanese wife.

The following year Kate's brother Herbert John died and she inherited part of his share of their parents' estate, some £748. Her sister, Mrs Chapman, inherited a similar sum. Percy would come into his inheritance either on his marrying – an unlikely eventuality – or on his reaching the age of twenty-one. (His nineteenth birthday would have been on the 18th December 1881.) If he died unmarried or before his majority, Kate, like her sister, would receive £1,500.

Lamson had already received a trouble-free £748 and £1,500 from the John family. Only the crippled Percy John, whose condition was steadily worsening, stood between Lamson and a further £1,500. Any spasms of conscience he may have had while contemplating the youth's murder were quickly anaesthetised by the enormous injections of drugs – particularly mixtures of morphine and atropine – Lamson was giving himself.

In 1880 Lamson bought a medical practice in Bournemouth. Despite the high proportion of well-to-do, hypochondriacal, retired people in that town Lamson failed to make a financial success because of his drug addiction, which was on such a massive scale that bailiffs were more frequent callers than patients. Finally his home was sold up.

His coachman, Charles Taylor, declared that from the moment he was employed by Lamson he realised the doctor was out of his senses. He was subject to childish fears and fancies, and quite unable to converse reasonably.

'If he had to attend a patient he frequently didn't go, but would tell me that he had just been. One morning he came out of the house and said to me, "Taylor, I shall summon you. I am an officer of the army and I have had threatening letters that they are coming here to kill me".' Lamson made Taylor promise to carry a pistol – which he did not do, of course.

The wonder is that Lamson had any patients at all. One mid-morning he fired a pistol out of a second-floor window for no reason that he could give. On another occasion he claimed that he had been called out at night to a patient at an address he couldn't find, and when he returned home he was attacked by two men, but he managed to run away from them.

In a statement that has the strong odour of hindsight Taylor added, 'On more than one occasion I told my fellow servants that Mr Lamson ought to be in a lunatic asylum, and I told them that I believed before six months he would be in one.' More importantly Taylor said, 'I have not the slightest doubt in the world that while I was in the service of Lamson he was insane, and totally irresponsible for his actions.'

According to an acquaintance who saw Lamson daily in Bournemouth for a year before he left for America, 'His eyes had a fitful and nervous look, as if he were in fear of a phantom . . . He would frequently go along quickly, then suddenly stop, turn back and branch off in another direction, crossing the road backwards and forwards without rhyme or reason. Not only so, but he constantly made the wildest and most outrageously improbable statements with an apparent air of sincerity.'

In March 1881 Lamson's father, the Rev. William Lamson, had a ministry in New York. He wrote to Gustavus S. Winston, medical director of an insurance company, asking him to see his son and give him professional advice for an excessive use of morphine to relieve pain. Dr Lamson went to America in April, 1881, and met Winston, who found Lamson beyond any help he could give.

The Lamson family in America had already had its fair share of problems before Dr Lamson's arrival. His grandmother, Lucretia Lamson (an unfortunate name for an ancestor of a poisoner) was a patient at the brutally-named Bloomingdale Asylum for the Insane. Lucretia Lamson suffered from senile dementia. Her brother, Lamson's grand-uncle, died in the asylum after suffering from dementia. However, they were both old, seventy-six and eighty-seven years of age respectively, which was considerably more than the average life expectancy of the period.

One of Lamson's aunts was another patient at Bloomingdale, suffering from hallucinations, incoherence, sleeplessness and other symptoms. In retrospect, and with the benefit of modern knowledge it seems she was suffering from post-natal depression, less charitably called puerperal mania at that time. It was popularly believed then that a nursing mother needed alcoholic drinks to have a good supply of milk. Even in an Asylum for the Insane alcohol was hardly a recommended treatment for depression. This aunt died in the asylum at the age of thirty-one.

Today we can see that there was nothing in these cases to suggest that there was any strain of hereditary insanity in the Lamson family, if indeed such a thing exists. But having three blood relations dying in a lunatic asylum might well have made an impression on the already seriously disturbed Lamson.

He went to stay with friends of his father, the Reverend Irving McElroy and family, Rector of Rouse Point, New York. They had met him in 1877, and now found him changed beyond recognition.

The account of Lamson's behaviour in New York State would have been considered wildly over the top in

a work of fiction about a drug addict. While staying with
the McElroys he rarely got up before midday. He was
always flushed, his eyes were dull and heavy, he moved
around unsteadily like a drunk. He constantly complained of headaches and dizziness. In the rector's
house, what time he didn't spend lying on a sofa dozing
or trying to read or carry on a conversation, he spent in
his room injecting himself with a mixture of morphine
and atropine. In a rare moment of lucidity he explained
that he preferred aconitine but it was unobtainable
locally. Once he was so dazed he tried to wind his watch
with a cigarette. On another grimmer and less farcical
occasion he almost killed himself drinking laudanum –
an opium mixture – in mistake for chlorodyne, which is
an alcoholic solution of chloroform and morphia, a
remedy for diarrhoea.

Because of his staggering walk, flushed appearance
and wild behaviour whenever he did manage to go out, it
was generally accepted in the locality that Lamson was
mad. But there was more than drug addiction affecting
Lamson. He was suffering from the effects of a chest
wound received during his war service, and frequently
he had fits of coughing up blood.

Reverend McElroy was glad to see the back of
Lamson, he said: the responsibility of looking after him
was too demanding. McElroy and his family were
constantly afraid that Lamson might do serious damage
to himself or someone else while he was under the
influence of drugs.

Lamson returned to England on the *City of Berlin* in
July, 1881, still addicted to morphine, and still desper-
ately short of money. During the voyage he borrowed £5
from the ship's surgeon, the unfortunately-named Dr
William Corder, namesake of the murderer of Maria
Marten in the Red Barn. A contemporary report says
Lamson 'helped' Dr Corder. One cannot help speculat-
ing whether he prescribed aconitine for any of the

patients on board.

On Saturday the 27th August, Percy John, accompanied by his sister and brother-in-law, Mr and Mrs Chapman, arrived in Shanklin, Isle of Wight, for a short holiday at a boarding house owned by a Mrs Sophia Joliffe. Lamson was with them but didn't stay in the house. The following evening, as late as nearly nine o'clock, he went to a chemist's shop in High Street, Ventnor, and bought three grains of sulphate of atropine, one grain of aconitine, some eau de Cologne and shaving soap.

A day or so after that, Lamson gave Percy John what he said was a quinine pill. The boy was taken ill the same evening. 'I feel as if I'm paralysed all over,' he said to Mrs Joliffe as he lay in bed.

The following morning he spent a long time in the lavatory – so long, in fact that his sister and Mrs Joliffe peered through the keyhole to make sure he hadn't fainted. Mrs Joliffe's evidence in cross-examination at the trial took the prosecution by surprise: she told the court something about Percy John that not even William Bedbrook, the proprietor of his school was aware of, as we shall see.

After spending most of July and August in England Lamson made another trip to America, on the *City of Brussels*, but this was no more successful than the first visit. A little more than a month later he returned to England as sick and as insolvent as ever.

On the 27th October Lamson went to see William Stevenson, Editor of the *Bournemouth Observer*, whom he knew and to whom he also owed more than one hundred pounds. A lot of people Lamson got to know wound up being owed money by him. Lamson asked Stevenson for a case of surgical instruments he had left with him, a travelling rug, and five pounds. Stevenson generously let Lamson have them.

Despite his own desperate financial situation Lamson

was helpful and as generous to friends as he possibly could be. On several occasions he lent money to John Law Tulloch, a medical student, and when John Tulloch's brother William asked Lamson for a loan, he raised the wind by pawning the surgical instruments he had recovered from Stevenson and a gold hunter watch. If the pawnbroker's other clients in Mortimer Street W1 were like Lamson it must have been a lucrative business. He lent Lamson only five pounds on the surgical instruments and the watch, which were never redeemed. Lamson gave this money to William Tulloch.

When it was that Lamson began to formulate his plan to poison his brother-in-law Percy John we cannot know. However, before he pawned his possessions to lend money to William Tulloch, on Sunday the 20th November Lamson tried to buy aconitine at the chemists Bell & Co., then of Oxford Street. John Stirling, an assistant, refused to supply him with a grain of it on Lamson's own prescription. Why Stirling refused is uncertain, because some days earlier he had filled Lamson's prescription for a mixture of morphine and atropine for his own use, and he was ready to give him digitalis – used as a heart medicine and poisonous if taken in excess – but had none in stock. When Lamson asked for aconitine Stirling said he should get it where he was better known. Perhaps by this time Lamson's appearance made him a bad risk for anything stronger than an aspirin.

[Some explanation concerning aconite and aconitine is required. Aconite is the highly poisonous plant known as Wolfsbane, Blue Rocket or Monkshood. The poison extracted from the plant is also called aconite; the active element of aconite is aconitine, and its action is caused by smaller doses than with any other drug. The drug was used mainly in liniments, but is seldom used today. One authoritative but somewhat dated reference book says 'Tincture of aconite, which is still kept in some households, should never be used without the sanction of a doctor.'

In the course of the Lamson trial there was some confusion over the name of the drug. In fact Percy John was killed by aconitine, although some witnesses spoke of aconite and of aconitia, which seems to be an elegant variation of aconitine.]

About the same time that Lamson visited the pawnbroker, he went to Allen & Hanbury, wholesale chemists, in Plough Court, Lombard Street. He asked the assistant, William Dodd, for a piece of paper and wrote out an order for two grains of aconitia [aconite], slightly less than half an ounce. He dated it and signed 'G.H. Lamson, M.D., Bournemouth, Hants.' Dodd looked up the *Medical Directory* and found Lamson's name and address in it.

During the trial Dodd was asked by Mr Harry Poland for the Crown to explain his criteria for judging whether a customer was a medical man or not.

Poland: Supposing I came in and gave you a name, Dr Brown, for instance, and called for aconitia, would you supply me?
Dodd: I should require you to write it down in my presence.
Poland: But if I did so?
Dodd: That would not be sufficient. It must be done in a formal manner, and I should require your name and address.
Poland: Suppose that I took a name out of the *Medical Directory*?
Dodd: If I was satisfied that you were a medical man I should let you have it.
Poland: How do you test the statement?
Dodd: The applicant must be well dressed and have a very respectable appearance.
Poland: Is there anything you satisfy yourself by that

the man is not an imposter?

Dodd: The only thing is the style of writing. *The writing of a medical man is characteristic.*

Plus ça change . . .

His own criteria satisfied, Dodd supplied the aconitine. Apparently, if Jack the Ripper had walked in and given the name of any doctor in the *Directory* he would have been served with aconitia, as long as he was shaved and sober. Charles Betts, another assistant, checked Dodd's weighing according to the firm's practice. After all, aconitia was 1s 3d per grain wholesale.

However, there was some doubt whether or not Lamson did buy aconitia or aconite that day, an uncertainty which his counsel, Mr Montagu Williams, exploited to the full. Dodd testified that when he read something in the evening paper on Monday the 5th December he spoke to Betts about it. Both men were under the impression that they had sold atropia (atropine) to Lamson. It was only later that they changed their minds and decided it was aconitia they had sold. Both Dodd and Betts were forced to admit that they couldn't remember the exact date or the day of the week it was that they sold the drug. Montagu Williams emphasised this heavily in his final speech for the defence. He called their evidence not only unreliable but also improbable. Even allowing for an advocate's tendency to hyperbolise, he had a point. Lamson, Williams reminded the jury, bought large amounts of atropia for his own use and the shop's sales book showed a sale of atropia at wholesale price to Lamson on Tuesday 29th November.

Two days after Lamson visited the pawnbroker and then bought aconitia – or atropia – he went to the American Exchange office in the Strand, where he asked them to change a cheque on the Wilts & Dorset

Bank for £15. They declined. Four days later, the 30th November, Lamson went to Ventnor where he continued to try to raise money with worthless cheques. This time he had more success. He went to a wine merchant's in the High Street and got the assistant to cash him a cheque for £10, then returned a quarter of an hour later. He persuaded the owner, Mr Price Owen, to tear up the £10 cheque and cash a new one for £20. One wonders whether Lamson's brass nerve was sustained by drugs or driven by desperation. Probably both.

The next day Lamson sent Owen a telegram, asking him not to present the cheque because he had drawn it on the wrong bank; and followed this with a suspiciously over-wordy letter of 'explanation' promising a new cheque. Of course, it never came.

Throughout November and for the first couple of days of December Lamson was staying in London at Nelson's Hotel, Great Portland Street. On the morning of Saturday the 26th November Lamson wrote one of his lengthy letters about money, this one to the proprietor, James Crichton Nelson, who apparently knew his parents. Lamson said that he needed urgently to go to see his wife because his little daughter was ill. He intended to bring his wife and child back to London to stay with him until he left for the Continent. Since he did not have time to go to the City to get the money for the journey, he asked Nelson to lend him £5 until he returned with his family that evening.

Perhaps to reassure Nelson about his credit-worthiness Lamson asked to be given an extra room, and to have collected from the left luggage office at Euston station 'a large trunk which contains a quantity of silverplate and household valuables, worth a considerable sum'. Nelson was unimpressed: he did not lend him the fiver.

The tragedy was approaching its climax. In fact it was

a double tragedy, for the murderer was no less a tragic figure than his victim. The tempo of Lamson's activities increased sharply as he struggled to escape from the quicksands of his financial problems.

On Thursday the 1st December Lamson called on John Tulloch, the medical student to whom he had lent money on several occasions, at his home in St John's Wood. Tulloch must have been a little surprised to see Lamson, for they hadn't met since the previous April.

'I'm staying at Nelson's Hotel,' Lamson mentioned, and added that he was going to Paris the next morning. However, he turned up at Tulloch's lodgings again at 1.30 p.m. the next day and they had lunch together. Lamson said he had postponed his Paris trip until that evening, and they both went to Lamson's hotel where Tulloch helped him pack. Lamson's behaviour was as erratic and irrational as ever. While the two men were doing the packing Lamson suddenly said he would run down to Wimbledon to see his brother-in-law, and if he could catch a train afterwards, he would go on to Paris.

Lamson and Tulloch went to Waterloo where they put Lamson's luggage into the cloakroom, and travelled to Wimbledon. Tulloch waited in a pub opposite Percy John's school until Lamson returned, ostensibly from the school, some twenty minutes later.

According to Tulloch's original version of their conversation Lamson said, 'I've seen the boy and he's not very well. The curvature of the spine is getting worse, and the boy generally isn't in a good state of health.' By the time Lamson came to trial at the Central Criminal Court, the Old Bailey, Tulloch had been subjected to considerable press interest and comment about the case, and it seems to have affected his memory. This time he testified that Lamson told him, 'I've seen my brother-in-law, and he's much worse. I don't think he'll last long.'

'What about your trip to Paris?' Tulloch asked.

'Mr Bedbrook [proprietor of the school] is a director of one of the Continental lines to Paris, and he told me it's as well I didn't go tonight. There's a bad boat on the service.'

All this was complete fabrication. Lamson didn't even go to the school, and certainly Bedbrook had no connection with the railway service. The only element of truth in his statement was that he didn't think Percy John would live long. Lamson himself was going to see to that.

Lamson now set out on an extended pub crawl. In addition to trying to drown his worries in alcohol, he had to get some money somehow. The two men returned to town and went to the Comedy Theatre in Panton Street. After the show they crossed the road to Stone's Public House. Lamson wrote a cheque for £12.10s, made out to Tulloch, and asked him to get it cashed for him. They first tried to cash it at the Adelphi Hotel in Adam Street, just behind the Savoy Hotel, but had no success. So they drove to the Eyre Arms in St John's Wood, near Tulloch's lodgings. The landlord there, a Mr Perrot, knew Tulloch and was unusually accommodating: he cashed the cheque. Tulloch handed over the money to Lamson, who then left him after arranging to meet at the Adelphi Hotel the following day, Saturday the 3rd December.

They met at between three and four o'clock. Tulloch went with Lamson to see him off on his trip, but he was too late for the train. 'I'll go in the evening,' Lamson said. In the meantime, inevitably, they went to a pub, The Horse Shoe. When it came to paying, they discovered that one of the bags of money Perrot had given them on the Thursday for the cheque contained copper instead of £5 silver. The two men returned to the Eyre Arms and changed the copper for a £5 note. They stayed drinking for a while, and Lamson finally left Tulloch at about six o'clock.

Lamson now set off to murder his brother-in-law.
Percy John was expecting a visit from Lamson: the
previous day he had received a letter from him.

> Nelson's Hotel, Great Portland Street
> London, December 1, 1881.
>
> My dear Percy,
>   I had intended running down to Wimbledon to
> see you today, but I have been delayed by various
> matters until it is now nearly six o'clock, and by
> the time I should reach Blenheim House you
> would probably be preparing for bed. I leave for
> Paris and Florence tomorrow [Lamson's father
> now had a ministry in Florence], and wish to see
> you before going. So I purpose to run down to
> your place as early as I can, for a few minutes
> even, if I can accomplish no more. Believe me,
> dear boy, your loving brother,
>   G.H. LAMSON

Lamson turned up at Blenheim House at five to seven
on that fatal Saturday, the 3rd December. He was
carrying a black leather bag. Bedbrook met him in the
hall, but failed to recognise him at first because he was
very much thinner.

'You've changed a great deal since I saw you last,'
Bedbrook remarked.

'I've come to see my brother-in-law,' Lamson told
him, and Bedbrook sent for Percy John. Bedbrook led
Lamson through the drawing room into the dining
room on the first floor while Walter Banbury, one of
the pupils who was an intimate friend of Percy, carried
him from the basement.

As Banbury came into the dining room Lamson said,
'I thought you would have been in India by now.'
(Banbury was due to go into the army.) He turned to
Percy. 'Why, how fat you're looking, Percy, old boy.'

'I wish I could say the same of you, George,' he replied with some concern. Banbury then left the room.

'Would you like some wine?' Bedbrook asked politely.

'Thank you. I think I should like to take some sherry.'

Bedbrook knew that Lamson had a particular fondness for sherry and served him a large claret-glassful. There was some desultory conversation, and Lamson asked for some sugar.

'These wines contain a large amount of brandy, and sugar destroys the alcoholic effects,' Lamson explained.

'Really? I thought it was the contrary,' Bedbrook replied, but rang for some sugar nevertheless.

Mrs Bowles, the matron, brought a basin of caster sugar. Lamson put some of it into his sherry with a spade spoon and stirred it with his penknife, which was hardly *de rigeur* even in middle-class society. Next Lamson opened his black bag and took out a Dundee cake and some sweets. At the trial Bedbrook testified that Lamson cut the cake with his penknife, but there is convincing evidence that the cake was *already* cut, and there can be no doubt that this was the case. Lamson, Percy John and Bedbrook all ate cakes and sweets at the time Lamson was there.

After some more small talk Lamson said, 'Oh, by the way, Mr Bedbrook, when I was in America I thought of you and your boys. I thought what excellent things these capsules would be for your boys to take nauseous medicines in.' He produced two boxes of capsules from his bag and passed one to Bedbrook. 'I'd like you to try one, to see how easily they can be swallowed.' This sort of gelatine capsule is commonplace these days, although they were something of a novelty then.

Bedbrook took one of the unwrapped capsules from the half-full box. The warmth of his hand made the capsule quite soft and he found he could swallow it without difficulty. Meanwhile, Lamson was filling another capsule with sugar from the bowl. This one was from the second box, Bedbrook believed, although he could not be sure. Lamson held the capsule between his fingers and said, 'If you shake it like this it will bring the medicine down to one end.' He passed it to Percy John, who was within arm's length, saying something like, 'Here, Percy, you're a swell pill taker. Take this, and show Mr Bedbrook how easily it can be swallowed.'

The boy put the capsule on the back of his tongue and swallowed it.

'That's soon gone, my boy,' Bedbrook observed.

Almost immediately Lamson said, 'I must be going now.' It was about 7.20 p.m. Bedbrook looked at a timetable and saw that the next London train was at 7.21 p.m. Although Blenheim House was less than a minute's walk from the station Bedbrook suggested that Lamson should stay a little longer and catch the 7.50 p.m.

'I can't, because I have to catch a train at London Bridge at eight o'clock for the Continent. I'm going to Florence via Paris.'

Yet Lamson dallied for another minute. 'You'll miss the train if you don't go at once,' Bedbrook warned.

'I intend to go to Florence for a few months for the benefit of my health, and then return and settle down in England,' Lamson said.

At last he said goodbye to Percy John. Bedbrook accompanied Lamson to the front door, remarking, 'I think the boy's curvature of the spine is getting worse.'

'I don't think he can last long,' Lamson said prophetically, with the benefit of inside knowledge. He caught his train at Wimbledon, and later that night he left London for the Continent.

Bedbrook returned to the dining room where there were two other visitors that evening, two young ladies who played and sang for about ten minutes. He escorted them out, leaving Percy John on his own. While Bedbrook was away Walter Banbury joined Percy and stayed for about five minutes. Lamson had left the two boxes of capsules and the remainder of the sweets and cake on the table. Banbury swallowed one of the capsules without any ill effects.

So there were two people who took capsules from the boxes and swallowed them without coming to any harm. The remaining capsules were subsequently analysed and found to be harmless, yet the prosecution concentrated on trying to prove that Percy John was killed by a poisoned capsule – somehow. Quite *how*, though, they couldn't say.

Next Bedbrook returned to the dining room, and this time Percy John complained of feeling ill. 'I feel as if I had an attack of heartburn,' he said, then added significantly, 'I feel as I felt after my brother-in-law had given me a quinine pill at Shanklin. I think I'd like to go to bed.'

Joseph Bell, another pupil, was sent for. He carried Percy John upstairs and sat him on his bed. Percy was still complaining of heartburn. Bell went downstairs and told Mrs Bowles, the matron, that Percy John was unwell.

Before she arrived on the scene Alfred Godward, an assistant master at the school, found Percy John alone in the bathroom, on the floor, vomiting and in great pain. 'My skin feels all pulled up,' Percy said pitifully, 'and my mouth is very painful. I took a pill my brother-in-law gave me.' He added, 'It was a quinine pill.' He repeated it a number of times, and said the same things after Mrs Bowles arrived at the bathroom. He also said 'I took one [quinine pill] at Shanklin and was nearly as bad then.'

During the trial the prosecution introduced evidence of quinine pills that Lamson had sent to Percy from

America, and the fact that some of them contained aconitine. This helped to prove murderous premeditation on Lamson's part, and that he intended to use aconitine as the means for murder. However, there was absolutely no evidence that Lamson gave Percy John a quinine pill on the day he died. The prosecution did not suggest that he did, nor did anyone who was in the room with Lamson and Percy John mention a quinine pill. So, when the young man mentioned the 'quinine' pill his brother-in-law gave him, he must have meant the capsule with the sugar in it. Although the pills sent from America might well give rise to a suspicion that Lamson was trying to poison Percy John from a distance, they have no direct relevance to the events of the 3rd December and the method Lamson used to poison his brother-in-law.

Alfred Godward picked up Percy John in his arms, took him back to his bedroom, undressed him and put him to bed. Mrs Bowles gave Percy some brandy and water, but it did nothing to ease the awful pain he was suffering. Alexander Watt, the school's classics master, joined Godward in Percy John's bedroom. The eccentrically named Dr Other Windsor Berry, a local medical practitioner, was a guest in the school at the time and Bedbrook asked him to attend Percy John. Bedbrook met Dr Berry, explained the situation and took him up to Percy's bedroom. It was now about five to nine.

By that time Percy John's condition had deteriorated. The pain had increased and he was still vomiting. He managed to tell Berry that he felt that the skin of his face was being drawn up, his throat was constricted and he couldn't swallow.

'Did your brother-in-law ever give you a quinine pill before?' Berry asked.

'Yes. At Shanklin.'

'Did it make you ill like this before?'

'Yes, but not so bad.'

'Did your brother-in-law know it made you ill like this?'

'I can't say.'

Dr Berry had frequently seen Percy John before and considered that his health was generally good apart from the paralysis of his legs. Now he had no idea what was wrong with the young man. He had some white of egg beaten up in water, and Percy was able to swallow a little of it between bouts of vomiting. Berry also prescribed hot linseed poultices to be applied to the abdomen, but they did not relieve any of the symptoms. Percy John was throwing himself about on the bed so violently that it took several people to hold him down on the bed to prevent him injuring himself.

After Berry had been with Percy John for a half an hour or so he was told that Dr Edward Little was in the house and had him sent for. The two doctors consulted and decided on a morphia injection. Berry went out for some five or ten minutes to fetch a hypodermic syringe and the drug; when he returned Percy was no better. At that time no one – except Lamson – realised that the young man had been given a fatal dose of poison.

Berry gave a subcutaneous injection of a quarter of a grain of morphia near the region of the stomach, and half an hour later, at about 10.30 p.m., Percy John's symptoms diminished to some degree. Another half an hour later they had become just as agonising as they were before, so Berry injected a further sixth of a grain of morphia, with no immediately apparent effect. Shortly afterwards Percy drifted into semi-consciousness and became incoherent. His breathing and heart-rate steadily slowed. He was given the standard remedy of the time, brandy and water, but he died after another twenty minutes, at about 11.20 p.m.

It was patently obvious that Percy John had taken 'something of an irritant nature into his stomach', to quote Dr Berry. He and Dr Little collected some of the vomit the young man had brought up. It was to prove a significant piece of evidence.

At 11.30 a.m. the next morning Bedbrook went to the police station to inform the police of the death and its circumstances. An Inspector John Fuller was put in charge of the case. He didn't go to Blenheim House until about 9.30 p.m. that evening: today a small posse of police and forensic science experts would have charged round there without a moment's delay. Fuller took away the boxes of capsules, the remains of the Dundee cake, sweets, crystallized fruits and a sample of the caster sugar Lamson had put into the capsule he gave Percy John. Incomprehensibly, Fuller didn't take away the rest of the Dundee cake for another couple of days, two pills wrapped in tin foil two days after that, while the sherry was left in the Blenheim House dining room for nine days after Percy John's death before it was taken for analysis! It is not difficult to imagine what a modern defence counsel would have made of all that.

Doctors Little and Berry, together with Mr Thomas Bond, an FRCS and Lecturer in Forensic Medicine at Westminster Hospital, carried out a post-mortem examination of Percy John on Tuesday the 6th December. They came to the somewhat negative conclusion that there were no signs that Percy John's death was not the result of natural causes.

The case was taken over from Inspector Fuller by Inspector Butcher of Scotland Yard. On Wednesday the 7th December he went to see William Chapman, Lamson's other brother-in-law, and the following morning Fuller sent a Sergeant Moser to Paris. It seems that the sergeant had a free jaunt to Paris, for on the same day Lamson turned up at Scotland Yard with his wife and asked to see Inspector Butcher.

'Mr Butcher?' Lamson asked.

'Yes.'

'My name is Lamson; I am Dr Lamson, whose name has been mentioned in connection with the death at Wimbledon.'

Politely Butcher said, 'Will you be seated?'

'I've called to see what is to be done about it. I considered it best to do so. I read the account in the public papers at Paris and came over this morning. I have only just now arrived in London. I am very unwell and much upset about this matter, and I am not in a fit state at all to have undertaken the journey.'

Butcher contacted Chief Superintendent Williamson, telling Lamson that he would have to remain for a while. While they were waiting for Williamson to decide what was to be done – a simple enough problem, one would have thought – Lamson 'conversed on various subjects'. According to Butcher, Lamson then said – a little confusingly, if he was correctly reported – 'Where is the delay? I thought I would come here and leave my address. I'm going into the country, to Chichester, so that you would know where to find me and attend the inquest. I have travelled from Paris via Le Havre and Southampton; I went over via Dover and Calais.'

Butcher saw Williamson again, and called Lamson into another room.

'Your case has been fully considered, and it has been decided to charge you with causing the death of Percy John. I thereupon take you into custody, and charge you with causing the death of Percy Malcolm John at Blenheim House, Wimbledon, on the 3rd December.

'Very well,' Lamson answered with apparent calm. 'Do you think bail will be accepted? I hope the matter will be kept as quiet as possible for the sake of my relations.'

'You will now be taken to Wandsworth Police Court,' Butcher told him, 'and before the magistrates. The question of bail will remain with them.'

Butcher took Lamson to Wandsworth in a cab. During the journey Lamson said, 'I hope it will be stated that I came to Scotland Yard voluntarily, and that I came from Paris on purpose.'

'Certainly,' Butcher replied. At Wandsworth he searched Lamson and listed his few pathetic possessions. They consisted of a couple of letters, an envelope with his Paris address, a pawnbroker's ticket for a case of surgical instruments and a gold watch, a cloakroom ticket and a chequebook upon the Wilts and Dorset Bank. All the money Lamson had on him amounted to 7½ francs and 6½d (2½p) in bronze.

Butcher went to Euston Station with the cloakroom ticket and retrieved Lamson's box. Among the unremarkable objects in it was a notebook which contained a description of the effects of vegetable poisons.

> Effects of acrid vegetable poisons when swallowed – Soon after swallowing any of these poisons there is felt an acrid biting, more or less bitter tasting to the mouth, with great dryness and burning heat. The throat becomes painfully tight, with a sense of strangling, distressing retching, vomiting and purging, and pains more or less severe in the stomach and bowels ensue, and those are succeeded by a quick and throbbing pulse, oppressed breathing and panting, a tottering gait as if the patient were intoxicated, alarming weakness, sinking and death. Sometimes there are convulsions, more or less severe, acute pain, causing plaintive cries, with stiffness of the limbs. The several poisons of this class vary much in the violence of their effects.

So Lamson knew only too well what a ghastly death he was sentencing Percy to.

He was brought before the magistrates at Bow Street Police Court (as it was then known), on Friday 30th

December, charged with the wilful murder of Percy John. He appeared in the small upper court, which was crowded with a rich cross-section of the public. The *Daily Telegraph*'s snobbish reporter referred to them as, *inter alia*, 'the common class, street Arabs, the rough element, tag-rag and bobtail, men who loaf about the streets and do nothing but ask for alms and drink . . . ' Well, even today the Bow Street regulars could hardly be mistaken for the patrons of the golden horseshoe in the Royal Opera House just across the road.

Lamson himself was fairly dishevelled at this time, and it was obvious from his appearance that he was hard up. He also seemed to be quite unconcerned with the court proceedings: he took much more interest in the motley mob crowding the public part of the courtroom. Of course, he had not yet shaken off the effects of his prolonged heavy drug-taking: he was still quite spaced out.

Lamson's trial at the Central Criminal Court, Old Bailey, opened a little more than two months after his Bow Street appearance, on Wednesday 8th March, 1882. The court was packed to suffocation long before 10.30 a.m. when the trial was due to begin. This was the former Old Bailey, stuffy, smelly, ill-lit and ill-ventilated, described by one leading advocate in the course of his final speech for the defence in another trial as 'utterly unfitted for the administration of justice and a disgrace to the richest municipality in the world.' Nevertheless, many barristers crowded into the court to follow what promised to be the most sensational case of the age, and fashionable women dressed as if for the theatre managed to find seats on the public benches. Would-be spectators waited outside the court building with no hope of getting inside, and the crowds increased with every day of the trial.

The judge was Sir Henry Hawkins (later Baron

Brampton), considered to be one of the finest criminal judges of the times. Sitting on the bench with him were a couple of Aldermen of the City of London – one of them an MP – the Recorder, the Sheriff and Under-Sheriff and several Middlesex magistrates. They were all carrying the traditional bouquets of flowers which were originally believed to ward off 'gaol fever' which was thought to be carried by the prisoners. Long after the imaginary threat of gaol fever had been proved groundless the judges still found the bouquets useful: they frequently pressed the bunches of flowers to their noses to kill the awful odours of close-pressed unwashed bodies. Also on the bench with the judges and magistrates was the black-clad chaplain. If his presence wasn't enough to fill the prisoner with foreboding, there was the small square of black cloth which the presiding judge placed beside him. This was the black cap.

The Crown in the Lamson case was represented by the Solicitor-General (Sir Farrer Herschell), Harry Poland and E. Gladstone. Montagu Williams led for the defence, with Mr (later Sir) Charles Mathews and Mr W. Robson. Both Poland and Mathews subsequently became Public Prosecutors. Some of these barristers were real heavyweights of the courtroom. The young Marshall Hall – later to become probably the greatest legal exponent of over-the-top eloquence – used to go to hear Poland and Williams in action. Mathews, too, became one of the great forensic orators. He had a high-pitched, not particularly pleasing voice, but it was impossible not to listen to him. However, all this was in the future at the time of the Lamson trial.

The 29-year-old Lamson was the object of enormous speculation and there was a buzz in court when he entered the dock, guarded by an unnecessarily large number of prison officers. He was dressed in a black frock coat, black tie and, curiously, black kid gloves.

He looked intelligent and sensitive, although he was quite pale, which made his dark eyes seem all the more piercing. He had a moustache and a short, dark beard. It was hardly surprising that he looked drawn with dark rings under his eyes. In prison during the ten weeks since he was arrested Lamson had undergone an involuntary 'cold turkey' cure of his drug addiction: his supply of morphine and atropine had simply been cut off like turning a tap. This process must have exacted a heavy toll.

Initially counsel for the Crown were in some difficulty. At the time there was no chemical test for aconite or aconitine, only for vegetable poisons in general. The first medical witnesses were quite hopeless under cross-examination as the following selection of questions and answers will show. The first witness is Dr Other Windsor Berry, who was the first doctor called to Percy John's bedside.

> **Montagu Williams**: . . . you said that you had not seen a case of poisoning by vegetable alkaloid.
> **Berry**: No.
> **Montagu Williams**: Are you acquainted with a book called 'Fleming on Aconitine'?
> **Berry**: No.
> **Montagu Williams**: You say you know nothing of aconitine proper?
> **Berry**: That is so . . . I have no experience with aconitine . . . I describe aconitia as an irritant vegetable poison, but I have no knowledge of it.

Next is Dr Edward Little, who was called in by Dr Berry.

> **Little**: I have had no experience in cases of death caused by vegetable poison . . . I have some knowledge of aconite and its preparations, but none of aconitine.

This last answer shows a certain confusion, since aconitine is the active principle of aconite.

Even Dr Thomas Bond, a Fellow of the Royal College of Surgeons and Lecturer on Forensic Medicine at Westminster Hospital, was led into making admissions which should have diminished his credibility.

> **Montagu Williams**: How many cases have you seen of death by aconitine?
> **Bond**: I have never seen one, unless the present is such a case . . . I really do not know anything about aconitine.

The judge, probably without meaning to, emphasised Bond's lack of knowledge of aconitine in an exchange with Montagu Williams.

> **Mr Justice Hawkins**: He [Bond] says he knows nothing at all about it . . . I have taken his [Bond's] answer like this, 'I do not know anything about poison by aconitine, so that I cannot say one way or the other.'

There was another setback for the prosecution case with the evidence of Mrs Sophia Joliffe, at whose boarding house in Shanklin Percy John stayed with his sister and brother-in-law, the Chapmans. The Crown tried to establish that Percy John could not get up and down stairs without help. So, on the day of his death he could not have gone upstairs to his room on his own where he had the quinine pills sent from America, some of which were laced with aconitine.

However, Mrs Joliffe soon put that right, and her evidence seemed to have taken Bedbrook and the others at Blenheim House by surprise. All these years they had thought that stairs were an impossible barrier for Percy.

Mrs Joliffe: The deceased slept in a room on the ground floor. The closet was not on the same floor. He used to manage to get up and down stairs . . . I do not know how he got up and down the stairs; I never saw him. I think he used to crawl on his hands and knees, I am not sure.

This was confirmed later in the trial by William Chapman, Percy John's brother-in-law. He told the court:

He [Percy] went from his bedroom up to the landing. He could go upstairs quicker than you or I could; he travelled upstairs by his hands. There was no difficulty in his crawling about to get from place to place. He could get upstairs without difficulty . . .
. . . He propelled himself with his hands from step to step backwards, seating himself from step to step.

So far the prosecution case had as many holes as a Gruyère cheese. The 'expert' witnesses had admitted knowing little or nothing about the poison from which Percy John had died, and nobody had managed to explain how Lamson had managed to sneak poison into the capsule of sugar. However, there is little doubt that there was strong prejudice against Lamson which was overcoming any lack of evidence.

And then Dr Thomas Stevenson stepped into the witness box. He gave evidence like a man hammering nails into a coffin lid. He was very nearly the perfect witness, certain of his facts without being dogmatic and with an encyclopaedic expertise in his subject. The experienced and wily cross-examiner Montagu Williams probed searchingly for the smallest gap in Stevenson's knowledge, but could find no way through: Stevenson did not give an inch under cross-examination. His associate in his analyses was Dr

Auguste Dupré, PhD, Fellow of the Royal Society and
Lecturer on Chemistry and Toxicology at Westminster
Hospital, and Chemical Referee to the Local
Government Board. Although Dupré was entitled to
call himself Doctor because of his PhD degree, he was
not a medical doctor, and this fact gave Montagu
Williams the opportunity to score his only point off
Stevenson.

Stevenson announced himself as a Doctor of
Medicine, Fellow of the Royal College of Physicians,
London, Fellow of the Council and Institute of
Chemistry, Lecturer on Medical Jurisprudence and
Chemistry at Guy's Hospital, and Examiner in Forensic
Medicine at London University. He also admitted to
having a large experience in analytical chemistry, and
particularly toxicology. During the previous ten years
he had been employed by the Home Office in making
analyses in cases of supposed poisoning. All of which
must have seriously impressed the jury.

In his necessarily long and detailed testimony
Stevenson explained that he (and Dupré) analysed
Percy John's body fluids, vomit and several of his
viscera – duodenum, intestines, liver, spleen, kidneys,
etc. – and found alkaloid extracts in them. He injected
some of the extract into mice, which killed them. He
then injected aconitine into other mice, and they died
in exactly the same fashion. The only way he could
identify the alkaloid as aconitine was by taste. Some of
the effects of this most powerful poison can be gauged
from Stevenson's evidence about his tests on the
extracts.

> Though placed on the tongue, there was a
> sensation of a burning of the lip, although the
> extract [of aconitine] had not touched the lip. The
> sensation was of a burning tingling, a kind of
> numbness difficult to define, salivation or a desire

to expectorate, and a sensation of swelling at the back of the throat, followed by a peculiar seared sensation at the back of the tongue, as if a hot iron had been passed over it or some strong caustic applied . . .

Stevenson later described the tests on the quinine pills, laced with aconitine, that Lamson had sent Percy John from America. He took one twenty-second part of a grain and divided it into four parts for testing separately by himself, Dr Dupré, and an assistant, and for microscopic examination. A grain is .002229oz, so Stevenson took for himself .000026oz, or something like forty thousandths of an ounce.

I . . . placed it on my tongue. I felt the bitterness of quinine, followed by intense burning on the tongue, tingling and soreness of the tongue. The sensations were the same in character, but more severe in form than those I had already experienced.

The judge intervened here with three questions.

Hawkins: Before you leave this part of the case I should like to know how long the symptoms lasted after tasting?
Stevenson: Seven and a half hours.
Hawkins: And that after taking a meal?
Stevenson: Yes.
Hawkins: The effects, then, did not pass away for seven and a half hours?
Stevenson: That is so, my lord.

Montagu Williams was faced with an impossible task in constructing a defence, particularly in view of Stevenson's evidence, but he made a Herculean effort. He began with a multi-pronged attack on Stevenson. He tried to cast doubts on Stevenson's expertise as far as aconitine was concerned, and he got him to agree that aconitine was used legitimately as a treatment for various ailments; then he attempted to establish that the symptoms found at the post mortem were consistent with causes of death other than aconitine poisoning. He opened with a broadside:

> **Montagu Williams**: Have you been present at any case of acknowledged aconitine poisoning?
> **Stevenson**: No. There has never been one, so far as I am aware, in this country.
> **Montagu Williams**: Nor at a post mortem examination?
> **Stevenson**: There has only been one abroad.
> **Montagu Williams**: You found your opinion, then, upon the taste test, your experiments on mice, and your knowledge from reading of aconitine poisoning?
> **Stevenson**: Yes, from my knowledge of aconitine poisons, that is, substances from which aconitine is extracted, and from reading.

Montagu Williams got a number of admissions from Stevenson: aconitine was used in medicines in Britain, France and Germany, and a French chemist's in Haymarket sold it as a patent medicine. Then came a rather testy set of exchanges as Montagu Williams referred to a medical magazine.

> **Montagu Williams**: Do you agree with this, that 'aconitine diminishes sensibility and has been used in various painful diseases'?
> **Stevenson**: Yes.
> **Montagu Williams**: Have you heard of its use in typhoid fever?
> **Stevenson**: Aconite or aconitine?
> **Montagu Williams**: Aconitine.

This was a curious answer by Stevenson, and it re-emphasised the uncertainty concerning aconite and aconitine at the time. It prompted a letter to *The Times* during the trial, which certainly would not have been published today while a trial was on.

> To the Editor of *The Times*.
>
> Sir,
>
> Having had experience regarding 'aconitine' and made many scientific experiments with this vegetable poison at the Chemical Laboratory of the University of Breslau, in Germany, where I also had the opportunity of observing the symptoms of poisoning by this alkaloid, I take the liberty to state that the article known as 'Morson's Aconitine, pure' (known on the Continent as 'English Aconitine, Napellin, Acraconitin or Pseudo-aconitine) is very different from the real pure aconitine. It differs toxicologically as well as in its constitution from pure aconitine. As the above-stated fact has not been mentioned by the scientific experts in a notorious case now before the public, I think it my duty to call attention to it.
>
> DR. FERDINAND SPRINGMUHL.
>
> 15, Gower-street, W.C.

To return to Stevenson's reply to Montagu Williams' question:

> **Stevenson**: I have heard of its use in fevers generally.
> **Hawkins**: Not specially in typhoid cases?
> **Stevenson**: No, in fevers generally, but not specially in typhoid cases.
> **Montagu Williams**: Do you agree –
> **Hawkins**: May I ask from what you are reading?
> **Montagu Williams**: *The Journal of Medicine*, No.27, March 1882.

The Solicitor-General objected, pointing out that the article had been written since the proceedings against Lamson were instituted.

Montagu Williams: But not with a view to this case. The journal is edited by Dr Phipson, who is an acknowledged authority.
Solicitor-General: It is something written in a medical journal within the last day or two.

Dr Stevenson now joined in. He said coldly, 'Dr Phipson is not a doctor of medicine.'

Montagu Williams: Then I will put the question generally. Have you heard of its use internally in several cases of fever?
Hawkins: He says 'I have heard of its use in cases of fever, but not in cases of typhoid fever'.
Stevenson: I have never heard of its being used in typhoid cases proper.
Montagu Williams: Have you heard of its uses in cases of pleuro-pneumonia?
Stevenson: Yes. In very minute doses . . .

Stevenson got in a dig with a final word, which clearly annoyed Montagu Williams.

Stevenson: I have read that in a journal not edited by a medical man.
Montagu Williams: But sink the journal, and suppose the question is from me. You have heard of its use in cases of pleuro-pneumonia?

Stevenson was not going to be shut up, but for this once Montagu Williams won the round.

Stevenson: Yes, I have read of it in an anonymous article in a journal edited by a man who is not a medical man.
Montagu Williams: I am sure you do not mean to

throw a doubt on your collaborator, Dr Dupré.
He is not a medical man?
Stevenson: He is not.

Montagu Williams next asked Stevenson to explain the
exact method by which he extracted the alkaloid
substances from the specimens. The answer was
enough to make the layman's head spin. The process
involved evaporation, washing and filtration, treatment
with rectified spirit, tartaric acid, absolute alcohol,
ether, carbonate of soda, chloroform, and oil of vitriol.
After urine, vomit and distillations of intestines, livers,
kidneys and spleen had gone through all that chemical
torture the jury may well have thought it was hardly
surprising that the result was enough to make the
tongue burn and kill mice.

Montagu Williams had obviously done his homework
very carefully. His questions were aimed at getting
Stevenson to say he didn't know, or at least flustering
him and making him look uncertain in front of the jury.
Stevenson was too good: his knowledge was clearly
wider and more up-to-date than that of Montagu
Williams' adviser. This was obvious during the
cross-examination concerning the taste test of the
traces of alkaloid found in Percy John's body.

> **Montagu Williams**: You say that this was aconitine?
> **Stevenson**: Yes.
> **Montagu Williams**: Was it not characteristic of anything
> else?
> **Stevenson**: No, nothing else that I know of.
> **Montagu Williams**: Do you not expect to find
> something of the same kind of effect with veratria?
> **Stevenson**: No. I have tried that on the tongue, and
> there is a difference.
> **Montagu Williams**: A marked difference?
> **Stevenson**: Yes.
> **Montagu Williams**: What do you say as to delphinia?

Stevenson: It is more like atropia than aconitine. There is more the bitterness I tasted some years ago.

Montagu Williams: Is it more bitter than aconitine?

Stevenson: Morson's aconitine, which is most pure, has little or no bitterness, whereas most alkaloids have a bitterness.

Justice Hawkins: What is the real difference?

Stevenson: There is more of astringency about aconitine – that is, its immediate effect, and this is quite distinct from the effects produced by delphinia.

Montagu Williams: Do you say it differs from pepperine?

Stevenson: Yes. We all know the effects produced by pepper.

Montagu Williams: That has a bitterness?

Stevenson: Yes, but you get the burning sensation at once.

Montagu Williams took another path, but this, too, proved to be a dead end.

Montagu Williams: Do I understand there is no special oil for aconitine?

Stevenson: Yes.

Montagu Williams: Is not phosphoric acid a test?

Stevenson: Yes, but not by those who have studied aconitine recently.

Montagu Williams: It has been looked on as a test?

Stevenson: Yes, no doubt. But I have made experiments in connection with this case with pure aconitine, and find it is not a reliable test. I could get no results from it.

Montagu Williams: Do you know this book?

Stevenson: Yes. It is by Flückner.

Montagu Williams: He gives the reaction?

Stevenson: Quite so, but it is to German aconitia that he refers, and that is very different to English.

Montagu Williams: Does he not refer to the English aconitia as well as to the German?

Stevenson: I don't see reference to English aconitia. Perhaps you will point it out to me if he does.

Having slammed that door, Stevenson then bolted it by adding: 'If he does say so, I should disagree with him.'

There was really nothing Montagu Williams could do for Lamson, but no one could have made a more powerful final speech for the defence. He spoke for nearly two days, and many contemporary barristers considered it to be one of the finest speeches he ever made. One colleague remarked to Charles Mathews as they left the court, 'I have never before been so moved in my life.'

There seems to be little in the flat, unemotional, printed report of Montagu Williams's speech to justify this assessment; but this is true of many written versions of great forensic orations. Indeed the manuscript version of classic plays can appear dull and unexciting to the unpractised eye and mind. Marshall Hall is universally acknowledged to have been the greatest of courtroom orators, and yet the records of many of his speeches hardly reflect it. I have spoken to people who heard him in court and they all mentioned the overwhelming presence of his personality and the magnetic quality of his voice which vividly coloured his words – not to mention his ability to plead for his client with tears of emotion running down his cheeks!

In Montagu Williams' time some barristers made speeches as passionately as any dramatic actor, and we can safely assume that Montagu Williams was not short of histrionic ability. There are a couple of passages in his speech on behalf of Lamson which are indicative of the Montagu Williams technique. In the first he went out of his way to butter up the judge, for want of a more vulgar expression. Reading it today makes the toes curl with embarrassment, but no one seems to have commented on it at the time.

Gentlemen, juries have made mistakes; judges have made mistakes, and although judges tell juries – and tell them earnestly and sincerely – for the judges of this country are one of its brightest ornaments . . . they tell juries . . . not to take any expression of opinion from them, because the responsibility rests with the twelve men who have to try the case. Yet, gentlemen, in my humble opinion, when you come to consider that our judges are in many cases elevated to the bench from being the most successful of advocates and the highest ornaments of advocacy in their profession, you must feel that it is difficult for a judge, or any human being who has been a successful advocate and who has been one of the brightest orators of the age, entirely to divest himself of oratory . . . the tones that have long charmed never lose their charm . . .

From that syrupy flattery Montagu Williams went on to refer to the moving spectacle of Lamson's wife, who went to the dock at the end of each day of the trial and held his hand for a moment before he was taken away.

Gentlemen, I now come to what is to me the most painful part of my duty. I have told you that you have a life of a fellow-creature in your hands. In reality you have a trinity of lives in your hands. You have three people to consider. This man has a wife. Who stood by him in his hour of poverty? That wife. Did you notice her on the first day? A thin, spare figure came up to that dock and took him by the hand, saying by her presence, 'Though all men be against you, though all the world be against you, in my heart there is room for you still.' Gentlemen, they say that women are inferior creatures, but in the hour of retribution it may be said of women; 'What pain and anguish wring the brow,/A ministering angel thou.'

Gentlemen, if the prisoner be convicted, and his

life be sacrificed, what a legacy is there for her!
What a reward for all her true nobility, and for all
that is best and softest in life – a widowed home, a
cursed life, and a poor little child never to be
taught to lisp its father's name, its inheritance the
inheritance of Cain!

That beats *East Lynne* hollow.

Although Montagu Williams raised all sorts of issues
about Percy John's general health because of his
deformity, of how aconitine was used as an ointment to
calm pain and as a medicine, these were irrelevant. The
case really boiled down to two simple questions: Did
Percy John die from aconitine poisoning? and if so,
who gave it to him?

The Solicitor-General's final speech for the Crown
and the summing-up by Mr Justice Hawkins – 'one of
this country's brightest ornaments' – were superfluous.
It was clear that the jury had long since made up their
minds that Lamson was guilty. They did not bother
their heads with *how* Lamson got his brother-in-law to
take the poison. They were out for only half an hour
before returning with their verdict of 'Guilty'. When
Lamson was asked whether he had anything to say why
the Court should not give judgement according to law
he replied firmly, 'Merely to protest my innocence
before God.'

Lamson was taken to Wandsworth Prison, where the
execution was due to take place on Sunday the 2nd
April. However, a group of Lamson's friends tried to
establish that Lamson was – or had been – insane. As a
result of their efforts US President Arthur cabled the
Home Secretary, Sir William Harcourt, asking for the
execution to be postponed. Sir William granted a
postponement until the 18th.

Four days before this second date a great packet of
affidavits arrived from America. Other affidavits from

people in England who knew Lamson well were also sent to the Home Office. So that the authorities would have time to consider them all a second stay of execution until the 28th was granted.

The Americans who sent affidavits were Dr Charles Vonklein, Reverend Irving McElroy, Mrs McElroy, O.L. Barbour, counsel-in-law, Miss Kate Barbour, Mrs Florence Schuyler, Dr W.H. Hall, Miss G.P. Williams, Dr G.S. Winston, Mrs Winston. Some of what they had to say about Lamson has been mentioned at the beginning of this chapter. The Home Secretary decided that the affidavits were not sufficient grounds for commuting the death sentence.

The day before his execution Lamson sent a letter to a friend in which he confessed to murdering Percy John. Part of the letter read:

> . . . Then came my long period of imprisonment at Clerkenwell, and, while there, necessarily the total deprivation of the drug I had so long been accustomed to. With great mental and physical suffering was the weaning accomplished, leaving, however, strongly perceptible results. Then the fearful ordeal of the trial, the awful shock of the sentence, and the sojourn in the condemned room here, face to face with death, cleared away all clouds from my mind and now, I believe I can truly and solemnly say . . . that in my right and normal state of mind the compassing and committing such a crime as that for which I must die would have been utterly and absolutely impossible, and altogether foreign to my whole nature and instincts . . .

Which is probably true.

At about 8.50 a.m. on Friday the 28th April the Under-Sheriff, the Deputy Governor of Wandsworth prison, the surgeon and four warders arrived in Lamson's cell to escort him to the scaffold, which was in the prison courtyard. Fortunately for the unhappy man the scaffold and the newly-prepared grave were not visible to him and he walked quite steadily in the middle of the grim procession. It was led by two warders carrying white wands and the prison clergyman. Next came Lamson, with a warder at each side, followed by the Deputy Governor, the surgeon and several more warders.

Marwood, the executioner, his straps over his arm, was waiting within the inner gates. Marwood held up his hand and shouted 'Halt!' And it was now that Lamson seemed fully to realise his situation. He staggered and nearly fell, but a warder helped him keep his feet, at least for the moment, for he was trembling uncontrollably. While some warders helped Lamson keep upright Marwood strapped his arms.

'I hope you won't hurt me,' Lamson said piteously.

'I'll do my best not to hurt you. I'll be as gentle as I can,' Marwood replied.

The procession moved on again, the two warders half-carrying Lamson to the gallows and up on to the scaffold itself. The warders stood on either side of the trap, holding up the shaking Lamson as his legs were bound and the hood placed over his head. Meanwhile the clergyman was reciting the Lord's Prayer, but the sharp noise of the opening trap interrupted him before he could finish it. Lamson's body was allowed to hang for an hour before it was taken down. Dr Wynter, the prison doctor, subsequently testified at the formal inquest that death had been instantaneous and was due to apoplexy, which seems to strain the usual meaning of the word.

There remains the question of how Lamson managed to get the aconitine in the particular capsule he gave to Percy John.

Of course, he didn't.

As we said at the beginning of this chapter, his

method of poisoning his brother-in-law had extreme subtlety and the applied psychological expertise of the master magician. The business with the capsules and the sugar was a conjuror's ruse to distract attention from the real trick. It hoodwinked everyone who was physically and emotionally involved in the affair at the time. We can see more clearly what happened from a distance, under the hard light of objectivity.

Lamson turned up at Blenheim House with a cake that was *already cut*. This is certain, although Bedbrook said Lamson cut it at the table. He got it wrong – understandably, given the high drama of the moment. Lamson had prepared the cake, not the capsule, by injecting aconitine into a raisin or cherry. He handed the cake round himself, and made sure that Percy John got the poisoned slice. He could easily have identified it by doctoring the end slice, or a slice with two almonds on the top, for example.

Even in the very unlikely possibility that Bedbrook was right and Lamson did cut the cake at the tea table, he still could have ensured that Percy got the piece of cake with the poison in it by having some identifying sign on it – like the two almonds, or a cherry.

He was too clever for his own good. It went over the head of the prosecution counsel, the judge, and the jury. But the jury simply didn't like him and rightly found him guilty on the strength of instinct and not reason.

DR ROBERT BUCHANAN

Silence is golden.
Carlyle

Some men . . . are mad if they behold a cat.
Merchant of Venice

A furious itch to talk . . .
Somerset Maugham

And a rogue is married to a whore.
Kipling

You can lead a whore to culture,
but you can't make her think.
Dorothy Parker

A potentially perfect murder, a kitten badly mistreated in a scientific experiment, a brassy madame of a bordello, a disgruntled minder, an investigative journalist of the Jimmy-Cagney-press-card-in-the-hatband school, a jury given doses of morphine in court by counsel and a defence lawyer counsel who combined the more colourful characteristics of the fictional Perry Mason and the real-life Marshall Hall were all elements of the case of Dr Robert Buchanan. It was like something dreamed up by a feverish scriptwriter with scant concern for believability.

And, as we shall see, the case also had a vital lesson for all would-be killers.

Dr Robert Buchanan was a mild-looking, sad-eyed man in the Crippen mould. He was short and weak-looking to the point of being puny – and even his moustache was weedy and straggly like a plant grown in perpetual shadow. Yet he had a strong sexual drive and the twisted strength of purpose to commit murder for gain. He was not a very nice man.

He very nearly committed a perfect murder, but he panicked badly and gave himself away a dozen times over with his recklessly incautious remarks and behaviour.

At the age of twenty-four, shortly after he qualified, Buchanan emigrated to America in 1886 with his wife Helen, who was an attractive young woman with a pale complexion and auburn hair. According to some reports she was a decorous-looking woman, but although she may not have been as sexually active as her husband, she seems to have had a promiscuous streak.

Buchanan hung up his shingle – put up his brass plate
– at a rented house, 267 West Eleventh Street in what is
known now as Greenwich Village, in Lower Manhat-
tan. He gradually built up a practice and a reputation as
a sober and respectable young man. However, his Dr
Jekyll-type character had a minor Mr Hyde side as well.

Buchanan, a Scot, had a weakness for spirituous
liquors. By day he lived an outwardly respectable life
seeing patients, although it appears that his treatment
of some of his younger women patients was unorthodox
in its intimacy. By night he frequented bars and low
haunts. First stop on his pub-crawl circuit was a nearby
saloon and restaurant owned by a Richard Macomber.
The two men met in 1898 in a real estate office owned
by a Robert Gibbons. He introduced the 35-year-old
Buchanan to Macomber as a fellow Freemason.
Macomber was an interesting character, and was to
become Buchanan's closest confidant. He was in
business for a while, including running a dairy, where
he was charged a couple of times with selling milk that
had been adulterated with water. He sold that business
and went into the Salvation Army for a year or so. He
left and bought his bar with the money from the sale of
his previous business.

They became friendly, not only because of their both
being Freemasons, but because Macomber was
flattered to have Buchanan, a doctor and a man of
some social standing, as a regular. In Macomber's
opinion Buchanan's presence in the bar gave it some
class – which gives a fair indication of the quality of the
place.

The two men were joined by a retired English Army
captain, William Doria, who lived in Newark, a not
very salubrious suburb of New York. Buchanan and
Doria shared a liking for strong drink and the sort of
women that the French describe as having light thighs –
presumably because they fly apart easily. One night in

1890 Doria took Buchanan on the wearisome journey
by train and ferry to a bordello in Halsey Street,
Newark. The house was run by a Mrs Anna Sutherland,
known to the clientele as 'Mrs S'. It boasted four girls,
if 'boasted' and 'girls' are the correct words. Some
reports suggest that there were ten whores in the house,
but this seems unduly flattering and unlikely. It was a
successful and prosperous establishment, though,
well-furnished and with a 'company' carriage and
horses worth $1,200.

Buchanan patronised the working members of the
quartet in turn for some time before his enthusiasm for
them began to droop. Nevertheless, he regularly
continued to drag out to Newark to spend time with
Anna Sutherland, which puzzled Doria for a while.

It was true that Buchanan claimed he was treating
Mrs S. for a kidney complaint, but this didn't explain
why he passed long hours alone with her. It was difficult
to believe that their relations were anything more than
strictly mutually professional. After all, she was twice
Buchanan's age and it would take an effort of will for a
young man to find her tempting. She had been married
three times before – not that this would necessarily
make her less attractive to a man – but she was fat,
vulgar, drank, had crudely dyed hair and a Crom-
wellian wart on her nose. Not to mention that she was a
bawd. Still, she had *some*, easily quantifiable, qualities
to commend her.

In November 1890, Buchanan confided in Doria.
'I've got a good thing going down there in Halsey
Street. The woman has heaps of money. And it doesn't
cost me a cent to go there,' he added cannily. 'She's
stuck on me and I think I'll marry her.' Doria took this
as a case of the liquor talking and thought nothing of it
at the time.

The first inkling that Buchanan was serious came
when he divorced his wife while she was out of New

York. He paid a lawyer named Gibbons $1,000 to secure the divorce, and the money was provided by Anna Sutherland. The grounds for the Buchanan divorce were adultery. This was pretty rich considering Buchanan's paid-for philandering and dalliance with some of his women patients. It was well-known that on one occasion Helen Buchanan had come downstairs from their living quarters to find her husband and a woman patient fornicating on the floor of his surgery.

As we have said, it is possible that the fair Helen was no stranger to promiscuity herself. When Buchanan was asked who the man was with whom she had the adulterous affair, he said that it wasn't a question of one man, but several. Sauce for the goose . . . However, anything that Buchanan said has to be treated with some reserve. Nevertheless, there must have been some proof of adultery for Buchanan to have got his divorce.

'I'm finished with marriage forever,' Buchanan told his friends when his divorce was granted. Prudently he did not go so far as to include celibacy.

On the 25th November Buchanan's intentions became unmistakable. He called on Macomber at his home at 297 West 12th Street. After some desultory conversation Buchanan said, 'I've got a wealthy woman patient in Newark and she's stuck on me. She wants to make me her heir because she has no living relatives. Will you come over there with me tomorrow and witness her will?' Macomber agreed.

Buchanan, Doria and Macomber went to the Halsey Street house the next evening, the 26th. Doria, of course, knew what the place really was, but apparently Macomber had no idea. He took Mrs Sutherland to be the respectable woman Buchanan said she was. Either Mrs S. was a consummate actress, or, more likely, Macomber wouldn't recognise a lady if one kicked him. And presumably the whores had been given the night off.

Doria and Macomber witnessed Mrs Sutherland's will. In it she left everything to her husband, whoever he might be at the time of her death. If she died unmarried her not inconsiderable fortune would go to her 'beloved friend and physician' Dr Robert Buchanan. The only other legacies were $50 each to a brother and sister. The little doctor had stitched up things very nicely. And if Macomber was puzzled by the conflict between Buchanan's statement that Mrs Sutherland had no living relatives and the bequests to the brother and sister there is no record of his raising the matter with Buchanan.

Three days after this Buchanan told Doria, 'I'm going to marry Mrs S. She's got a power of money.'

'You're drunk,' Doria retorted. 'You can't marry *her*.' He tried to dissuade Buchanan, but he wouldn't listen.

'I will marry her,' he repeated. 'She's got lots of money.'

Doria gave up. He didn't want to fall out with Buchanan, and subsequently he went with him and Mrs Sutherland to the house of a minister, Davis W. Lusk, at 124 Elm Street in Newark, and was a witness to their marriage on the 29th November, 1891.

They all returned to the Halsey Street house where Doria and Buchanan celebrated with some wine. The new Mrs Buchanan, however, was a teetotaller and refused to drink, even on her wedding night. This evokes the curious image of the bordello-keeper saying virtuously, 'I don't touch the demon alcohol. What sort of woman do you think I am?'

The doctor's vow that he was done with marriage forever had lasted for only seventeen days following his divorce.

When Macomber heard of Buchanan's marriage he congratulated him, but Buchanan denied that he was married, despite the fact that Doria had witnessed the ceremony. He tried to keep up this pretence for some time, telling his other friends that Mrs Buchanan was only a housekeeper.

Doria was a good friend of Buchanan for some time, but later in their acquaintanceship Doria severely cooled off towards him. Buchanan met a young woman named Lyman whom he seduced. After they had been lovers for some time he wanted to get rid of her. Doria was sick at the time and Buchanan was treating him.

'You ought to settle down,' he advised Doria, who wasn't enchanted by the idea. Buchanan persisted. 'I know a nice girl who will do for you.' He introduced Lyman to Doria, and some three weeks later they were married. Later Doria found out, or at least suspected, that Buchanan had foisted the woman on to him. At the time of Buchanan's arrest *The World* reported that Doria was the principal witness against Buchanan.

Soon after his own wedding Buchanan left his new bride to arrange her affairs in Newark while he hurried to New York where he negotiated the purchase of the house in Greenwich Village that he had been renting. Much of the money for it came from his wife. Without delay he then moved his mother and his daughter Gertie into the house.

Back in the now deserted Halsey Street brothel there was an elderly man named James Smith who lived in the basement and acted as caretaker and dogsbody. He received no fixed salary, or percentage of the house's take. When he needed money he went to Mrs Sutherland, who gave it to him. Smith was to prove himself a dogged nuisance to Dr Buchanan.

Buchanan's marriage to Anna Sutherland badly galled Smith for two reasons. First, for some time he had wanted to become her fourth husband himself, but it was a hopeless ambition. She turned him down because, she said, she would never marry a man 'who lived off girls'. Coming from the madam of a brothel that was a bit rich.

Second, the new Mrs Buchanan's decision to retire from peddling prostitution and leave Newark for Greenwich Village meant that Smith was out of a job and a home, and although he claimed to be a hatter by trade, in fact he was unemployable. He drank excessively, and had been treated for alcoholism. Smith hated Buchanan, for he believed that the young doctor had married Sutherland only for her money. It was a fair guess which needed no great insight.

Eventually Mrs Buchanan quit the house in Halsey Street and went to live with her husband. It appears that Buchanan persuaded her to bring all the bordello furniture with her. It must have made a very interesting-looking doctor's home and surgery.

As the saying goes, you can't make a silk purse out of a sow's ear. The transition from keeping a brothel to being the ostensibly respectable wife of a doctor was rather too much for the new unblushing bride. Her behaviour was an example of fact outdoing fiction: it would have been considered exaggerated even for someone in a 'Carry On' film. At a tea party she gave for some of the doctor's women patients she regaled them with *osé* anecdotes and salty stories which went down like a lead anchor. And old habits die hard. Mrs Buchanan greeted her husband's male patients unconventionally with 'Hello, dearie, what'll it be? Blonde or brunette?'

Mrs Buchanan's behaviour outside the matrimonial home was no better. Buchanan used to take her with him to Macomber's bar where she startled even the unfastidious regulars. According to Macomber she was loud and coarse. She could stand at one end of the bar on a busy night and be heard cursing above all the noise at the other end. Buchanan stopped taking her with him to the bar and ate many of his meals there alone. So it didn't take long for Buchanan to become overtly fed up with his wife. He persisted as long as he could

with the fiction that Mrs Buchanan was his housekeeper, admitting the truth only to Doria, who had
been at the ceremony and subsequent celebration
anyway.

For her part, it is clear that the constrained,
bread-and-butter existence of housewife to the doctor
soon palled on Mrs Buchanan after the noisier, more
boisterous and spicier lifestyle of madam of a bordello.
Her impossible desire for respectability was being
bought at too high a price: her wimpish-looking
husband was a closet brute. His treatment of her and
the way he bled her of her money was too much even
for her to bear.

Doria had been visiting the unhappy couple from
time to time, and Mrs Buchanan had written to him
regularly complaining that her husband was ill-treating
her. They all met at a lawyer's office in Newark
concerning a claim for commission from Mrs Buchanan
over the sale of a house – not the disorderly one. While
they were there Mrs Buchanan told Doria she'd had
enough of Buchanan's behaviour and she had decided
to return to the Halsey Street house and resume her old
business.

'Nearly all my money has been spent by that
scoundrel. I must go back,' she said forcefully.

Doria didn't think much of the idea. 'If you come
back to Newark and run the house again it'll ruin
Buchanan's professional and personal reputation.'

'Tough bloody luck,' was Mrs Buchanan's attitude. 'I
can't live with that fellow. If he don't like it he can get a
judicial separation.' With which she stalked off.

Buchanan, who could sense that something was
going on, came over to join Doria. 'I advised her
against it, but Mrs Buchanan intends to come back to
Newark and open up the house,' Doria reported.

'– – – – her!' Buchanan exclaimed inelegantly, using
a word his wife must have heard frequently in the

course of her business. 'I'm not going to be disgraced
by her in my profession and family standing.'

'Well, you're not supporting your wife or doing
anything for her,' Doria pointed out.

'– – – – her!' Buchanan repeated. 'She shan't go back
to that house!'

He was right there.

Buchanan had a bad case of wind up. He feared –
and with good reason – that if his patients, instead of
considering his wife highly eccentric, discovered her
true background he would lose his practice. By this
time Buchanan had advanced in his public life: he had
become a police surgeon and a Commissioner in
Lunacy. He achieved this despite having the noisy,
vulgar albatross round his neck and being a drinker
himself, and he didn't want to lose it all. He tried to
spread the story that his wife was the daughter of a
Philadelphia banker. It was a claim that was received
with a certain reserve.

In addition to his other very considerable short-
comings, as we have seen, Buchanan was also an active
lecher. Quite soon after his marriage to Sutherland,
Buchanan started running around with what a
prosecuting counsel later described rather coarsely as
'younger and fresher women'. Three of them were
named Hazel, Blanche and Sadie. A fourth, Maggie
Young, was a very attractive young woman who lived in
Little Twelfth Street, and from all accounts was – to use
an expression of the times – no better than she ought to
be, and probably not even as good as that. Buchanan
told her that he was unmarried and divorced, and the
woman living at his West Eleventh Street home was his
housekeeper. As we shall see, Maggie Young figured in
what would have been a quite remarkable incident in
most court cases, but this was only one of a whole host
of bizarre events in Buchanan's extraordinary trial.

At about this time, in 1891, there was a famous

murder trial in New York of a young man named
Carlyle Harris. Buchanan's subsequent case was to
echo with a number of similarities. Harris was also a
(recently qualified) doctor, who wanted to rid himself
of an inconvenient wife. As Buchanan was to do later,
he tricked his spouse into taking a fatal dose of
morphine.

Harris, member of a well-to-do bourgeois family,
married Helen Potts because it was the only way he
could get her into bed. Helen was attractive – and
moral – but she was definitely from the wrong side of
the tracks, and according to all reports, her mother was
a sight to be seen. At the time Harris was only a
medical student, dependent upon his grandfather for
his tuition fees and living expenses. So Carlyle Harris
persuaded Helen to keep the marriage secret until he
qualified as a doctor and could afford to be
independent.

Helen Potts Harris became pregnant, precipitating a
whole series of critical events. Harris talked her into
letting him perform an abortion on her, which he
botched. She was taken ill, went to the country and
gave birth to a stillborn child. She then returned to New
York.

Mrs Potts was now putting pressure on Harris to tell
his family about Helen, and go through a proper church
marriage with her. It was then, the prosecution were to
allege, that he formulated the plan to kill her.

Harris came up with one of his bright ideas. He
arranged for Helen to go as a boarder to a finishing
school for young ladies, to make her more polished and
acceptable to his family when he announced their
marriage. Since her abortion, Helen had suffered from
recurrent headaches. He wrote out a prescription for
capsules of a standard quinine–morphine mixture. Of
the four he gave her, he had emptied one and filled it
with pure morphine.

Helen collapsed after taking this capsule. Three doctors were brought in and diagnosed morphine poisoning because her pupils were contracted to pinpoints. They fought in vain to save her life and assumed that the druggist who had prepared the capsules had made an error.

The secret Harris-Potts marriage was kept from the coroner, Louis Schultze, who did not order a postmortem. His verdict was accidental death. Schultze was the coroner involved in Buchanan's case.

Ike White, a reporter of *The World*, owned by the celebrated Hungarian-born Joseph Pulitzer, discovered that Harris had been secretary of the infamous *Neptune* club, which was reputed to stage orgies on the premises. According to White, girls were seduced by plying them with ginger pop laced with whisky. White's story in *The World* stirred up a public outcry, and a postmortem of Helen Potts Harris was ordered.

Ike White was the journalist whose investigations and subsequent stories prodded Schultze into ordering an autopsy on Anna Buchanan, leading to Buchanan's arrest. The judge at Harris's trial was Recorder Smyth; he presided at Dr Buchanan's trial. The principal expert witness in the case was Dr Rudolph Witthaus. He also testified for the prosecution against Buchanan.

The Harris case was the source of a great deal of talk and speculation in Macomber's bar. Naturally Buchanan, as the bar's resident sage, was asked his opinion. Harris was a bungling fool and an amateur, Buchanan declared contemptuously. He obviously didn't know how to disguise the symptoms of morphine poisoning. Inevitably Buchanan was asked, 'Do you know how to do it?'

'Yes, a way has just occurred to me. Every acid has its neutralizing base and every chemical agent its reagent.' Undetectable poisoning was easy for the knowledgeable, Buchanan declared.

On another occasion he was overheard to say of his wife, 'I'll dump her some day. It's an easy matter for a doctor to get rid of someone if he wants to.' They were the sort of remarks that people remember.

Meanwhile, stories of domestic rows and discord between the Buchanans became known outside the immediate family circle. The doctor was a heavy drinker, and he was very loose in the mouth when he was in a bar. He once said 'I wish I'd never married her. I wish I'd never had anything to do with her at all.' Later he told Macomber, 'That old housekeeper of mine will drive me crazy. I'm going to dump her. I'm going to get rid of her. I'm getting tired of her.' He followed this up by telling his friends that his 'housekeeper' was continually quarrelling with him. He was going to get rid of her without any trouble, he said darkly. It was true that she had given him money, but he was going to dispose of her one way or another.

Ungallantly he told Macomber on another occasion, 'Her face is enough to drive a man crazy or to drink' – not that he needed any prompting for that – 'Scandal or not, I'm going to get rid of that old chromo.'*

Dr Buchanan finally decided to translate thought and desire into action. He began to prepare the ground – almost literally – for disposing of Mrs Buchanan II. His first step was to move his mother and daughter out of the Greenwich Village house. Then he started a campaign of disinformation.

He reminded his friends that he had treated 'the old woman' for Bright's disease, or nephritis.

(These days it is known that nephritis is a group of

---

* Buchanan's use of the word 'chromo' is interesting. Eric Partridge's *A Dictionary of Slang and Unconventional English* has the following entry: **chromo**. Abbreviation of *chromolithograph, -ic*, 'in use shortly after 1850' (*OED*) 2. A prostitute: Australian: since ca. 1925 (*BAKER, Australian Slang, 1942*).

I have not seen any reference to 'chromo' meaning 'prostitute' as early as 1892.

several different diseases of the kidneys, and the name Bright's disease has largely dropped out of use.)

'She can't live long. She's sure to die,' he announced in Macomber's bar. And in case that hadn't properly sunk in, he added, 'She's sick now and can never get better. Go and see her once in a while and keep her in good humour. She's sure to peg out in less than six months.'

It seems that Buchanan was arrogantly full of self confidence at this time. After all, he had successfully prised a near-fortune away from a madame of a bordello, a class of person not known for gullibility or generosity. He had been successfully bedding a number of 'younger and fresher women', he was successful in his profession, and he had a lot of sycophantic, admiring drinking companions who helped bolster his ego.

He intensified his preparations for the murder of the old chromo. Quite coolly he told Macomber, 'That old woman threatens to poison herself if I insist on breaking it up. I said, "I wish you would. You know where my poisons are kept. You couldn't please me better than by taking morphine. It'd be the best thing for you and for me".'

In March of 1892 Buchanan apparently could stand being with his wife no longer. He told his friends he was going to Edinburgh to study, but he wouldn't take Mrs Buchanan with him even though she had threatened to cut him out of her will if he left without her. Despite this threat – perhaps he knew that Mrs Buchanan wouldn't be able to carry it out – on the 1st April he bought a single ticket for a ship leaving on Monday the 25th.

The Thursday before he was due to leave Buchanan told his friends that Mrs Buchanan had been taken so seriously ill that he'd had to cancel his trip. He had arranged for a nurse, Mrs Childs, to take care of his wife. Later the ubiquitous Ike White discovered that

Buchanan had cancelled his passage on the 11th, *ten days* before his wife fell fatally ill.

The next day Buchanan called in Dr Burnett C. McIntyre. He arrived at two o'clock to find Mrs Buchanan hysterical and suffering from contraction of the throat. He prescribed 'a small nervine: eight grains of chloral with eight grains of bromide of sodium, syrup of ginger and water, a teaspoonful of which to be taken every two hours.' McIntyre's prescription called for a two-ounce bottle of the nervine, so if Mrs Buchanan had gulped the whole lot down in one go it would not have killed her.

One hour later the nurse, Mrs Childs, and a Mrs Brockway – wife of a dentist who was going to take a house from the Buchanans – called in to see Buchanan. They walked into the sick room just as Buchanan was giving his wife something from a spoon. When she got it down, he more or less forced another on her. Immediately afterwards she grabbed an orange and tore off a piece of it with her teeth, grimacing as if the medicine she had just been given had a bitter taste. Buchanan subsequently said that he was giving her the nervine prescribed by Dr McIntyre, although the nervine was slightly sweet, not bitter, and the dose was once every two hours.

Some ten or fifteen minutes after Buchanan had given his wife the two spoonfuls of whatever it was, she fell into a deep sleep. Dr Henry B. Watson was called in, and Buchanan gave him a history of the case. When he said that his wife had kidney trouble, Watson immediately diagnosed uraemic poison, known today as uraemia. He gave her an injection of digitalis. A few minutes later Dr McIntyre returned and consulted with Dr Watson. To satisfy themselves that Mrs Buchanan was really suffering from uraemia, they tested a specimen of her urine with nitric acid, but there was no albumen present, which ruled out uraemia.

The two doctors conferred and came to the conclusion that Mrs Buchanan's coma was caused by a reaction to the chloral she had been given because of 'some peculiarity of her constitution'. In other words, what we would call an allergy today.

'What have you given her?' Doctors Watson and McIntyre asked Buchanan.

'One dose of your medicine,' Buchanan answered innocently.

McIntyre could think of nothing else to do than treat Mrs Buchanan for the chloral she had been given. For two hours he rubbed her and 'irritated' her, as he said, with the crude procedure of constantly slapping her about the face with a wet towel, and then with his hand, to bring her back to consciousness. This rough and ready method also happened to be the treatment for morphine poisoning.

McIntyre and Watson left their patient at about seven o'clock, and returned a couple of hours later. They were still uncertain of the cause of Mrs Buchanan's coma. They were wavering between ascribing it to a reaction to the chloral, to a narcotic, or to some third cause. It would take very little to make them decide in favour of any one of the possible causes, and Buchanan was able to steer them in the direction he wanted.

'Gentlemen, I want to disabuse your mind of the idea that this woman is suffering from the effects of chloral. Dr Janeway has been prescribing much larger doses than that for her and she has become used to it. She has become used to it and cannot be idiosyncratic to its influences.' Which left as possibilities narcotic poisoning or some other cause.

For the moment the scales teetered gently in the balance. Then Buchanan followed up with, 'Gentlemen, the woman's father died of cerebral apoplexy or cerebral haemorrhage.' The symptoms of cerebral haemorrhage were exactly the same as those displayed by the unfortunate Mrs Buchanan, and the scales came down with a resounding bang in its favour. Relieved of having to take an uneducated guess at what was wrong with Mrs Buchanan, McIntyre and Watson settled for cerebral haemorrhage as the cause of her illness and subsequent death.

In fact there was no Dr Janeway who had prescribed large doses of chloral for Mrs Buchanan; and her father didn't die of cerebral haemorrhage. His fatal complaint could not have been further removed from his brain: he died of a gangrenous foot.

Mrs Buchanan died at three o'clock the following afternoon. Charles Benedict of Carmine Street was the undertaker who was called in. At six o'clock that same evening an employee, George Bender, called at the house and spent a couple of hours embalming Mrs Buchanan's body. He injected into the brachial artery of the right arm eight pints of 'Utopia' embalming fluid manufactured by Dollis & Huckle of Brooklyn. Another eight pints was injected into the navel.

At the time of his wife's death the widower was out with Macomber on a pub crawl. After he returned home and learned of his wife's decease Buchanan rushed round to Macomber's bar to drown his sorrows. Or maybe it was to celebrate. 'My God,' he told Macomber. 'I can't stay in the house with that dead body. I'm going to a hotel. I wouldn't stay there for a thousand dollars.'

The doctor did his grieving – such as it was – in Macomber's bar. He didn't allow his anguish to delay him in making funeral arrangements. He fixed them up that same night in the bar, and while he was at it he invited a number of his drinking pals to the funeral. They reciprocated by offering to carry the coffin.

Anna Sutherland Buchanan was whisked off to Greenwood Cemetery, Brooklyn, on Tuesday 26th

April 1892. Apart from Buchanan no relative, friend or former employee from the Newark brothel was present at the service; only Macomber and the boozy pallbearers from his bar were at her burial.

The recently bereaved husband told Macomber that a great load had been lifted from his shoulders; he had expected a rumpus but 'Providence had interfered' and so his troubles were over. As we know now, he was being seriously over-optimistic. The two men returned to Greenwich Village together. On the way Buchanan stopped the carriage in Brooklyn and again in New York to have a few drinks. 'After this trying ordeal we had better stop and take something to revive our drooping spirits,' he said, which was breathtakingly hypocritical even by his standards.

The carriage was paid off at the corner of Eleventh Street and Sixth Avenue. Macomber walked up Sixth Avenue with Buchanan, who eventually left him to see a lady he knew named Mrs Albro, who lived in Sixteenth Street. Buchanan didn't say why he was going to visit her, and Macomber didn't ask why. He could guess.

Later that day a professional nurse, Gretchen Maas, met Buchanan with Macomber at number 70 Seventh Avenue, a house with a marked shadow of dubiety over its reputation and that of one or two of its inhabitants. Mrs Maas, whose husband was frequently away on business for long periods, had known Buchanan for some three years or so. Macomber originally introduced them. Buchanan seemed to have revived his drooping spirits successfully enough, for when he told Mrs Maas 'I have just come back from a funeral after burying my sister,' – he really found it difficult to admit that Anna was his wife – she replied, 'You feel mighty jolly over it.'

'They all have to die,' Buchanan said philosophically, if not heartlessly. While he was in the house Buchanan tried to kiss one of the women who was living there. She pushed him off with little ado.

Buchanan enthusiastically continued restoring his spirits for the next few days. On the following Saturday he sent a note to Macomber asking him to join him and Doria in the back room of Duffy's Saloon at Eighth Avenue and Fifteenth Street. Buchanan asked Macomber to come out with him 'to places where there were girls', but Macomber pointed out that he had work to do.

'All right, we'll meet again at seven,' Buchanan said. When Macomber met up with the two men they were both drunk, but not too drunk to visit several saloons.

To all intents and purposes, Buchanan was now home and dry. His albatross of a wife was dead and safely buried, her death certified as being due to cerebral haemorrhage; her remaining money – some $18,000 – had been willed to him and he had got his hands on her jewels, which he showed to his boozing companions. All he had to do was to stay calm and behave normally, or at least, what passed for normally with him. In fact, as we shall see, he spectacularly lost his cool.

This was because the disgruntled James Smith was doing his best to stir up trouble for Buchanan. He went to the coroner, Dr Louis Schultze, and accused Buchanan of having killed his wife. Schultze should order an autopsy, Smith said, but the coroner was a firm believer in non-intervention and *laissez-faire*. In any case, an elderly rumpot of a former caretaker in a house of ill-repute was not the sort of person who was going to stir him into action.

Whether Smith sought out Ike White of *The World*, or whether White had the good fortune to bump into Smith as he came grumbling out of Schultze's office as some commentators say is unimportant. The fact is that these two very different elements did meet, and their coming together set off a thunderous reaction. When Smith told White his story, it must have set the journalist vibrating with excitement at its potential, with its never-failing ingredients of mystery, murder and sex. Lots of sex. Smith began to dig in the fertile ground of Macomber's bar and other of Buchanan's haunts; he interviewed Buchanan himself. These enquiries by the most celebrated – or notorious – investigative journalist of the day and his articles in *The World* put extra strain on Buchanan's already taut nerves.

Soon after the second Mrs Buchanan died, Buchanan went to see his first wife, Helen, in Halifax, Nova Scotia. According to her, he told her nothing about his second marriage. He simply said that he was lonely and was missing her. He asked her to forgive him and to marry him again. Three weeks after the death of Mrs Buchanan II, Buchanan, declaring himself to be a bachelor, made Helen Mrs Buchanan III. As a wedding gift he gave Helen a pair of diamond earrings, without bothering to tell her that he had taken them from Mrs Buchanan II before she died.

To Helen Buchanan's considerable surprise, although Buchanan apparently hated New York he insisted on returning there because he had important business in that city. If that wasn't enough to make her think, Buchanan first installed her in a boarding house under the name of Read, and then in the Hotel Hamilton at 125th Street and 8th Avenue, under the name of Frazer. Whether Mrs Helen Buchanan was naive, genuinely fond of her husband, in financial straits or plain submissive like an English Victorian wife, it is difficult to say.

When Buchanan was asked, he firmly denied that he had married Helen again. That was mildly eccentric, perhaps, but stories by the tirelessly inquisitive Ike White in *The World* about Mrs Buchanan's death pushed Buchanan into actions which were either imprudent, self-incriminating or wildly bizarre to the point of unbelievability – sometimes all three.

As the stories began to appear in *The World* Buchanan went into a sort of semi-hiding. Instead of going to his usual haunts, mainly Macomber's bar, for a period Buchanan went uptown to Dorsch's saloon wearing a different disguise every day, including on one occasion a pair of green goggles. He couldn't have drawn more attention to himself if he'd blown a whistle and waved a flag.

He stopped a stranger in the street and asked him if he had heard any gossip about a doctor having poisoned his wife. When at last he returned to Macomber's bar he told his drinking companions that he was sure that people were saying he had poisoned wife number two. 'Do you really believe I could do a thing like that?' he asked plaintively.

'Of course not,' they reassured him; but Buchanan was generating so much smoke that even his friends couldn't help thinking that there must be some fire somewhere.

Buchanan was now running around like a frightened gerbil in a cage. He told Macomber, 'That man Smith is sore on me because I cut him out. It's getting hot for me. I'd better skip out till this thing has blown over.' Macomber didn't want to give his friend any advice until Buchanan had consulted a lawyer, so they went to see his Newark lawyer, Herbert W. Knight.

Buchanan asked the lawyer about the countries which had extradition treaties with America.

'Doctor, you're in no danger. The physicians have certified that she died of cerebral haemorrhage. That has nothing to do with poisoning,' Knight replied.

'No, but Smith has made a charge that she died of poison. *If they dig up her body they'll find her full of poison.* Coming so soon after the Carlyle Harris case they'll say I poisoned her and I'll be put on trial for my life.' Buchanan claimed that Mrs Buchanan had been a 'morphine eater', and that is why an autopsy would reveal the presence of poison in the body.

After some more talk Knight recommended a New York counsel, Charles E. Davison, who was one of the lawyers in the Carlyle Harris case. Perhaps Buchanan would have been better advised to go to a lawyer who had been on the winning side.

On the way back from Newark to New York Buchanan took off his glasses because he was afraid he was being shadowed and he thought he would stand less chance of being recognised. Rather bitterly he said to Macomber, 'If I'd only looked ahead I'd have got the old woman cremated, and then the – – – –ing newspapers and the District Attorney's office could go – – – –.' Rather primly, newspaper reports of the trial said 'Buchanan uses bad language.'

Macomber tried to cheer up Buchanan, who eventually said, 'Well, Dick, I don't think she died of cerebral haemorrhage. I think she took a dose of morphine.'

'But the symptoms weren't of morphia poisoning.'

'Ah, but a little belladonna would counteract that.'

When Macomber repeated that conversation at the trial, *The World* reported, 'There was a hush in the courtroom so that you could hear the clock ticking.' Well, no one had dropped a pin.

One night soon after the visit to the lawyers Buchanan feared that a story about him was going to appear in the next day's paper. He rushed to the newspaper building with an old friend from Nova Scotia, Henry Warren, who had called to see him during a visit to New York. The two men waited from midnight until the first papers came off the press at 3 a.m. Buchanan grabbed one and turned the pages feverishly looking for the non-existent story. Momentarily relieved, he told Warren, 'It looks like they investigated and didn't find anything and dropped the matter.'

Nevertheless, Buchanan decided to go to the cemetery to see that Mrs Buchanan was safely six feet under. He went in mid-morning with the long-suffering Macomber and Lawyer Davison. The ostensible reason for the visit was to see if the grave had been turfed over yet.

When they got to the cemetery Buchanan had a terrible shock: the grave had been opened. 'My God!' he exclaimed in horror. 'They've been here already and dug her up!'

They were at the wrong grave. When they found the correct one, it was untouched.

This didn't calm Buchanan for long, and he was soon back in his state of quaking terror. He instructed Davison to pay a man a dollar a day to go to inspect the grave daily. At the same time he was convinced that his house was under surveillance and he made arrangements for a suitcase to be smuggled out so he could make a dash off to Milwaukee and evade the man shadowing him. He made a break for it, but farcically missed the train, had second thoughts and went home. He decided to go to Detroit instead, but that was another journey he didn't make.

He arranged to get news of any developments by telegraph, sent to him under his assumed name of Read, using coded messages. If there was no move to exhume Mrs Buchanan and the whole affair was blowing over the telegram would read: 'Will ship goods immediately'. But the moment that the first spadeful of earth was turned over on the grave the message would be: 'Can't ship goods', which would be the signal for Buchanan to get even farther away from New York. Even Sir Walter Scott's 'Oh what a tangled web we weave/When first we practise to deceive . . . ' badly understated Buchanan's frantic scurrying around.

The World's Ike White and another journalist named

Roeder had been rushing around as busily as Buchanan and with much greater effect. White took the results of the extensive enquiries to the coroner Dr Schultze, who conferred with the Assistant District Attorney, and a postmortem was ordered. Mrs Buchanan's body was exhumed, and taken to Selle's Morgue, just outside the gates of Greenwood cemetery. The body was in an excellent state of preservation because of the embalming process that George Bender had carried out.

The initial autopsy was performed by Dr Henry P. Loomis. Also present at the exhumation and post-mortem were Charles Benedict, the undertaker, George Bender, the embalmer, and Dr Watson, who took notes.

Loomis was a leading pathologist although he was only thirty-two years old. At the trial he testified he had carried out something like two thousand autopsies. He had a familiar report to make: he could find no natural cause of death – and Mrs Buchanan had healthy kidneys: she was not suffering from Bright's disease.

A subsequent minute examination of the brain – more than 150 sections of the brain were taken – proved that there had been no cerebral haemorrhage or any disease of the brain. When he first saw the body the celebrated chemist Professor Rudolph Witthaus lifted the eyelids to confirm the presence of morphine. He expected to find even after all this time that the pupils were contracted. He was severely taken aback when he discovered they were of normal size. This presented the State with a serious problem. Although it was evident that Buchanan had poisoned his wife, the State could not prove it unless they could explain how he had managed the trick of concealing this vital symptom.

Ike White heard that Buchanan was on his way back to New York. He persuaded Schultze to leave Mrs Buchanan unburied for another day, and that night he went to Macomber's saloon to meet Buchanan. Eschewing any thoughts of subtlety he planned to make Buchanan drunk enough to give away his secret, but Buchanan was a practised drinker who could out-drink even a journalist.

It was Buchanan's thick spectacles that betrayed him. They made his eyes look markedly larger. This jogged White's memory of a boy at school who had been given belladonna drops to enlarge the pupils for an eye examination. Although it was late at night White rushed off to Dr Schultze and roused him. It was not difficult for White to persuade the coroner to order a test for belladonna on Mrs Buchanan's body.

None was found in the stomach, but the eyeballs gave a positive reaction (although the principal prosecution witness was unable to state categorically that he had found atropine in the body). Even then the inertia-prone Schultze was undecided about making a move, but when he heard next morning that Buchanan had been warned by the private detective of the exhumation and was going to flee, he at last cranked up the machinery of the law and Buchanan was arrested.

Because of the part played in Buchanan's arrest by *The World*'s Ike White, the newspaper took an enormous interest in the trial. Articles in *The World*, before the trial even began, would have been well outside the confines of British law. The paper outlined the case against Buchanan, quoting at length long extracts of witnesses' affidavits; comment and specu- lation were mixed, with headlines like 'Buchanan's Bad Day'; 'Macomber's Damaging Testimony Unshaken by Cross-Examination'. Text of the evidence included phrases like 'The judge gave his ruling with a calm smile . . . '

It was an extraordinary newspaper. Verbatim quotations of the court proceedings (and small ads) were printed in minuscule type of sixteen lines to the inch! It must have been a popular paper with opticians. Advertisements for bizarre products abounded. Typical of them were: 'LYDIA E. PINKHAM'S VEGE-TABLE COMPOUND for complaints of women'; 'COMPLETE MANHOOD and How to Attain it'; 'WEAK MEN, Instant Relief. Cure in 15 days. I will send a prescription to develop weak organs; a sure cure for Lost Vitality, Impotency, Nervous Debility, Varicocele, &c.' The advertiser offering this magic cure was an L.S. Franklin, *Music Dealer*.

The trial of Dr Buchanan opened on Monday 20th March, 1893, before Recorder Smyth. Leading for the State was District Attorney De Lancey Nicoll, with Francis L. Wellman and James Osborne. Defending Buchanan were the experienced Charles W. Brooke and the young William J. O'Sullivan, who would make his name in this, his first major murder trial. Before becoming a lawyer, O'Sullivan had been a physician, and he concentrated on cross-examination of the scientific and medical expert witnesses.

In newspaper accounts of the Buchanan trial O'Sullivan is constantly described as young. Yet in contemporary portraits he appears staid and middle-aged. His hair is parted in the middle and he sports a large moustache and pince-nez; he is dressed as conservatively as a diplomat at a reception.

The first week was spent in choosing a jury, and more than two hundred were rejected by one side or the other until they reached agreement on the final dozen.

The District Attorney outlined the case for the prosecution, which was largely circumstantial and seemingly rather tottery, although reports in *The World* were shaded to make it appear more solid, and coloured to make it more titillating.

Macomber and Doria – whom the newspaper insisted on calling Buchanan's 'chums' or 'cronies' – were among the first witnesses. They testified to much that we have already outlined. Next came James Smith (the disgruntled dogsbody/caretaker from the Halsey Street brothel). He was described by *The World* as a well-built man with a bushy, red beard and a strong, intelligent face. The quality of his testimony (and his character) is revealed by the report of the following exchange during his cross-examination by Mr Brooke.

> The witness denied that he had even been in any inebriate asylum. . . . Witness finally admitted he had consulted a physician who had recommended him to go to the Essex County Lunatic Asylum, and that he had gone there for two or three weeks, paying his own board.
> Q. Were you there as an inebriate? A. No.
> Q. What were you being treated for? A. For alcoholism.

It was Smith who started the whole process against Buchanan. He was an unlikely Nemesis.

Early in the trial the State produced a witness who aroused in *The World* reporter a state of lubricious excitement – and had a similar effect on many of the other people in court as well, it is quite clear. This was the aptly-named Maggie Young, one of the 'younger and fresher women' mentioned earlier. The newspaper's unnamed court reporter described her as 'a very pretty young girl'. He wrote:

> Miss Young will never have a better time at a Union Hill [where she lived] sociable than she appeared to have had during her brief examination yesterday. She had bright green feathers in her hat and light brown eyes beneath it. She said that Buchanan in the month of April last year – the month that Mrs Buchanan died – made love to her.

The expression 'make love to' did not have the same meaning it bears now. She could equally well have said that Buchanan made advances to her.

Maggie Young's testimony had Buchanan's lawyer Charles Brooke bouncing up to object strenuously to the admission of her testimony. Whether Buchanan made love to her or not had nothing to do with the charge; the District Attorney's motive was to show Buchanan's heartlessness in going about with young girls while his wife was dying, Brooke declared with some justification. The argument between District Attorney Nicoll, Brooke and Recorder Smyth waged for some lively minutes.

> During all the arguments Maggie Young appeared to enjoy the fuss made over her. She made eyes at the Recorder, at Mr Nicoll and at Mr Brooke. She smiled coyly on the artists who were sketching her joyous face.

(According to *The World*'s reports throughout the trial, there were a lot of 'coy smiles', 'calm smiles', 'serene smiles' and 'broad smiles'. On one occasion the prosecution lawyer Wellman was reported as replying 'with a sneer on his face', and on another he 'cried with almost a yell of triumph' during a cross-examination. The paper's whole attitude to reporting the trial had all the even-handed objectivity of a football report in the home-town newspaper.)

> Finally, after she had told all about the doctor's advances to her on Little Twelfth Street, the Recorder, with a smile even broader than Miss Young's, decided that her testimony had better be stricken out and told the jury to forget it.

Smyth had let Maggie Young do her little act purely for light relief and because she was attractive. The episode may have amused and titillated the majority of the

court and the spectators, but it was badly unfair to
Buchanan, guilty or not.

Then came another crony, George F. Dale. *The
World*'s reporting of this witness typifies its attitude and
style:

> George F. Dale, with his long black mustache
> exquisitely curled and a combination of red and
> white roses in the lapel of his coat was the next
> witness . . . He gave his testimony in an easy,
> fluent way but dropped his h's in such abandon
> that the Recorder threatened once to clear the
> court-room if the people could not suppress their
> merriment. Mr Wellman asked Dale if he
> remembered any conversation with Buchanan that
> he might have had during the winter before Mrs
> Buchanan's death. Dale said he remembered one
> particularly.
>
> Q. When was it?   A. It was somewhere about
> December 12 1892.
>
> Q. What was it?   A. He told me he was going
> to get rid of his 'ousekeeper and pay her off.
>
> Q. Intimate any trouble he was having?   A.
> He said 'The old 'ag is driving me crazy.'

Later the paper reported:

> . . . the witness went on to say that he
> remonstrated with his friend [Buchanan] and told
> him 'not to be 'arsh on 'er'.

The weekend followed this day's evidence. *The World*'s
Sunday edition carried a most extraordinarily biased
and prejudiced feature article entitled 'CONVICTING
A MURDERER; How the Various Workers in the
District Attorney's Office prepare the Case.' It
eulogised the prosecuting team, outlined how they
worked, commented on their successful presentation of
the people's case against Buchanan, underlined the

weight of some of the evidence and previewed some of the expert testimony yet to come. The article concluded:

> It is understood that De Lancey Nicoll [the District Attorney] will sum up the case of Robert W. Buchanan for the people. If so, no one will have to be reminded that it will be a masterpiece.

The real forensic struggle began with the expert evidence, and in his cross-examination of the state's doctors and scientists O'Sullivan was quite brilliant. Even *The World* praised him extravagantly on a number of occasions. However, O'Sullivan did go on at some length at times to the point where the Recorder threatened to hold night sessions to get through the trial.

Wellman became so irritated with O'Sullivan's persistence that during his cross-examination of Dr Loomis 'Mr Wellman, who had kept his impatience well bottled up all day, put his hands in his pockets, walked up and down the inclosure where the attorneys are penned up and smiled . . . ' It seems a fair bet that it wasn't a happy smile.

The prosecution had their own moments. District Attorney Nicoll took *eleven-and-a-half minutes* to ask one question of 1,230 words of a Dr George Peabody. It was an hour and a half before he got his answer because of the strenuous objections of the defence lawyer Brooke. The question was a lengthy résumé of Mrs Buchanan's last day before her fatal illness and her medical history, and called for an opinion as to her cause of death. Dr Peabody obliged by saying he was sure it was due to morphine poisoning.

Much of the technical evidence was fairly dull and apparently largely incomprehensible to the jury. There were, however, some dramatic moments which captured the interest of the jurors and the spectators in the stuffy, overcrowded courtroom.

Professor Witthaus, a very highly qualified and experienced chemist, an impressive-looking figure with a surprisingly quiet voice, explained how he had found approximately one-tenth of a grain of morphine in Mrs Buchanan's body, from which he calculated that she had been given a fatal dose of some five or six grains. He gave in gruesome detail some experiments he carried out on frogs in his test for the morphine. Next, to observe the effect of atropine on the eyes he carried out experiments on a kitten which were as horrifying as anything done these days in laboratory experiments on rabbits' eyes to test the effect of shampoos and cosmetics. Perhaps it would have sounded a little less inhuman if Witthaus had used a cat instead of a kitten. The atropine had the effect of dilating the kitten's pupils, Witthaus declared.

O'Sullivan's penetrating and skilful cross-examination was aimed at getting Witthaus to admit that liquids formed by putrefaction, cadaveric alkaloids, would give the same reaction as morphine in tests. Witthaus demurred, but O'Sullivan scored a notable point when Witthaus had to admit that he could not swear that there was atropine in Mrs Buchanan's body. In other words, there was no *proof* that Buchanan had administered atropine to his wife to neutralise the symptom of pin-point pupils. O'Sullivan's duel with Witthaus earned the first of *The World*'s enthusiastic compliments.

There were certain elements of *grand guignol* in the trial. Dr Loomis produced a wax model of a human brain to explain the examination procedures he had carried out on Mrs Buchanan's brain. The next prosecution witness was Dr T. Mitchell Prudden, Professor of Pathology at the College of Physicians and Surgeons, and director of the Pathological College at the institute. The defence laid a trap for him and Prudden fell in with a clatter that must have discomforted him for a long time afterwards. He rejected a human brain handed to him by O'Sullivan for demonstration as unsuitable as 'a caricature of a brain', and took the wax model provided by the prosecution instead. Unfortunately for Prudden the defence's wax 'caricature' was a real, preserved human brain, an error which seriously undermined his credibility.

Mr Wellman went some way to repairing the damage during his cross-examination of Dr Arthur W. Wolff, a defence expert witness. First he produced the preserved brain that Prudden had taken to be a wax model. Then, like a conjuror performing a trick, he whisked away a cover from a plate. It contained a fresh human brain that had been removed that same morning. Wellman asked whether he didn't consider the preserved brain to be a caricature of this fresh brain.

'I certainly don't,' Wolff replied firmly. 'Every part that's in that brain [the fresh one] you'll find in that one. That's a brain that God Almighty made and so is this one.'

The trial had not finished producing its surprises and its light relief. It was widely said that a defence witness, Professor Scheele, was going to challenge Mr Wellman to a duel. Scheele was a powerfully-built German student with a sabre scar across his ear and nose, who had already fought some twenty-eight duels. The imagined slight was that Wellman had suggested that Scheele was only an apothecary.

It was only one of O'Sullivan's jokes, but it caused a commotion. 'Really,' said O'Sullivan when he was asked whether he was going to be one of the professor's seconds, 'I was so afraid the professor would jump down and tear Mr Wellman up that I kept my hand on the wicket every moment ready to interfere.'

He added, 'Please correct the statement that I said Mr Wellman was no gentleman. I said that, you know, merely to quiet the professor. I could never say that Mr Wellman wasn't a gentleman. Professor Scheele knows a lot about fencing and ptomaines and all that, but you can't expect him to catch on to American ideas of things in the short time he has been here . . . He won't hurt Mr Wellman,' said O'Sullivan reassuringly.

After that light interlude came the major shock of the case. In many trials the defence produces expert witnesses who declare that the prosecution's witnesses had got it all wrong, and they give convincing-sounding arguments to sustain their own opinions. The statement and the experiments in court of Professor Victor C. Vaughan, who gave evidence on behalf of Buchanan, were more than convincing: they were sensational. With the court's permission he turned the courtroom into a chemical laboratory with white-coated assistants and scientific equipment.

As we have said, O'Sullivan's case was that cadaveric alkaloids – the result of natural decomposition – had triggered the chemical tests for morphine although no morphine was present in Mrs Buchanan's body. Dr Vaughan added the test reagent to a saucer containing morphine, which gave the characteristic pink colour. The prosecution's experts had declared that morphine and only morphine would produce this result. Then Vaughan added the reagent to a saucer containing no morphine, only cadaveric alkaloids from a corpse, and got exactly the same colour.

He had exploded the worth of the prosecution's tests. The shock waves were felt well outside the courtroom and outside the United States: it was a major story in newspapers all round the world.

If the defence had left it at that – if they *could* have left it at that – almost certainly Buchanan would have been acquitted. Unfortunately for him, although fortunately for justice, the defence could not stop there: they were haunted by the spectre of the Carlyle Harris case. It was generally accepted that Harris's refusal to give evidence on his own behalf was the deciding factor of his conviction. Curiously, this ran contrary to the English experience of accused persons going into the witness box. Before the introduction of the Criminal Evidence Act of 1898 the accused was not allowed to give evidence. For a few years afterwards, most prisoners in capital cases who elected to do so were found guilty and would have done better to keep their mouths shut. In Harris's case, nevertheless, the New York public apparently expected him to testify.

Buchanan, obsessed with the thought that Harris's failure to testify had ensured his conviction, insisted against the advice of his highly experienced counsel Charles Brooke on having his say. Until now he had been almost a peripheral figure in the trial, very much a supporting player, almost a non-speaking extra. At last he took centre stage and everyone's attention was focused on him.

His performance was a disaster.

The Assistant District Attorney Francis Wellman tore him to shreds; he led Buchanan into contradictions and manifest lies. He mumbled and stuttered; he often put his hand to his mouth as if to try to stop the words coming out. Merely to read the transcript of Buchanan's pitiful testimony is embarrassing.

Nothing could save him, although O'Sullivan tried by interrupting Wellman's final speech and generally making a nuisance of himself to the point that the Recorder severely admonished him on numerous occasions. O'Sullivan must have felt a mixture of sympathy for Buchanan because of his awful state, and of frustration at watching all his brilliant defensive work being demolished by the man it was meant to save.

There was yet one more farcical scene to be reported. The previous Monday, on his way from the court back to the prison where he was being held, Buchanan met a friend. The two men and prison guard John J. Lynch, known as 'Happy Jack', who was in charge of Buchanan, went into a saloon at the corner of Elm and Leonard Streets where they had drinks. 'Happy Jack' returned Buchanan to the prison some three hours after the court had adjourned. The guard was sacked from the service.

The jury were out for twenty-eight hours and four minutes, coming back at 11.24 p.m. on Wednesday, 26th April 1893, to return a verdict of 'Guilty of Murder in the First Degree'. *The World* was exultant. 'BUCHANAN IS GUILTY!' declared its headline.

There was one more *coup de théâtre* to come.

Mrs Helen Buchanan was waiting in an outer office when she heard the verdict. She screamed and fell to the floor, recovered quickly, sprang to her feet and rushed out into the corridor. She made a break for the stairs leading to the basement and tried to throw herself down. Two young men who were standing nearby prevented her.

The distraught young woman kept crying out 'Oh! My Bob! Where is he?' One is irresistibly reminded of Mrs Lamson's loyalty to her husband.

On the street Mrs Buchanan broke away from her escort and ran down Chambers Street. Two park policemen caught her by the fire station. Her friends called a cab and bundled her inside while she was still screaming.

The World ran a brief editorial the next day, criticising the American judicial system. The article concluded:

> Under the laws of criminal procedure in New York, even [Buchanan's] conviction does not insure his punishment, while at the very best his punishment must be postponed for months and perhaps for years.

Buchanan spent two years on Death Row at Sing Sing,
awaiting the results of his appeals and his pleas for
clemency. On 2nd July 1895 he died in the electric
chair.